# STRATEGY *in* TURBULENT TIMES

*How to Design a Strategy That Is Robust and Future-Proof*

# KURT VERWEIRE

Lannoo
Campus

# CONTENTS

D/2023/45/59 – ISBN 978 94 014 9039 9 – NUR 800

Cover design: Joost van Lierop
Interior design: Gert Degrande | De Witlofcompagnie

LannooCampus Publishers is a subsidiary of Lannoo Publishers,
the book and multimedia division of Lannoo Publishers nv.

LannooCampus Publishers
Vaartkom 41 box 01.02        P.O. Box 23202
3000 Leuven                 1100 DS Amsterdam
Belgium                     Netherlands
www.lannoocampus.com

*Kurt Verweire, Koen Tackx & Walter Van Dyck*

Chapter **3** **STRATEGIZING IN TURBULENT TIMES** **75**

Chapter **4** **CHAPTER OF THE CAMEL – CORE RESILIENCE** **115**

Chapter **5** **CHAPTER OF THE SALMON –**
CORPORATE INNOVATION **155**

Chapter **6** **CHAPTER OF THE CHAMELEON –**
CORE TRANSFORMATION **195**

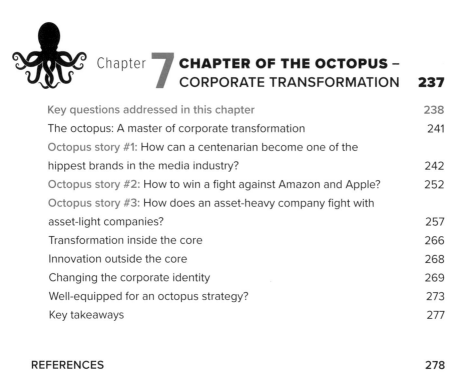

Chapter **7 CHAPTER OF THE OCTOPUS –**
CORPORATE TRANSFORMATION **237**

# Acknowledgments

Strategy is a fascinating topic. As a faculty member at Vlerick Business School, I've had the pleasure to work with many executives and management teams and witness the power of strategy. But I've also noted how many companies struggle with it and fail to use it to their advantage. For a long time, the focus has been on building a competitive advantage—which essentially is about beating your competitors. Today, many strategy authors believe that competitive advantage is a relic from the past and that you need new recipes to win. Managers tell me that the traditional competitors are no longer their biggest nightmare. The world has become more turbulent and disruptors are attacking from many different corners. Some management authors even wonder if we are experiencing the end of competitive advantage? Even the biggest strategy thinkers disagree on this topic.

Over the last five years, I've spent a lot of time thinking about strategy in turbulent times: What are the typical strategy recipes for dealing with turbulence? Is strategy in turbulent times different from the traditional strategic thinking, focused on competitive advantage? Does it replace it or should it be seen as a complement? I've tried to find answers to these questions—not just theoretical ones, but also answers that are practically relevant. So, I went out and read management books and articles, studied numerous cases, and did many interviews with managers to find out how they approached this topic. I was surprised by the lack of coherence in the academic theories, models and practical recommendations. There are so many different frameworks and toolkits and there is so much contradictory advice that managers no longer see the forest for the trees.

*Strategy in Turbulent Times* is my synthesis on this important strategic topic. It captures my most important insights and recommendations on how firms should deal with turbulence, disruption, and disturbance. Writing this book was a very interesting journey that has broadened my strategic insights significantly. During that journey, I got a lot of help and support from many organizations and individuals.

I am deeply grateful to my Vlerick Business School colleagues Koen Tackx and Walter Van Dyck for the great discussions on the Turbulence Strategy model—which has become the central model of the book—and the role of corporate foresight in the new strategy process. I am also grateful to my colleagues from the Vlerick Strategy Department for sharing ideas on the turbulence topic: thank you Carine Peeters, Martin Weiss, Kerstin Fehre, Filip Abraham, Leonardo Meeus, Philippe Haspeslagh and Esha Mendiratta. And I also acknowledge the valuable input from Bjorn Cumps, Stijn Viaene and Miguel Meuleman—also Vlerick Business School colleagues—when writing some of the case studies for this book.

I've been able to discuss the topic of turbulence in strategy with many managers in my strategy courses—their input was a true source of inspiration. I've had sessions with companies from many different industries—including postal services, construction, healthcare and pharma, IT, publishing, financial services, education, food manufacturing, and retail. These sessions have helped me tremendously in validating the new models that are presented in the book. I want to thank two companies in particular—KBC and NowJobs (and its corporate parent, House of HR)—for their openness on how they dealt with turbulence. Thank you Johan Thijs, Erik Luts, Sigrid De Wever, Katrien Dewijngaert, Karin Van Hoecke, and Barak Chizi from KBC, for your openness, sharpness, and bright insights. You taught me that business model innovation should not necessarily be an external activity and that tugboats sometimes work better than speedboats. And thank you Frédéric Pattyn, Eline David, Peter Ingelbrecht, and Lindsay Demuynck from NowJobs/Accent Jobs/House of HR to share what it means to be in the driver's seat of a new corporate venture in a large corporation.

I am deeply indebted to Marije Roefs and Niels Janssens, editor and publisher at LannooCampus, and Anna Rich and William Wright to have a thorough look at the manuscript and make the necessary adaptations.

Finally, I want to sincerely thank my wife, Lieve, for all her patience, support, and understanding during this entire research project. You tolerated and accommodated my countless sudden urges to write and never became bored with my endless stories about turbulence, disruption, and the animal kingdom. I promise, from now on, I'll keep these stories for my students and participants and won't bother any longer.

# CHAPTER
# 1

## the future isn't what
## it used to be

# Key questions addressed in this chapter

What is turbulence? And why should you worry about it?

Do we really live in more turbulent times, or is this whole discussion 'cool-sounding nonsense'?

What are the typical strategic responses to turbulence?

Does a turbulence strategy replace the traditional strategy models?

# What if competitors are not your biggest nightmare?

Some weeks ago, I got a phone call from a CEO who had received some bad news; despite great results the year before, his contract had been terminated. Sometimes this happens—the job of a top executive is tough, and managers who take that job must accept the uncertainty that goes along with it. This call was a bit different, though. Appointed as the first external CEO in the 280-year history of a timber importer, he had inherited a family business that had struggled with profitability for years. But in 2021, the company achieved a record year in revenues and profitability—the Covid-19 crisis turned out to be a blessing for the company. One year later, euphoria had given way to disillusionment: the war in Ukraine exposed the fundamental weaknesses in the company's business model. The ban on Russian timber deprived the company of half of its supply and revenues. The result was a big loss, so big that the family decided to sell the company to a smaller but more resilient competitor.

This story is quite familiar to anyone who reads contemporary management books. The world is changing faster and becoming more complex than in the past. Strategies and business models expire faster than ever before, and change is the only constant. We just went through one of the most impactful global health crises in recent memory, while geopolitical tensions are now leading to high levels of economic uncertainty. Technological revolutions will continue to change our lives, and people's needs and demands will further evolve... The future ain't what it used to be.[1]

Organizations can build sophisticated strategies to beat their competitors. But sometimes your competitors are not your biggest nightmare. Natural disasters, geopolitical events, broken supply chains, economic volatility, or the arrival of disruptors with new business models might at times have a more profound impact on your performance. Unfortunately, the common strategic models offer little help for dealing with those particular challenges. That's why many strategy researchers and consultants believe the time of traditional strategic thinking is over. The new ideas about strategy are best summarized in Rita McGrath's book *The End of Competitive Advantage*: to win in volatile and uncertain environments, executives need to learn how to exploit short-lived opportunities with speed and decisiveness.[2] Strategy is no longer about finding a favorable position in a well-defined industry and exploiting a long-term competitive advantage; it's about building dynamic capabilities to cope with changing conditions and turbulent times.[3]

What does all this mean in practice? How should your company strategize in a world full of surprises? Unlike many other management authors who propose a particular tactic to fight turbulence—for example, launch a new business model, strengthen your resilience, or embrace agility—I think this challenge deserves a more comprehensive strategic answer. Rather than immediately jumping to conclusions and implementing some appealing initiatives, I believe it's necessary to first ask yourself a series of strategic questions: What are the issues that your company is facing? What strategic options do you have to tackle turbulence? What is the best strategic choice, given your organization's capabilities? And how to best implement this turbulence strategy?

In this book, I will show you how to build such a comprehensive answer to turbulence. Let's kick off by examining what turbulence is and looking at the evolution of turbulence over the last few decades.

# What is turbulence?

Organizations face a lot of turbulence. There can be turbulence in your boardroom or in your management team. Or there's turbulence amongst your employees because of some unpopular decisions that your management team has taken. Or there's turbulence because you're involved in an acquisition, especially when your company is the target company. But that's not the turbulence I cover in this book. This book concerns *environmental turbulence*—the turbulence that you encounter in your industry or broader business environment and that can have a significant impact—negative or positive—on your organization's performance. The industry environment consists of your major buyers and suppliers, your competitors, potential new entrants in your market and your substitutes—companies from another industry that offer products or services with similar benefits. (The typical example of a substitute for an airline company is a railway company.) The broader business environment—also called the macro environment—consists of all of the external influences that affect a company's strategy and performance.[4] Strategists generally look at 6 major macro influences: Political, Economic, Social, Technological, Ecological, and Legal (generally captured as the acronym PESTEL).

**ACADEMIC FOUNDATIONS.** People often refer to the VUCA acronym when talking about a turbulent environment, Volatile, Uncertain, Complex, and Ambiguous. The VUCA concept was first used in the mid-1980s by Warren Bennis and Burt Nanus to describe how the world had become more vulnerable after the end of the Cold War.[5] The term gained wider recognition and popularity in the business and leadership domains.

But strategists talked about turbulence long before the VUCA concept was born. Frederick Emery and Eric Trist had already introduced the concept of environmental turbulence in 1965 in a study that defined 4 types of organizational environments, of which the 'turbulent field' was the most challenging.[6] Over the years, strategy scholars have come up with different operationalizations and measurements of environmental turbulence. In academia, researchers define a turbulent environment as one that is dynamic, complex, and unpredictable.[7] Dynamism describes the frequency and intensity of change in the environmental components—such as the change in inflation or interest rates (economic component) or the rate of technological change (technological component).[8] An environment can be static/stable versus dynamic/unstable. Complexity means that there are many issues and factors that cause the change. The relationships between these issues and factors are difficult to understand and it's not clear which factors are most important in the decision-making process. Predictability represents the uncertainty and ambiguity regarding the cause-and-effect of the change.[9]

I define turbulence slightly differently as a huge shock or a fundamental shift in the industry or broader business environment, with a potentially significant impact on a company's performance, or even its survival. Turbulence doesn't have to persist long for it to have far-reaching implications on your firm's performance.

**MANY SHAPES OF TURBULENCE.** Turbulence can take many shapes and you can classify turbulence in different ways. Figure 1 highlights 4 different ways to look at turbulence.

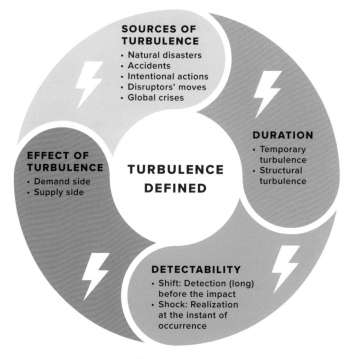

**Figure 1** • Classifications of turbulence

First you can look at the sources of turbulence. MIT Professor Yossi Sheffi distinguishes between natural disasters, accidents (mostly caused by safety violations or noncompliance), intentional actions (sometimes called 'issues'—examples include strikes and boycotts by stakeholders, and terrorist attacks), disruptors' moves, and global crises (like the 2008 financial crisis or the Covid-19 pandemic).

A second classification considers whether the economic effects of turbulence are mainly situated on the demand or on the supply side. Demand-side turbulence leads to a significant loss of revenues—for example, due to reputational damage or a sudden drop in demand (as with the pandemic). Supply-side turbulence can lead to a loss in revenues (because you cannot meet demand) or to a significant cost increase. Whatever side is affected, the turbulence can lead to serious financial problems and threaten your firm's survival, as the introductory case demonstrated. Of course, turbulence can create more than just economic harm—think, for example, about your employees' health and safety. It's obvious that the wellbeing of your employees should be your primary concern.

A third classification introduces the concept of detection lead time, defined as the time between knowing that a turbulent event will take place and the first impact.[10] Detectability adds a time dimension to the turbulence discussion and helps to distinguish between turbulence as a shock or as a shift. If you can detect a disruptive event before the first impact, then the detectability is positive. The detection lead time can be lengthy—then we speak about long-term shifts or trends, like climate change. New disruptors arriving with new business models also fit in this category. When the detection lead time is small, disruptions arise after some short warning (hurricanes, for example). If the detection lead time is zero, then you realize the impact of the turbulence at the moment of occurrence. Turbulence strikes without warning and you experience a shock—for example, an earthquake in the middle of the night.[11]

The final classification considers the duration of the turbulence. Some turbulence is temporary: the anticipated duration is short (in practice, researchers consider 'short' to be less than one year). For example, one researcher considered the Covid-19 pandemic a temporary turbulence because 85% of the participants of his research project expected the impact to last one year or less.[12] Structural turbulence, on the other hand, lasts much longer—and sometimes you never go back to the original state.

**DISRUPTION VERSUS DISTURBANCE.** Turbulence can take many shapes and forms and this will influence your strategic response. I find it useful to distinguish between 2 forms of turbulence: 'disruption' and 'disturbance'. Turbulence through disruption means that your competitive landscape changes: new players enter your market and change the rules of the game with a fundamentally different value proposition and a different value chain. Academics and consultants often recommend doing business model innovation, a strategic move that implies setting up a new business with a fundamentally new value proposition. This is considered to be one of the toughest management challenges for incumbent firms and many really struggle with it.

But not all turbulence is caused by disruption. Some firms face a shock in demand or in supply because of a natural disaster or a severe accident. I call this disturbance. Here, the competitive landscape remains unchanged. Disturbance can have an equally significant impact on your performance. Just consider the financial crisis or the pandemic; these crises have seriously impacted the performance of many firms. The performance effect is different though. Firms suffer not because they haven't found an appropriate answer to the disruptors but because they lack the resilience and agility needed to deal with sudden shocks or longer-term shifts. It's important to add—and this is also one of the main messages of this book—that turbulence brings opportunities. Some firms thrive in turbulent times.

Developing a turbulence strategy without reflecting on the nature of the turbulence that you are facing is dangerous. Disturbance and disruption are very different phenomena which require different strategic responses. Table 1 presents the major differences between the 2 kinds of turbulence.

|  | Disruption | Disturbance |
| --- | --- | --- |
| Source of turbulence | Disruptors with new business models | Natural disasters, accidents, intentional actions, global crises |
| Effect of turbulence | Mostly on the demand and supply side | Mostly on the demand side or the supply side; sometimes on both |
| Detectability | Long detection lead time | Mostly shorter detection lead times, sometimes no detectability at all |
| Duration | Mostly structural turbulence | Sometimes temporary turbulence, sometimes structural turbulence |

**Table 1** • Disruption vs disturbance

# VUCA, VUCA, VUCA

*"It is not too much to say that, in these respects, more has been done, richer and more prolific discoveries have been made, grandeur achievements have been realized, in the course of the 50 years of our own lifetime than in all the previous lifetime of the race."*[13]

**MORE TURBULENCE?** Do you know the author of this quote? This quote gained fame not for the person who said it, but for the time it was said. It originates from an American scientific article from 1868, which described the technological revolution brought about by light bulbs, trains, and telephones. Roger Martin, one of today's most influential strategy thinkers, concludes that people always think the current time is more VUCA than any previous time. He goes one step further: he believes that the whole turbulence discussion is all 'cool-sounding nonsense'. Business can't stop talking about VUCA, VUCA, VUCA. But according to Martin, the world has always been VUCA—and in his opinion, the world is not fundamentally different than some decades ago. And if the notion of competitive advantage was relevant 20 or 30 years ago (in VUCA times), then it continues to be relevant today.

To make his point, he looked at the durability of advantage of the 20 highest market capitalization companies in America in 2022—from #1 Apple to #20 Pfizer. More than half of his list consisted of tech firms. Martin looked at the duration for which these companies have followed largely the same strategy with their core offering. What did he find? "The median duration of these advantaged strategies as of 2022 is a lengthy 36 years—over a third of a century! And that is the end of competitive advantage? Really?"[14]

**MORE TURBULENCE.** There is, however, academic evidence that turbulence has increased. A study by the Boston Consulting Group showed that, for a sample of almost 10,000 American public companies, the volatility of revenue growth and EBIT margins has increased significantly over the last 50 years—and for both parameters, it has more than doubled since 1960. BCG also checked the turbulence in competition by looking at the change in rankings. This volatility measure has also doubled since the 1960s.[15] The consulting firm also noticed a drop in the average age at death of public companies: the life span of corporations had nearly halved over just 4 decades—from almost 60 years in 1970 to a little more than 30 years in 2010.[16]

Donald Sull, a senior lecturer at the MIT Sloan School of Management, and formerly a professor at London Business School and Harvard Business School, reported similar findings.[17] He found that the average life expectancy of a firm listed on the S&P Index decreased from 90 years during the 1930s to less than 25 years by the late 1990s. Julian Birkinshaw, another London Business School professor, published one of the most recent empirical studies on turbulence. He analyzed to what extent the makeup of the Fortune 500 has changed in the last 25 years—a period that coincides with the rise of the internet. If the business world has become more turbulent, this should be reflected in the composition of the Fortune 500 list.

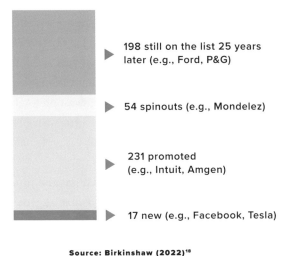

198 still on the list 25 years later (e.g., Ford, P&G)

54 spinouts (e.g., Mondelez)

231 promoted (e.g., Intuit, Amgen)

17 new (e.g., Facebook, Tesla)

Source: Birkinshaw (2022)[18]

**Figure 2** • Fortune 500 list in 2020

198 companies made it to the Fortune 500 lists of 1995 and 2020. 231 companies were promoted: these firms already existed in 1995, but they were not yet part of the Fortune 500 list. 54 firms were spinouts—companies that were part of a larger group but became independent. Only 17 new companies—companies that did not exist in 1995—made it to the 2020 list. And only 35 of the original Fortune 500 companies of 1995 went bankrupt. These are rather small figures, and Birkinshaw's conclusion was that there is less creative destruction than most people believe. Birkinshaw did find some significant churn in the technology, media, telecom, and retail industry (including restaurants and hotels), but most other industries had high levels of inertia and looked surprisingly stable.[19]

**MORE TURBULENCE EXPECTED.** Several studies indicate that obsolescence and renewal will appear higher on the corporate agenda in the future. James Allen and Chris Zook—both partners from Bain & Company and well-known strategy authors—ran more than 150 forums on growth and business building which were attended by some 3,000 CEOs in 35 countries. Here are some of their interesting observations: "65% of the CEOs predicted that in 5 to 7 years their firms' main competitors would be different from their main competitors today. 63% said that new competitors with new business models would pose a major threat to their firms' core business. The CEOs projected that in the next decade, 40% of the value their companies created would come from entering new markets and launching new business models. Clearly, the business landscape feels highly unstable to them."[20] A study with more than 4,000 CEOs by consulting firm PwC finds that 40% of them think their organizations will no longer be economically viable in 10 years' time. But are they spending enough time on business reinvention? According to PwC, the answer is no.[21]

**MY CONCLUSIONS FROM THIS RESEARCH.** What are my conclusions from all these studies? First, there is no denying the exponential growth of the large tech companies that have changed the business world—think Meta, Alphabet, Apple, Amazon, Tencent, and Alibaba. And it's clear there are also famous victims of disruption and disturbance—companies like Nokia, Kodak, Blockbuster, and Thomas Cook failed to adapt to a changing world. But I don't believe that turbulence creates death and destruction in every industry or for every company. The corporate world hasn't become a forest full of wildfires yet. We need a more nuanced view on this topic than the simplistic 'reinvent or die'. Vigilance is needed, but let's not forget that many firms continue to exploit their competitive advantage successfully.

However, there are times and situations in which you need to adapt to fundamental change. Whether turbulence comes as a shock or as a shift, you need to get ready and build an appropriate strategic response. If you consider the CEO surveys, turbulence may increase in the future. So this topic will be of even higher interest to many executives. Let's now take a look at all the possible options for dealing with turbulence.

# Many different turbulence recipes

In the last few decades, a lot of research has been done on turbulence and strategy, which has resulted in a broad set of strategic recommendations. Let's have a look at the palette of turbulence recipes.

**EMBRACE AMBIDEXTERITY: EXPLOIT AND EXPLORE.** This is by far the most popular advice. Respond to turbulence by splitting up your company into exploration and exploitation parts. Leaders understand that creating a new business and optimizing an already existing one are 2 fundamentally different management tasks. The challenge is doing both simultaneously—a tough and difficult job.[22] Nevertheless, if you want to continue your growth path in the future, you need to set up innovation initiatives that strengthen your core and at the same time launch transformational initiatives focusing on creating new offerings for new markets. Or as Steve Jobs put it: "It's not simply a choice between being in the navy or being a pirate. Established companies have to develop processes that allow their innovators to become pirates in the navy."[23] Most publications focus on the pirate part of the endeavor and provide recipes for established companies to tackle the exploration challenge.

You can do that in several ways. Many authors recommend creating game-changing ventures at startup speed—commonly referred to as business model innovations.[24] Corporate venturing is a related topic—it's a practice where a company sets up a separate organizational unit to launch exploration initiatives. The unit invests in new technologies and business opportunities arising within or outside the firm's boundaries, for long-term strategic or short-term financial purposes.[25] Corporate venturing fits in the new approach towards building more open and collaborative innovation models with new research and development partners.

**TRANSFORM YOUR CORE: REINVENT YOUR ENTIRE BUSINESS MODEL.** Some authors concentrate more on the navy than on the pirates. They admit that building new business models is important but believe that this is often not enough to counter the turbulence in the industry. Turbulence forces you to transform your core as well, in addition to building a new business model. One of the most convincing books on this topic is *Dual Transformation*, wherein Scott Anthony, Clark Gilbert and Mark Johnson introduce the notion of Transformation A and Transformation B. Transformation A is about repositioning the core business and adapting it to the realities of the disrupted marketplace. Transformation B covers the business model innovation outside your core. Key in making both transformations work is establishing a capability exchange, a very distinct way to build synergies between the two units.[26] I will come back to this interesting topic later in this book.

**PLATFORMIZE YOUR BUSINESS AND BUILD AN ECOSYSTEM AROUND IT.** Platforms are everywhere today and their success and phenomenal growth have received widespread attention. Platform companies like Uber, Airbnb, Alibaba, Google, Meta and Apple have become extremely powerful—a trend that continued during the Covid-19 crisis, when everybody started ordering goods and services on digital platforms. So, managers are wondering whether building a platform business with an ecosystem of partners is the next big thing to do.[27] But the shift from an integrated firm with a hierarchical supply chain to an ecosystem with largely independent partners working together to deliver integrated solutions is a tough one.[28]

**EMBRACE AGILITY.** Turbulence implies many shifts in the business environment. Some authors suggest building agility capabilities for your organization. Agility is the ability to see and capitalize on new opportunities.[29] These opportunities can be tactical—such as improvements in your existing value chain—or they can be strategic—e.g., entering a new market or acquiring an important competitor. There are many publications that provide you with useful advice on how to read and surf on the winds of change.[30]

**BUILD STRATEGIC RESILIENCE.** This topic is related to the previous one, but this literature focuses more on the downside of turbulence (as opposed to agility, which is more oriented towards the upside of turbulence). Organizations have always used risk management techniques to deal with uncertain events. But the risks that companies are facing today are larger, more impactful, and more unpredictable. Think about the Covid-19 crisis or the demand and supply shocks that we've seen in the last couple of years. On top of the health and supply chain problems, organizations are subject to many business challenges, societal uncertainties, geopolitical tensions, price volatility and cyberthreats. They need to plan for the unexpected and build up their response capabilities in advance.[31] That means screening the environment, building buffers, and adapting your business model—a key recipe in agility research too.

**ISSUE MANAGEMENT AND NON-MARKET STRATEGY.** Researchers like David Baron and David Bach argue that managers need to manage customers and competitors but also face issues that are raised by a broader set of stakeholders.[32] Some companies have run into serious problems because they neglected or underestimated the reaction of some impactful stakeholder groups. One of those companies was Shell UK, which decided in the early 1990s to get rid of its Brent Spar oil storage facility. In February 1995—after an extensive analysis that also incorporated the environmental effects of the options—the company decided to sink the Brent Spar at sea. That decision, however, elicited strong reactions, especially from Greenpeace, which mounted an energetic media campaign to influence public opinion. This led to a boycott of Shell products in Northern Europe, damaging Shell's profitability and brand image.[33]

Another famous example is United Airlines, which was severely attacked by a customer whose guitar was damaged during a trip. Check out the YouTube video 'United Breaks Guitar' that went viral and attracted millions of views in just a couple of weeks.[34] The airline company tackled this incident so badly that it lost $180 million—10% of its market value. Issue management is a management process for anticipating and taking appropriate action on emerging trends, concerns, or issues that could affect an organization and its stakeholders. Publications on issue management and non-market strategy provide useful advice on how to frame and address these issues as well as on how to do proper communications management.

**OPEN STRATEGY.** Some authors suggest adapting your strategy process, which is about how your strategy is made and implemented.[35] All too often, the strategy formulation process is restricted to a small elite of C-suite executives, which leads to unimaginative and boring strategies that are nothing more than copies of the competitors' strategies. If you involve a wider group of people from inside and outside the organization in your strategy discussions, you end up with much more creative and robust strategies. Firms should open up strategy just like they have opened up other areas of business, such as innovation and marketing. A recent book on this topic, called *Open Strategy*, has convincingly shown that this unusual way of doing strategy can bring surprising results.[36]

**SCENARIO PLANNING.** Finally, there are many publications on how to do strategy analysis in uncertain environments. When uncertainty is high, it's hard to apply the typical strategic planning process. How can you make sound predictions if you have no clue what the future will bring? Many strategy authors believe that it's useless to try to predict the future. Managers can then turn to scenario planning and other foresight techniques—tools that have been in use for a very long time but that have become increasingly popular. These tools help organizations imagine what could happen and then build appropriate strategic responses. There're many consultants and academics out there who help companies with this sensing and foresight process. And there are even entire strategic journals devoted to this topic.

**TOO MANY RECIPES?** This overview shows that there's no shortage of ideas and solutions for the turbulence challenge. But I guess you all agree with me that this list of recipes is overwhelming. There is no doubt that these publications contain a lot of useful information and rightfully challenge some of the traditional strategic thinking. But how can you reconcile all these different ideas into one strategic journey? Sometimes the advice is just contradictory: Should you tackle turbulence in the core or should you start building ventures outside your core? Should you focus on the upside or on the downside of turbulence? So many questions remain.

But I have a more fundamental problem with many of these concepts: they are mostly tactical responses. Turbulence, however, requires a more comprehensive strategic answer. Turbulence is a key strategic issue: it can have a profound impact on your company's performance, it needs substantial amounts of your firm's resources, and it requires your top management team to make fundamental decisions.[37] Strategic issues force you to make fundamental choices. You had best done some proper analysis before you choose among your strategic options. And finally, you will achieve good results only if you implement your strategy well.

## Are the traditional strategy models obsolete?

Strategy in turbulent times asks for a new theory on strategy, as the turbulence fundamentally changes the content of strategy analysis, strategy formulation, and strategy implementation. Does this new approach towards strategy make the traditional strategy models obsolete? I don't think so. It's not the end of competitive advantage yet. In my view, a turbulence strategy complements the existing strategy frameworks—it doesn't replace them. Strategists need to master a wider palette of strategy recipes. I would like to introduce a new concept—called 'strategy rocks'—to illustrate this.

**STRATEGY ROCKS.** Most fundamental strategic decisions deal with one of the following 3 main challenges: (1) How to win in your core business? (2) How to grow beyond your core? (3) And how to deal with turbulent times? I call these three challenges the three strategic rocks. Firms may face one challenge—typically the first one—but I've conducted strategy seminars where the management teams had to find answers to all three strategic questions. Let me tell you what the first two strategic rocks are about before we elaborate on the third one, which is what this book is all about.

**STRATEGY ROCK #1: HOW DO YOU WIN IN THE CORE BUSINESS?** This is the traditional view on strategy—often referred to as positioning or competitive strategy. You apply competitive strategy to a business unit—this can be a firm or a unit within a larger corporation with profit and loss responsibility and external customers. The main challenge here is beating your competitors. Before you decide about your competitive strategy, it's good to analyze the market environment and your own resources and capabilities. It's important to do that internal and external analysis along with a financial analysis. A combination of quantitative and qualitative information allows for much better insights into your current competitive position. After the analysis, the management team makes choices regarding your competitive arena—who your core customers are, and what your core products are—sometimes called your 'where to play'.

The second strategic choice focuses on your competitive theme—often called your 'how to win'. It involves a clear choice concerning your value proposition—what you promise to your customers—and your operating model—how do you configure your value chain to make your promise to your customer come true? In the early 1990s, Michael Treacy and Fred Wiersema argued that firms needed to make a choice between three operating models: customer intimacy, operational excellence, or product leadership.[38] Many managers ask me if that model is still relevant today. I can only confirm that I'm still using it extensively in my strategy workshops, and firms really benefit from making a choice with regard to one of the three models. This choice is important because it drives your strategy implementation efforts. Strategy implementation is about taking actions in line with your operating model. For example, customer intimacy firms implement a strategy differently to product leaders or operational excellence firms. The more you involve your employees in this strategy implementation journey, the more successful you will be. I've written extensively about strategy formulation and implementation in the core business in my books *Strategy Implementation* and *Six Batteries of Change.*[39]

**STRATEGY ROCK #2: HOW DO YOU GROW BEYOND THE CORE?** Some firms have growth aspirations that can't be matched by their core business. When you are a winner in your core, you can leverage your advantage in other markets and move into new adjacencies. Then your firm becomes a multi-business firm, also called a corporation. Multi-business firms have various business units, each of which needs to formulate and implement a business strategy. But you also need a strategy for the corporate parent, and that seems to be a challenging issue. The literature on corporate diversification shows that many corporate parents have destroyed value because they went after the wrong acquisitions or adjacencies.

Growing beyond the core requires that you make two new strategic decisions—commonly referred to as 'corporate-level strategy' choices.[40] The first one is which new markets to enter. Firms can usually enter various markets, so it's important to choose the best one(s). A related question is whether a firm should dispose of some business units because they no longer fit the portfolio. I call these decisions the 'shaping-the-portfolio' decisions. Again, ideally, this choice should be preceded by some strategy analysis. Key questions to address in this analysis phase are: which markets are most attractive? In which markets can you best leverage your corporate capabilities? How well do you know the markets that you're planning to enter? How related are they to your core business? And if you make acquisitions, what is the price you want to pay for the target?

The second strategic question deals with how to manage the multi-business firm: Do you want to be a loose confederation of business units—sometimes called a 'portfolio manager'—or do you want to pursue many synergies across the business units? In that case, you choose to be a 'synergy manager' or a 'parental developer'. Many companies struggle and haven't found an appropriate answer to this question—I've seen so much frustration with both corporate and business unit managers on failed synergies that I believe this topic deserves more attention in a corporate management team. (I refer you to the more specialized literature if you want to know more about this topic.[41]) Strategy implementation then is about making these adjacency moves and ensuring that the new business units fit in well in the corporate strategy by setting up the right systems and structures to pursue the synergy benefits that you are aiming for.

**STRATEGY ROCK #3: HOW DO YOU DEAL WITH TURBULENT TIMES?** This is the third key strategic challenge. Here too, you need to do a sound strategy analysis on turbulence, then build the right turbulence strategy, after which you start with your implementation initiatives. Let's examine this a little further.

# Towards a new turbulence strategy playbook

Strategy in turbulent times is fundamentally different from the two other strategy challenges. Unlike strategy for the core business, the focus is less on the direct competitors but more on the disruptors or other change drivers that can have a significant impact on your performance.

**SOMETHING FOR YOU?** Let's find out if turbulence strategy is something relevant for you.

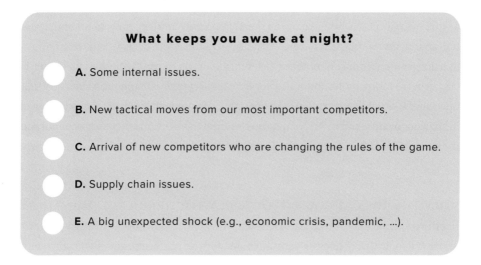

**What keeps you awake at night?**

**A.** Some internal issues.

**B.** New tactical moves from our most important competitors.

**C.** Arrival of new competitors who are changing the rules of the game.

**D.** Supply chain issues.

**E.** A big unexpected shock (e.g., economic crisis, pandemic, ...).

What keeps you awake at night? Every executive has some issues to worry about. What are your biggest concerns? If you've answered A or B, then you can probably stick to your strategy for the core—i.e., strategy rock #1. But if you have answered C, D or E, then turbulence is knocking on your door. In all of my turbulence strategy classes, I ask participants to score the level of turbulence on a scale from 0 (no turbulence at all) to 10 (hyper-turbulent environment). You would assume that in the current turbulent environment every participant gives at least a score of 7 or 8. But that's not always the case—I regularly have managers who only give a score of 2 or 3. This confirms what we said earlier: turbulence does not affect all industries equally—some industries are more turbulent than others. This means that in some cases, it's justified to go ahead with your current core strategy or with your growth strategy, without worrying too much about this whole turbulence thing.

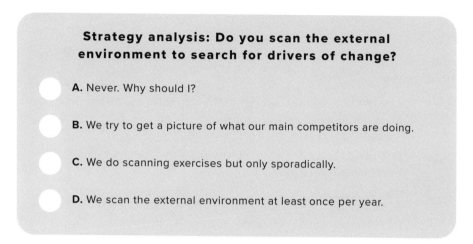

**Strategy analysis: Do you scan the external environment to search for drivers of change?**

**A.** Never. Why should I?

**B.** We try to get a picture of what our main competitors are doing.

**C.** We do scanning exercises but only sporadically.

**D.** We scan the external environment at least once per year.

Do you scan the external environment to search for drivers of change? The more you face a turbulent industry or business environment, the more you should systematically do scanning exercises. The goal of these analyses is not to explain your current performance, but to look into the future and spot directional shifts as soon as possible. This is called corporate foresight (or sensing): it's about detecting and interpreting weak signals in your business environment and imagining what these signals and potential changes could mean for your company. Such a sensing exercise is more of an imaginative than a pure analysis exercise—some people like it, others really hate it. You wouldn't be the first manager to feel very uncomfortable when making a trip into the future. Chapter 2 describes the crucial steps in this corporate foresight process so you can identify those change drivers that might have the highest impact on your future performance. You cannot build a good turbulence strategy if you don't have a good understanding of the fundamental drivers of change of your business.

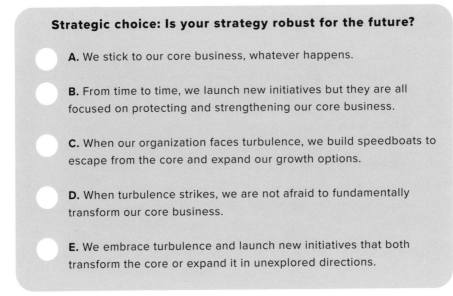

**Strategic choice: Is your strategy robust for the future?**

- **A.** We stick to our core business, whatever happens.

- **B.** From time to time, we launch new initiatives but they are all focused on protecting and strengthening our core business.

- **C.** When our organization faces turbulence, we build speedboats to escape from the core and expand our growth options.

- **D.** When turbulence strikes, we are not afraid to fundamentally transform our core business.

- **E.** We embrace turbulence and launch new initiatives that both transform the core or expand it in unexplored directions.

Strategy is about making choices. Turbulence also forces you to make choices that will help you remain robust for the future. What was your answer to the strategic choice question? Could you point to one answer? If that's the case, you might not be well prepared for the future. Because there's no standard answer for tackling turbulence: your strategic response really depends on the nature of the turbulence.

Chapter 3—which elaborates on this topic and is the core of this book—focuses on two strategy formulation questions: What are the specific choices firms should make when facing turbulence, and when to apply each choice? This chapter presents a new strategy framework for dealing with turbulence and presents four options for fighting disruption or disturbance, based on two dilemmas: Should you transform your core business, or can you stick to it? And do you need to engage in building new businesses, or can you thrive without such expansion initiatives?

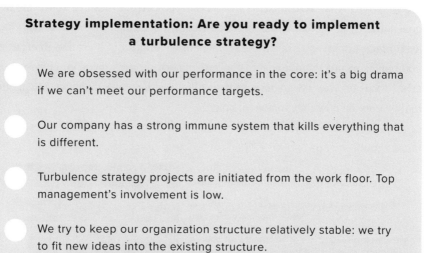

**Strategy implementation: Are you ready to implement a turbulence strategy?**

- We are obsessed with our performance in the core: it's a big drama if we can't meet our performance targets.

- Our company has a strong immune system that kills everything that is different.

- Turbulence strategy projects are initiated from the work floor. Top management's involvement is low.

- We try to keep our organization structure relatively stable: we try to fit new ideas into the existing structure.

- We find it very hard to fit in new employees who have the necessary skills to be ready for the future.

A strategy without implementation is useless. Many publications on turbulence describe how new players have become market leaders with new business models. Examples abound of new innovative offerings that are conquering the market. But all too often, those publications forget to describe how the companies moved from an idea to a successful business. This gives the impression that you just initiate an idea, and some months later, you can start harvesting. Of course, this is not how it works. And if you agreed with most of the statements here above, I'm afraid you will have a tough time implementing your turbulence strategy.

Chapters 4 to 7 explain what is needed to implement each of the four turbulence strategies. The different strategies require you to take a different set of initiatives to be successful, and they all have their own implementation challenges. Each chapter contains several case studies that illustrate the implementation journey in some more detail. You will see that there are some great stories of extraordinary companies and managers out there that can inspire you with examples on how to survive and thrive in turbulent times.

**HOW GOOD ARE YOU TODAY?** In a research project that I've started with my colleagues Geert Letens and Peter De Prins, we are collecting data about change and change effectiveness.[42] At the moment of writing, there were 284 international companies in our database. 8 questions (part of a much more elaborate change scan) focus on how companies deal with turbulence. Let's see how management teams score on how they tackle turbulence.

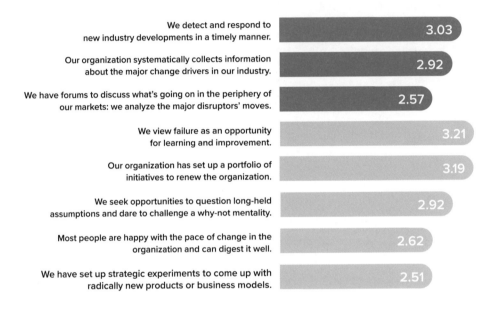

**Figure 3** • How well are companies dealing with turbulence?

The darkblue bars are strategy-analysis items; the lightblue bars deal with strategy-formulation and implementation issues. Scores range from 0 to 5.[43] On 5 of the 8 items, our respondents 'tend to agree' with the statements—they have a score close to or higher than three. But for the other three items, the scores are in the range of 2.5 to 2.6—indicating that these practices are not well developed yet. One could conclude that firms have started implementing some turbulence-strategy initiatives—but they need to do much more to be fully prepared for disruption and disturbance. Hopefully, this book gives you some practical insights and concrete tools to take up the challenge and build and implement more robust and future-proof strategies.

# Turbulence animal farm

When I was reading all those books and articles on disruption and disturbance, one particular observation drew my attention. I noted that there's a lot of reference made to animals. It's striking to see the analogy between the turbulence strategies of companies and the reaction of animals to the tough environments they live in. Some animals face environments that are even more threatening and hostile than the marketplaces in which businesses operate. But they have adapted well and developed a wonderful survival instinct. One study compared the companies' turbulence strategies with the animals' resilience strategies: lions fight back, seagulls take flight and move away from hostile environments, sharks constantly look for opportunities and threats, and bears go into hibernation, conserving energy to survive the tough (winter) times.[44] I'm not sure, however, how many companies will choose this latter strategy.

Other authors describe animals that have been extinct for millions of years or that are featured in fairy tales or fantasy novels. The unicorn is an obvious choice, of course, given the link with successful scaleups of $1 billion. But the dodo, the dinosaur and the phoenix have all returned to great fanfare in some new turbulence books.[45]

I will continue the tradition and provide you with a sneak preview of the animals that appear in this book. You can choose your favorite one. I admit, they are probably not the cutest animals in the animal kingdom, but I'm sure that this book will lead you to start appreciating them because they are truly amazing beings. Then, it's up to you to find out whether this animal also represents the appropriate turbulence strategy for your organization.

Let's start our trip into the wonderful world of strategic turbulence. I hope you will enjoy the ride!

**What's your favorite of the following four animals?**

 ◯ Camel

 ◯ Salmon

 ◯ Chameleon

 ◯ Octopus

STRATEGY IN TURBULENT TIMES

# KEY TAKEAWAYS

- The future isn't what it used to be: the world is changing but that does not apply to every industry.
- Turbulence can be defined and classified in many ways. In this book, I'll make a distinction between disruption and disturbance, two different kinds of turbulence that need to be tackled in different ways.
- Top strategy researchers disagree about whether we live in a more turbulent world today: is it really the end of competitive advantage?
- A turbulence strategy does not replace the traditional strategy frameworks on competitive strategy and growth strategy—it complements them.
- Turbulence should be addressed with a fundamental strategic answer, not some tactical initiatives. A comprehensive strategic answer consists of a proper strategy analysis, specific strategic choices, and strategy implementation. This book provides insights into each of these three topics.

# CHAPTER

# 2

# building corporate
# foresight

---

## Kurt Verweire & Koen Tackx

# Key questions addressed in this chapter

What is corporate foresight? And does it make sense to predict the future in a world full of uncertainty?

How do you build corporate foresight? What are the essential steps in a sensing process? And how does each step work out?

What are the typical biases that come along with a sensing exercise?

Is your organization ready to engage in systematic corporate foresight exercises?

STRATEGY IN TURBULENT TIMES

Managing turbulence requires new strategy recipes and approaches. In the past, managers had sufficient time to analyze the market, the customers, and the competitors, and to choose a strategy and then implement it. Once they established a competitive advantage, they could maintain it for years, even decades. However, a different skill set is required to survive and flourish in today's environment. Rather than being better at something, you increasingly achieve advantage by seeing and responding to changes in the market more quickly. The recent global developments affecting many industries have led many firms to be more attentive and vigilant to potentially surprising future events and trends. Today it's all about seeing sooner and acting faster.[46]

A key practice in the new strategy playbook is building corporate foresight. Corporate foresight is the firm's ability to interpret changes in the business environment and to develop insights into future alternative states that are based on these changes. Researchers also use the word 'sensing' to denote activities that aim at screening, interpreting, and acting upon key drivers of change in a company's business ecosystem. We will use those two terms interchangeably.

In this chapter, we present the crucial steps in the sensing process and describe the challenges and the typical managerial biases associated with looking into an uncertain future. We also provide some recommendations for organizing your foresight activities and a test to assess the foresight capabilities of your company. But we start off by elaborating on what corporate foresight is and what it's not. This is definitely needed because there are too many misconceptions and too many wrong expectations about building foresight.

# What is corporate foresight?

**WHAT'S THE VALUE OF AN ALMOST PERFECT BALL?** Many managers agree that their environment has become more turbulent—more uncertain, more ambiguous, and therefore more unpredictable. Many would pay a fortune to see what the future holds for them. Too many companies have been caught off guard by unexpected events, economic volatility, and disruptive innovations—and they blame themselves for not having predicted these changes.

That's why executives try to build a crystal ball to predict the future. But what are your hopes for your prediction results? Are you happy with a 50 percent success rate? Or should it be 90 percent? This reminds us of a quote by a researcher who served in the British Foreign Office from 1903 to 1950, charged with assessing the probability of occurrence of a military conflict: "Year after year the worriers and fretters would come to me with awful predictions of the outbreak of war. We denied it each time. We were only wrong twice."[47]

The point is that building foresight is not about prediction. In business prediction is an illusion anyway, as is confirmed by Lord John Browne, former CEO of BP: "Giving up the illusion that you can predict the future is a very liberating moment. All you can do is to give yourself the capacity to respond to the only certainty in life—which is uncertainty. The creation of that capability is the purpose of strategy."[48]

Corporate foresight is not about predicting what *will* happen but is about imaging what *could* happen. It's a process that is called 'sensing'—which is about identifying, observing, and interpreting the factors that induce fundamental change and taking appropriate strategic action to improve your company's long-term competitiveness. It is a very different process from the traditional strategy planning exercise, where managers work on concrete cases, supported by precise data, and work out detailed plans to allocate resources efficiently and effectively. It's a big challenge to systematically look ahead into an unknown future and to interpret ambiguous early warning signals. When an event has occurred or a crisis has arisen, things look obvious in hindsight. Then we wonder why we didn't see things coming. The signs are on the table, but it's difficult to connect the dots until the plot has unfolded. You may want to take a look at industry outlook reports for your company of 10 years ago. Or check your own annual report of that period and read the forward-looking section. Was the magnitude of the predicted events correct? Often some changes were largely overestimated, while others were largely underestimated.

A famous example in this respect is the Final Report by the United States Senate '9/11 Commission' that provides a full and complete account of the circumstances surrounding the terrorist attacks in 2001. That report explicitly stated that the 9/11 attacks were a shock, but they should not have come as a surprise. Across the American government, there were failures of imagination, policy, capabilities, and management. The most important failure, however, was the one of imagination. "We do not believe leaders understood the gravity of the threat."[49] If one of the most powerful countries with a well-established intelligence agency suffers from this problem, then it's no surprise that many companies struggle with this issue as well.

**MORE DIFFICULT THAN YOU THINK.** Building corporate foresight an exercise that is more difficult than you would expect. In 2007, the German Federal Armed Forces, better known as the Bundeswehr, wanted to set up a more formal corporate foresight process. In their search for the optimal model, they identified 150 foresight methods. Although many were similar in approach and only differed in names, their conclusion was that corporate foresight is by no means a standardized process.[50] There are many foresight models and sensing approaches to choose from, which makes it difficult for an outsider to choose the right one. So, the first challenge is to build a structured and good sensing process.

But that is not enough. Sensing requires you to look at the business with a fisheye lens.[51] This is a lens with an angle of 180 degrees (or even more), which allows you to see the edges of the view in as sharp a focus as that in the middle. You need such a lens because dangers increasingly come from the periphery of your market— the broader environment outside your focal competitive arena. However, that periphery is difficult to interpret and hard to scan.[52] Looking with a fisheye lens allows you to detect the weak signals of what could become important future trends, events, and shocks. The problem is that when you scan and interpret signals of emerging change, you inevitably have to cope with deep-seated cognitive biases that distort your view of the future. These biases limit the effectiveness of your foresight exercises.[53] We will discuss these biases later in this chapter.

Finally, building corporate foresight also requires discipline to prepare for the unknown. A sensing exercise is not a one-off event but a continuous activity. Organizations need to become vigilant and need to build a dedicated management system to develop corporate foresight capabilities. But most organizations find it hard to invest sufficient time and resources in this activity. In the final section of the chapter, we illustrate what is needed to build the organizational capabilities to become vigilant.

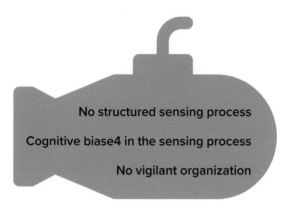

No structured sensing process

Cognitive biase4 in the sensing process

No vigilant organization

**Figure 4 ·** The challenges of corporate foresight

**DOES IT MAKE SENSE TO SENSE?** But before embarking on these various topics, it's worth asking the following questions: Does it pay off to invest in building corporate foresight activities? Given the fact this is such a difficult journey, is it worth making all these efforts?

Clearly, sensing is hot these days. It is an emerging field yet with a rich tradition that even goes back to the 1950s and the popularity has increased significantly.[54] There is no doubt that corporate foresight allows firms to see sooner and be more open to new developments and changes. And case studies show that organizations that embraced sensing have been able to take appropriate action in turbulent times. But despite the popularity of foresight activities in practice, there is a lack of longitudinal evidence that suggests that investing in foresight helps improving firm performance.[55] We know of one study by René Rohrbeck and Menes Etingue Kum, who investigated to what extent future preparedness in 2008 impacted firm performance in 2015.[56] Their results revealed that future-prepared firms—firms that have built corporate foresight practices in relation to the uncertainty in the industry—perform better than deficient firms—i.e. they are more profitable and their market capitalization has grown stronger.

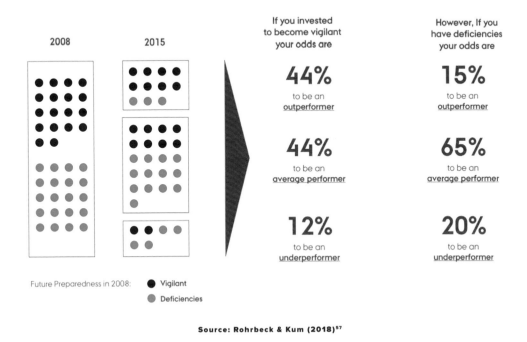

Figure 5 • Benefits from a high future preparedness

# Steps in the sensing process

In this section, we present a model that incorporates the essentials of sensing and foresight and that is practically useful. We've seen much more complicated and detailed approaches which are typically used by the more strategically experienced firms—still a minority in the business world. We've also seen that companies apply only part of the proposed sensing process. But to achieve the best results you need to address all four steps of the sensing process.

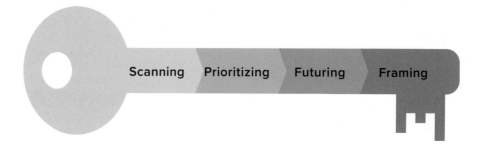

**Figure 6** • Key steps in the sensing process

**STEP 1:** Scanning—Identify change drivers that might affect future performance

How businesses operate today is often significantly different from how they operated some years ago. Some of these changes have gone unnoticed and were absorbed without any problem. Others were far more challenging and required fundamental changes in the company. And it's hthese latter that we remember, especially the ones that came as a real surprise.

The first step of a sensing exercise is to simply list all the uncertainties that you are noticing *around your company* and that may have an impact on your business— risks, trends, events, and whatever changes that might affect your company in the next 3, 5 or 10 years. The choice of the time frame depends on your industry. For example, technology firms typically use shorter time frames than energy companies. Don't just go after the change drivers that have a huge and immediate impact in the near future but also incorporate 'weak signals' in your scanning analysis. A weak signal is the first indicator of a change or an emerging issue that could become significant in the future. Typically, people tend to disagree about a weak signal's nature, timing, and impact. But from the moment you believe there is a chance that this signal could have a significant impact on your company's performance—positive or negative—it's good to include it in the analysis.

**WHERE TO LOOK FOR WEAK SIGNALS OF CHANGE?** Managers should reflect upon uncertainties in both the industry and the broader business environment. The broader business environment—also called the macro environment—consists of all the external influences that affect a company's strategy and performance.[58] Strategists generally look at six major macro influences: political, economic, social, technological, ecological, and legal factors—generally captured in the PESTEL acronym. The industry environment consists of your major buyers and suppliers, your competitors, potential new entrants in your market and the substitutes. The smart strategist will probably have recognized Michael Porter's five forces model, a model that is typically used to assess industry attractiveness.

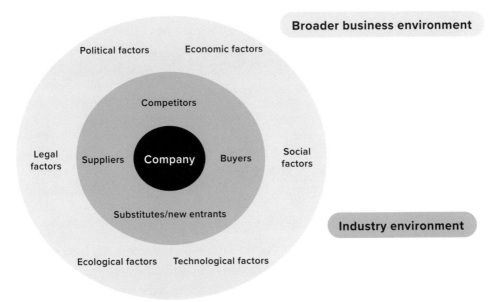

**Figure 7** • Where to look for uncertainties?

When managers start thinking about possible change drivers in both the broader business and the industry environment, they may come up with a much larger list than originally anticipated. For example, when PepsiCo did a sensing exercise to help fuel its strategic innovation pipeline, their scanning analysis revealed no less than 300 potential change drivers. This broad list was reduced to a list of 40 trends and uncertainties.[59] In our experience, companies identify between 10 and 30 change drivers. When listing the major key factors or drivers of change, explain why you include this particular change driver in the list. Furthermore, try to provide some evidence as to why this driver needs further management attention.

Some organizations spend a lot of time on this phase and run extensive interviews with managers from within the company and with external specialists, such as consultants, academics, government officials and various stakeholder groups. You can also do this exercise in a relatively short period of time by asking the participants to list their major uncertainties in a document. Obviously, you'll only cover the most easily and significant trends and uncertainties. Here, it's important that you include the items that only one or a few people mention in the list.

Companies with scouting teams whose responsibility is to screen and prepare may adopt a more formalized approach. Those teams do a lot of preparatory work, for example by doing extensive desk research on some key factors. Over time, you get more experienced when doing those exercises. Then you will also see how much time is needed to do a proper screening of the change drivers and check if you need more time to investigate them in more detail.

The more advanced firms take a systematic approach and build on previous exercises. Rather than doing one-off screening analyses, they build on the knowledge of the past and adapt the list of change drivers and issues. Some issues become clearer and less ambiguous, others are dropped off the list, and new ones are added.

**WHOM TO INVOLVE IN THIS EXERCISE?** It is important that senior executives are included in this exercise to ensure their views are captured and that they buy into the process. But in general, it is not always the highest-ranked manager who has the clearest view on uncertainties. Therefore, it makes sense to involve a broader group of employees from different departments, with different backgrounds. You can assign different teams to surface weak signals in various areas—for example, you can establish a technology team, a competitor team, and a customer team. The more diverse the team, the better. If you use a fixed scouting group, it's common to use a rotation system to ensure that there is enough fresh blood and innovative perspective in the scanning team. Cisco, the multinational technology conglomerate, uses an international scouting network to identify new technologies or technological trends. This international scouting network also invites experts from outside the organization to prevent biases from purely internal views.[60] This is a common and best practice: it's good to build strong external networks of experts, academics, and other specialists.

## STEP 2: Prioritizing—Focus your attention on the change drivers that matter

After you've compiled a list of uncertainties and potential strategic issues, the next step is to evaluate and sort them by level of uncertainty and the potential impact on the organization's performance. An organization can never address all emerging changes. Therefore, some prioritization is needed: paying attention to everything is equivalent to paying attention to nothing.

**WHAT IS 'HIGH UNCERTAINTY' AND 'HIGH IMPACT'?** An issue scores high on uncertainty if you don't know what will happen, when it will happen, and how it will affect your company' performance. High uncertainty items are often issues on which there is a lot of debate inside your company—often emotional. If one of your colleagues thinks something important may happen and another one thinks this is 'crazy,' then you have nailed a highly uncertain item. On the other hand, if the nature of the event or trend is clear and the impact can be estimated well, then uncertainty is low.

What is high impact and low impact can be assessed qualitatively, but you can also assign numerical values. For example, high impact could be 10 or 20 percent of your profits of the last three years. Or you can specify financial numbers: for example, high impact is more than 5 million EUR profit impact, low impact is less than 1 million, and then medium impact is 3 million EUR. Of course, these figures need to be finetuned to your particular situation.

**WHICH ITEMS SHOULD YOU PRIORITIZE?** The issues with high uncertainty and high impact are the 'key issues' or 'critical uncertainties' that need further examination. They deserve the highest priority in the foresight exercise. To use the full number of identified issues in the foresight process would lead to an overly complex and messy process.

Issues with a high impact and low uncertainty are 'givens.' You understand the nature of the change and the impact of the issue. Here the motto is: Just do it. Create a project team to address the issue, allocate resources, include the change in your budgets and plans, and follow up. Your company should take immediate action to maximize the positive or minimize the negative impact.[61]

The items that are 'out of scope' are issues with low impact and should be further monitored and examined. At this stage you don't need to devote further attention to them.

Figure 8 presents an Impact-Uncertainty Matrix of an energy company that identified 14 drivers of change. Five of those drivers emerged as key issues.

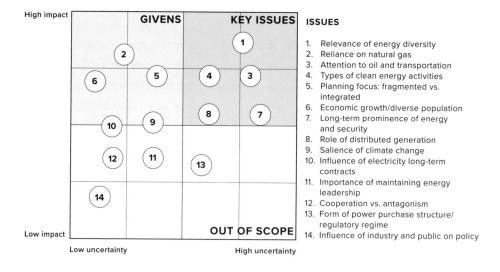

Source: Rhydderch (2017)[62]

**Figure 8** • Impact-Uncertainty Matrix at an Energy Company

Important to note is that the exercise requires continuous update not to lose relevancy. So did the German Federal Armed Forces create a Risk Assessment and Horizon Scanning tool in which participants were allowed to add or remove issues and to add descriptions and comments continuously. At regular time intervals, participants of the group were asked to rank the issues again. Some out-of-scope-issues became key issues, while key issues became givens or out-of-scope items. The result is a highly dynamic and continuous process where new information and insights are added to existing data and information, which increases the productivity of the sensing exercise significantly.[63]

## STEP 3: Futuring—Explore plausible futures

In the Futuring phase, the goal is to build a couple of plausible scenarios. Academics suggest not building more than 4 or 5 scenarios at the same time. The starting point is the Impact-Uncertainty matrix that was introduced in Step 2 but the focus now turns to the 'key issues.'

**FROM KEY ISSUES TO SCOPING OUTCOMES.** It's possible to examine each of those key drivers in great detail and to imagine two scoping outcomes per key driver. If you would have identified 10 key issues, you would need to conduct 10 analyses—which is a lot. In reality, most companies narrow their focus and restrict themselves to the two most fundamental key issues from the analysis—also called the 'critical uncertainties.' The goal is to build a 2-by-2 matrix that generates 4 different scenarios. Therefore, you choose the 2 key issues that have the highest impact on the company's future performance. In our example, that would be issue#1 and issue#3. If the 2 issues are strongly correlated to each other, then it's better to choose another key issue.

After you've identified the two most important key issues, you define two extreme scoping outcomes for each critical uncertainty. These outcomes are called 'scoping outcomes.' Recall that sensing is about imagining what could be possible, not what is likely to be possible. Therefore, our recommendation is to think wild: develop challenging yet plausible outcomes for both key issues. For example, if economic growth is a key issue for you, you may build a scenario where the economic growth is low or even negative, and another one where growth is high. We recommend specifying outcomes in quantitative terms. If that is not possible, you can use qualitative criteria, such as 'low' vs. 'high', 'weak' vs. 'strong', or any other set of opposing adjectives.

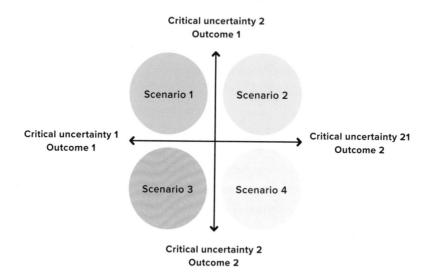

**Critical uncertainty 2**
**Outcome 1**

Scenario 1    Scenario 2

**Critical uncertainty 1**     **Critical uncertainty 21**
**Outcome 1**                **Outcome 2**

Scenario 3    Scenario 4

**Critical uncertainty 2**
**Outcome 2**

**Figure 9** • 2-by-2 scenario matrix

**BUILDING SCENARIOS.** Now, you're ready to start building your scenarios. It's common practice to first identify some salient characteristics of each scenario and come up with three to five bullet points or sticky notes per scenario.

Then you can build the narratives for each scenario. Ideally, divide into groups so that each group can work on one scenario. Describe how the critical uncertainties will materialize in each scenario. Don't restrict yourself to outcomes of the two key issues, but integrate all the other issues that popped up from the scanning and prioritization exercise and combine them in a consistent and possible future. Here are some questions that help you build your narratives:
- What is this future all about?
- How do the different uncertainties interact?
- How did you get there? What are critical events for each scenario that lead to the outcomes?

- How do various stakeholders act in this particular scenario?
- What are the outcomes of this scenario: what is the impact on key stake-holders? What will happen with customers, suppliers, competitors, and partners?
- Are the outcomes in each scenario supported by the evolution of current trends?
- And, for each scenario, what variables might serve as good indicators of the direction of change?

Our Vlerick Energy Center conducted a scenario thinking exercise with executives from the European energy industry. The objective was to explore who would lead the energy market in 2030. The work group identified two major key issues: the level of consumer involvement in energy choices and the decentralization of the energy resources, which resulted in the four scenarios presented in Figure 10. You can find a description of two scenarios in Figure 11.

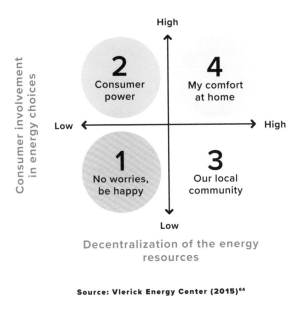

Source: Vlerick Energy Center (2015)[64]

**Figure 10** · Who will lead the energy market in 2030?

## SCENARIO 2: HIGH INVOLVEMENT, LOW DECENTRALISATION

# CONSUMER POWER

**This scenario imagines that the majority of consumers would continue to receive their electricity from a central national or international producer, and have very little inclination or reason to get more involved or produce electricity by themselves.**

Higher consumer involvement has occurred, however, because European energy policymakers finally saw their 'open' market vision come true and there are now many more suppliers available in the market, thereby keeping prices competitive and supply stable.

### OUTCOME

The DSO landscape is likely to remain stable, while the TSOs will have released part of their monopoly. Large-scale projects have been tendered for both on- and offshore, and this has consolidated the TSO market into regional clusters and has given opportunities for the strongest European players to get involved in other markets than their home turf while remaining on the same continent. Indeed, with TSOs now increasingly regulated, there are simply some projects they'd prefer not to get involved in—cross-border connections for example. This has led to other private companies stepping in to the breach, spurring competition.

## SCENARIO 3: LOW INVOLVEMENT, HIGH DECENTRALISATION

# OUR LOCAL COMMUNITY

**Ironically, this future scenario takes us back to a time when the electricity business first started, with many industrial and commercial customers producing their own electricity and heat.**

Not only has it been driven by the need for efficiency and cost savings, it's been growing out of necessity too, as energy shortages on a national level have become more or a regular issue.

### OUTCOME

Many of the latest 'power' innovations have been imported from outside Europe as the developing, once energy-poor countries, have 'leapfrogged' their way to a lower-carbon economy without passing through a phase of high-energy use, as North America, Europe and Japan did in the past.
The result is that DSOs have become the core providers of energy services, while TSOs continue to deliver back-up power for emergencies and contingencies. New players now take on a leading role, particularly as they have been able to import innovative solutions from around the world in a kind of reverse Innovation Revolution, as when the mobile money solution was imported from less developed countries 15 years ago.

Source: Vlerick Energy Center (2015)

**Figure 11** • Descriptions of 2 scenarios on the future energy market

Some companies take a lot of time to build and develop these scenarios. Corporate strategy departments often take the lead in such a scenario development process, script out the scenarios and even make video footage of each new future. If you want a nice example, check out Shell's most recent *Energy Transformation Scenarios*.[65] If you have less time and resources, you can develop the scenarios with the team members of the sensing exercise.

Once again, it's important to stress that building scenarios is an exercise in imagination, so there's not much guidance on how to proceed. There are just a few constraints. The first one is that scenarios should be plausible: the developments that are presented must at least be regarded as possible developments. Possible doesn't mean probable or desirable. It's not a problem to create a doom scenario.

A second element is that scenarios should be internally consistent. For example, if you have identified a scenario with high economic growth, then you should also expect rather low degrees of unemployment. Plausibility and consistency lead to credible scenarios.

Furthermore, it's great if scenarios are comprehensible and traceable: can you check whether a scenario unfolds or not? This means that scenarios must be detailed enough to be comprehensible without becoming overly complex.[66]

A final suggestion is to make scenarios memorable and vivid. It's good to give a name to your scenario. Use catchy titles that refer to film scripts or songs, for example, and avoid technical jargon. Here is what the work group at the Vlerick Energy Center did to make the narrative appealing: they created a newspaper article, dated 30 September 2030.

# THE DAILY NEWS

Monday 30 September 2030

## Europe lives through another weekend of power cuts

Blackouts causing a major rethink of the world's electricity supply market

With blackouts and the threat thereof now a regular occurrence, consumers – both private and industrial – are taking energy production into their own hands. Ever since the phase-out of nuclear power plants in the 2020s and the unresolved lack of regulatory certainty, capital markets have declined to invest in power generation technologies, resulting in significant under-capacity issues.

From a consumer's perspective, this has led to much lower trust in the legacy systems and so naturally there has been a rise in the number of microgrids and local generation, diversifying security of supply very much from region to region. This has been good news for local economic policy, as guaranteed energy – both generation and consumption – has gone hand-in-hand with rising local employment.

This trend has just been following the general trend in society over the last 15 years with decentralisation a major movement in many industries: for example much more food is now produced locally than in the past and increasing shares of our manufacturing are done locally using 3-D printers.

Unsurprisingly, with national producers (and the EU) unable to respond to the rising demand, local governments and large consumers have taken over the responsibility.

The result has been many more smart cities and community initiatives supported by publicly owned multi-utility network companies.

The resulting market means that every town and region now has different energy prices depending on the resources locally available. And this is now not just true for energy but for all local services (gas, telecom, water and waste collection for example) as in many instances they are bundled into one central but local service, run by the city or local government.

Lack of investment in central power plants has boosted new local power generation rates to new highs.

**Source: Vlerick Energy Center (2015)**

**Figure 12** • Making scenarios memorable

The end product of the Futuring step is several finished scenarios that present a vivid picture of how the competitive world could look like. Each scenario is a narrative exploration of an alternative future state. You can decide to present the scenarios to managers and employees in your organization and ask for their reactions. The goal is to create acceptance that the future could be very different from the current reality and that you might need to change your perceptions and assumptions drastically.

It's good to keep the scenarios general: you should not focus on your own company. This is what you'll do in the next step.

### STEP 4: Framing—Examine implications and brainstorm on potential reactions

In the final step, you examine the implications of each scenario for your business and brainstorm about possible actions. We propose to do that in two steps.

**EXAMINE THE IMPLICATIONS.** The first step of the framing process is to look for the implications of each scenario on your business and performance. If your performance is under serious threat, you may need to change your future strategy. But opportunities may arise too. So how do you look at the changes in the environment? What does the rise of veganism mean for your diary business unit? And how should business schools react to the rise of massive online open courses (MOOCs)? In framing, it's important to take a broad view before immediately jumping to conclusions.

**Figure 13** • Framing is opening up

Think about implications as both threats and opportunities. Many people see turbulence as an attack that must be met through defensive measures. But turbulence can open up new avenues for growth—not only for startups and disruptors but for established companies as well.

In addition, you can examine the implications of each scenario by focusing on your existing business. However, a new future can steer your organization into new ventures that are outside of your current core.

We use the framing template presented in Figure 14 to get a full list of potential implications per scenario. Open up and adopt an as wide as possible view on the implications of each scenario. This template investigates threats and opportunities inside and outside the core. It's irrelevant to look for threats outside the core.

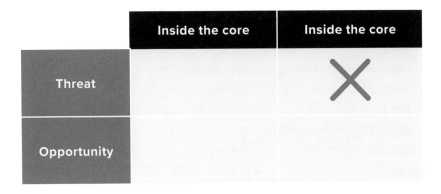

**Figure 14** • Framing template

When you examine the implications of a scenario, you can fill out the threat box by asking the following questions:

- Does the scenario create significant operational issues—e.g., in your operations or in your supply chain? Which issues do you expect?
- Do these operational issues increase your cost base significantly? Where and how?
- Or do they make your capabilities obsolete? Which ones?
- Will you experience a significant loss in revenues in the scenario? In what business lines?
- Which business lines have profitability issues?
- Which customer segments could we lose?

But it's important to consider new opportunities too, first in your core:

- Does the scenario create opportunities to add extra business lines to your product portfolio? Which ones?
- Can you address new customer segments in the changing environment? Will new customers be attracted by your products and services? Which ones?
- Which competencies can you develop to build new and better ways to serve your existing customers?

Finally, check whether a scenario holds promise to build a new business unit:

- Do the scenarios open up new markets for your company? Which ones?
- Which competencies are needed to target those new markets?

**DEFINE REACTIONS.** After you've identified threats and opportunities for each scenario, it's time to come up with a list of reactions. What actions could help neutralize the threats and leverage the opportunities? It's best to do this exercise per scenario and build a set of potential strategic responses. You can use the same framing template, as presented in Figure 14, but this time filled with concrete strategic and tactical actions. Strategic actions include rethinking your value proposition, targeting a new customer segment, adding a new product line, building a new business unit. Tactical actions—which take place at the operational level—marketing, sales, operations, logistics—could be setting up new marketing campaigns, changing your supply chain, or adjusting your pricing strategy.

As a final exercise, you can then take a step back and contemplate all of the different scenarios you've worked on. It's a useful exercise to identify the three or five most important strategic responses that pop up, irrespective of what scenario unfolds.

Note: this is a brainstorm exercise. Ultimately, the actions that will be adopted will be decided in the strategizing phase. We'll discuss this in chapter 3.

## Biases in the sensing process

In the previous section, We presented a four-step sensing process that helps identify the major sources of turbulence and we showed how to build scenarios around the critical uncertainties and key drivers of change. Such an exercise prepares you for potentially surprising future events. However, it's important to be aware of several traps and biases that inevitably sneak into the sensing process and that limit the effectiveness of your corporate foresight activities.[67]

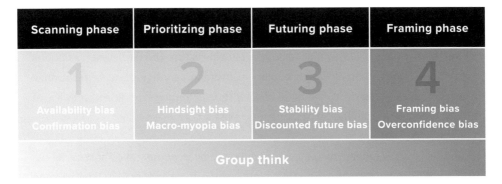

| Scanning phase | Prioritizing phase | Futuring phase | Framing phase |
|---|---|---|---|
| 1 | 2 | 3 | 4 |
| Availability bias<br>Confirmation bias | Hindsight bias<br>Macro-myopia bias | Stability bias<br>Discounted future bias | Framing bias<br>Overconfidence bias |
| Group think | | | |

**Figure 15** • Biases and traps in the sensing process

**TRAPS IN THE SCANNING PHASE.** In the Scanning phase you try to detect patterns and trends in the broader business environment that can point to change, discontinuities, or disruptions that may affect your business profoundly.[68] This analysis results in a list of uncertainties and change drivers. This process, however, is subject to biases. The most important one is the availability bias. There is evidence that experts and managers tend to compose this list based on trends actively discussed in the media and on social networks. The more some items have occurred in the past, the more likely they will be in your list.[69]

A second bias is the confirmation bias: this means that you pay more attention to the signals that confirm what you already believe while you tend to ignore the other ones. All this results in judgments that depend on the content of your memories and the fit with your mental maps rather than on objective data. This is not particularly helpful if you want to create a rich and open view of *all* drivers of change, not just the most popular ones.

One way to tackle this bias is to involve a broad set of people inside and outside the firm and to encourage everyone to have an open mind. Don't impose limitations on the number of potential change drivers. The filtering will be done in the next step.

**TRAPS IN THE PRIORITIZING STAGE.** It is one thing to identify emerging changes—you also need to interpret them. In the Prioritizing phase, you assess the uncertainty of the key factors and their potential impact on your organization's performance. This interpretation also has its challenges: how you assign scores on 'level of uncertainty' and 'impact' is subject to biases too. The hindsight bias points to the underestimation of the probability of events that we have never personally experienced and the overestimation of the predetermination and predictability of trends and events that have occurred in the past.

The other bias is macro myopia: the tendency to overestimate the short-term impact of a new change and to underestimate its long-term impact. Bill Gates warned us for the macro myopia bias: "Don't overestimate what will happen in the next two years, and underestimate what will in the next ten years."

One way to deal with these traps is to bring in as much quantitative data as you can and objectivity to come up with more precise assessments. If you don't have extensive means, ask people why they have come up with a particular change driver and ask for some evidence of the importance of the trend. Take some time to discuss in groups the scoring of each change driver on the Impact-Uncertainty Matrix (see Figure 8).

**TRAPS IN THE FUTURING STAGE.** The Futuring phase is where you build scenarios with possible futures. The challenge here is to overcome a natural tendency to assume that the future will look a lot like the past.[70] This is called the stability bias and is somewhat related to another bias: the discounted future bias. We all have a tendency to discount the future in favor of today. When building future scenarios, participants typically tend to feel more comfortable with building shorter-term rather than longer-term scenarios. This discounting the future leads not only to making inaccurate estimates of when events might occur, but also to using a narrower time horizon and the devaluation of long-term forecasts.[71] This challenge is difficult to tackle—involving 'creative' thinkers from outside the management might help, as well as pushing the scenarios to more extreme outcomes. This can be enhanced by making different people responsible for different scenarios.

**TRAPS IN THE FRAMING STAGE.** In the Framing stage, you examine the implications of each scenario on your business strategy and performance. In this last phase, it's good to be aware of the framing bias, which says that managers strive to keep what they have achieved. That's why they focus more on the threats than on the opportunities. There are advantages to emphasize threats: this leads to bigger commitment and more resource spend. Recall that step number one in any change book is to 'create a sense of urgency' by highlighting the bad news. But seeing a phenomenon as a threat also makes you retreat into the trenches rather than embrace the change. Therefore, it's good to not only have a list to tackle the threats but to also come up with a list of actions to grab the opportunities.[72]

Another challenge is the overconfidence bias which makes managers overly optimistic about planning and launching the actions and underestimate the chances of failures. Managers are sometimes inclined to choose the scenarios they deem most likely and focus their action list solely on them. Check out that you have created action plans for all scenarios, not only for what you consider the most likely one.

**GROUPTHINK.** During the whole sensing process, it's important to pay attention to the impact of groupthink. Groupthink describes a phenomenon of self-censoring diverging opinions when a group is focusing on getting consensus.[73] Groupthink can be dangerous. In the early stages, it can lead to too much focus on particular key drivers and scoping outcomes. But it can also play out in the scenario building phase when people with initially opposing ideas about the future discuss possible scenarios in an all-too-harmonious way. The danger is that groupthink can result in more extreme decisions because of one-sided arguments. Of course, we are not suggesting that every scenario exercise should result in ferocious fights in which every member tries to impose his or her ideas on the other team members. But finding a balance between looking for contrast and opposites and ensuring a constructive process is sometimes quite challenging, yet crucial when doing corporate foresight exercises. Experienced facilitators can be of great help here.[74]

# Building a vigilant organization

Building corporate foresight should be a continuous activity, not a one-time event. In turbulent times, you can gain an edge only when you routinely watch for, evaluate, and respond to weak signals from outside the comfort zone of the traditional business environment. This requires that you turn your company into a vigilant organization. Just like the city of New York—which never sleeps— such an organization is always awake and ready to move. But becoming a vigilant organization is a challenging job that goes beyond building a well-structured sensing process. Companies like Shell, BBC, and Siemens have put a whole management system in place to support their foresight activities. I've identified five building blocks of such a foresight management system, which are presented in Figure 16.

**Figure 16** · The five building blocks of a foresight management system

---

STRATEGY IN TURBULENT TIMES

**STRUCTURED SENSING PROCESS.** Vigilant organizations have put a well-structured, continuous sensing and foresight process in place. This sensing process is driven by the top management team's desire to have good continuous input for regular strategy discussions about the longer term. Otherwise, it will probably not engage in such a foresight exercise.

There are an increasing number of companies building strategic radars to identify change drivers and potential discontinuities. While such a scanning and prioritizing phase may start broad, it's quite common to evaluate and dig deeper into some of these forces and uncertainties to better understand what is really going.[75] In addition, vigilant firms do not just track those uncertainties but build narratives to describe what the future could look like. This puts changes in the environment into a larger perspective and forces managers to consider multiple plausible futures and check the potential impact on the organization's strategy.

In vigilant firms, these sensing exercises are not autonomous initiatives of some individuals with an interest in corporate foresight. The outcomes of the foresight exercises are integrated in strategic reports and discussions in the strategic planning process. Some organizations use the sensing insights to experiment with new initiatives to learn about new markets via accelerator and venturing programs.

In summary, the core of a vigilant company is a sensing process that complements the traditional strategic planning process. Those companies devote significant resources to it.

**FORMAL ORGANIZATION STRUCTURE.** This foresight process is embedded in a formal organization structure. It is important to set up a dedicated unit responsible for the coordination of the sensing activities. This unit may have links with the Strategy, R&D, or Marketing Department through formal meetings or dedicated task forces. Only with the establishment of a formal organization will people be 'forced' to do those foresight activities—an activity that will otherwise be postponed indefinitely.

It's a good idea to assign the scanning task to managers and employees from different functional backgrounds. And to involve people from different organizational levels who don't have to conform to authority. Those employees are more likely to identify challenging signals in the environment and might come up with fresher ideas because they are less constrained by the organization's culture and hierarchy.[76]

Another building block of a formal structure is the cultivation of an external network, composed of industry or technological experts, consultants, or any other gatekeepers who can inform your company about new trends, developments, and drivers of change. An external network favors a more unbiased outside-in view; sometimes it takes a fresh pair of eyes to see things in a different perspective.

**OPEN AND EXPERIMENTAL CULTURE.** A formal organization structure should be complemented by an open culture. And that open culture in turn is created by a vigilant leadership team that encourages a broad focus that goes beyond the core market. Only when the top team stresses the importance of vigilance will the rest of the organization be mobilized to pay attention to exotic business models, crazy competitors, and remote or emerging markets.[77] Leaders should put sensing and foresight activities on the company calendar and practice them publicly.

Vigilant companies stimulate curiosity and openness, a trait often not present in hierarchical organizations characterized by political games among managers. They establish a culture that is respectful of ideas outside the dominant logic and mainstream concerns of the company. They try to 'manipulate people into being open-minded' and get employees enthusiastic about company-wide challenges that put the firm on new, unexplored tracks. Information sharing across borders is common and stimulated, and employees are exposed to entrepreneurs and people with different worldviews. This challenges the workforce to think out-of-the-box. Employees are continuously challenged with inspiring cases and best practices. Creating such a culture of openness and experimentation requires new stories and conversations that celebrate employees who venture out, collect data about new trends and developments, and map the new reality that exists.[78]

**HIGH-QUALITY EXPERTS.** Leaders play a crucial role in making a company more vigilant. But vigilance should not be limited to the leadership team. It's equally important to incorporate sensing into human resources practices.

Firms that want to thrive in turbulent times should invest significantly in foresight training to create awareness and to build sensing skills with as many employees as possible. It's good to train people in the typical scanning and futuring methodology and help them to develop peripheral vision.

HR practices also include selection. Hiring for vigilance means looking for individuals with a wide network and ability to reach out to many different stakeholders, who can listen well and see patterns in complex data. Hire people who are open to new ideas and who are not afraid to experiment.[79] Go after employees who are curious, open-minded, and passionate, and have a deep and broad knowledge. And don't forget to put incentives in place to reward scanning for change. It's not always the highest-ranked manager who has the most developed foresight skills.

**FORESIGHT DATA SYSTEM.** The last component of a vigilant company's foresight management system is a powerful knowledge and data system, which is probably one of the most challenging components to manage. A sensing exercise involves collecting a lot of data about events and potential drivers of change. If you make this a recurrent process, it's more effective if you can work on data you've collected in the past. So, it's essential to reflect on the quality of your competitive intelligence systems and your customer databases. To what extent do they allow you to identify and reflect on new phenomena and unusual observations? And to what extent have your employees found their way to those databases? Or do they remain a hidden secret in your company?

Table 2 provides you with a checklist to assess your foresight and vigilance capabilities.

| STRUCTURED SENSING PROCESS | STRONGLY DISAGREE | NEITHER AGREE NOR DISAGREE | STRONGLY AGREE |
|---|---|---|---|
| 1. In our strategy discussions, we regularly discuss what could happen in the longer term (> 3 years). | 1 ○○○○○ | | 5 |
| 2. The organization continuously scans for trends and changes in the broader business environment (i.e., outside our industry). | 1 ○○○○○ | | 5 |
| 3. Our organization regularly uses scenario thinking to guide our strategy process. | 1 ○○○○○ | | 5 |
| 4. The management team uses the outcomes of the foresight exercises in our strategic discussions and/or planning process. | 1 ○○○○○ | | 5 |

| FORMAL ORGANIZATION STRUCTURE | STRONGLY DISAGREE | NEITHER AGREE NOR DISAGREE | STRONGLY AGREE |
|---|---|---|---|
| 1. In our organization, there is a dedicated team focusing on corporate foresight which has the resources and mandate to coordinate long-term sensing activities. | 1 ○○○○○ | | 5 |
| 2. Our organization assigns scanning and prioritization tasks to managers and employees from different functional backgrounds. | 1 ○○○○○ | | 5 |
| 3. Via corporate foresight platforms or dedicated taskforces, our organization involves people from different levels of the organization in the scanning process. | 1 ○○○○○ | | 5 |
| 4. Leaders in our organization encourage the construction and maintenance of a network of external partners, including experts, consultants, and other gatekeepers who provide input on trends and changes in the business environment. | 1 ○○○○○ | | 5 |

| OPEN AND EXPERIMENTAL CULTURE | STRONGLY DISAGREE | NEITHER AGREE NOR DISAGREE | STRONGLY AGREE |
|---|---|---|---|
| 1. Leaders in our organization recognize the importance of the foresight activities and are strongly involve themselves. | 1 ○○○○○ | | 5 |
| 2. In our company, information is shared freely across functions and hierarchical levels. | 1 ○○○○○ | | 5 |
| 3. In our company, we cultivate an environment that is open to new ideas and worldviews. | 1 ○○○○○ | | 5 |
| 4. In our organization, we regularly share stories and conversations that celebrate employees who venture out, collect data, and map the new reality that exists. | 1 ○○○○○ | | 5 |

| HIGH-QUALITY EXPERTS | STRONGLY DISAGREE | NEITHER AGREE NOR DISAGREE | STRONGLY AGREE |
|---|---|---|---|
| 1. People involved in foresight and sensing have a broad knowledge reaching beyond their own domain. | 1 ○ ○ ○ ○ ○ | | 5 |
| 2. When hiring, we look for people who are curious, open-minded and passionate, and have a strong external/internal network. | 1 ○ ○ ○ ○ ○ | | 5 |
| 3. The organization invests significantly in foresight training to generate awareness and skills among as many employees as possible. | 1 ○ ○ ○ ○ ○ | | 5 |
| 4. We have incentives from senior management in place to encourage and reward a wider vision. | 1 ○ ○ ○ ○ ○ | | 5 |

| FORESIGHT DATA SYSTEM | STRONGLY DISAGREE | NEITHER AGREE NOR DISAGREE | STRONGLY AGREE |
|---|---|---|---|
| 1. The quality of data about events and trends at the periphery is excellent: there is a broad and timely coverage. | 1 ○ ○ ○ ○ ○ | | 5 |
| 2. We have employees whose role is to document, update, and manage the observations about environmental changes. | 1 ○ ○ ○ ○ ○ | | 5 |
| 3. There is a proactive communication throughout the organization about events and trends and this information is easily available to many. | 1 ○ ○ ○ ○ ○ | | 5 |
| 4. There is a formal data system where foresight information is stored and can be consulted. | 1 ○ ○ ○ ○ ○ | | 5 |

**Table 2** · Is your organization ready for corporate foresight?

Calculate your scores per building block and check whether or not you are ready to start sensing and foresight activities. Scores range from 4 to 20.

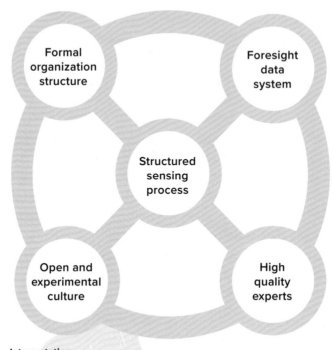

| Scores | Interpretation |
|--------|----------------|
| 4 - 7 | Problematic – Hardly any foresight at all |
| 8 - 11 | Weak – Improvement needed |
| 12 - 15 | Good – On track |
| 16 - 20 | Strong – Vigilant organization |

**Figure 17** • Is your organization vigilant?

# KEY
# TAKEAWAYS

- A key element in strategizing for turbulence is building corporate foresight. This is the capability to interpret changes in the business environment and to develop insights into future alternative states that are based on these changes.
- Corporate foresight is not about predicting what will happen but about imaging what could happen. And this is more complex than you think.
- Building corporate foresight can only occur if you have a good and well-structured sensing process in place. The sensing process consists of 4 steps.
- The first step is Scanning, which is about identifying uncertainties and drivers of change that might affect your future performance.
- After you've made up your list of uncertainties, you need to focus attention on the key issues, those change drivers that are highly uncertain and very impactful. That is the Prioritizing phase.
- In the Futuring phase, you build scenarios based on the 2 most impactful key issues—which are called the critical uncertainties.
- In step 4, you examine the implications of each scenario on the company, and you identify appropriate (re)actions.
- In this sensing process, it's important to be aware of some cognitive biases and traps that are potentially present in each step.
- Finally, vigilant firms build an entire management system around this sensing process. This management system consists of a formal organization structure, an open and experimental culture, high-quality experts in the entire organization, and a good and accessible foresight data system.

# CHAPTER

# 3

## strategizing in
## turbulent times

—

Kurt Verweire, Koen Tackx &
Walter Van Dyck

# Key questions addressed in this chapter

How can you react to the various sources of turbulence?

Is it better to play offense or defense when fighting turbulence?

What do camels, salmon, chameleons and octopuses have to do with turbulence strategies?

How important is business model innovation as a turbulence strategy? And what do we mean with business model innovation?

What are the four turbulence strategies? Which strategy should you apply, and when?

In the previous chapter, we described the sensing process in greater detail. By now, you have decided on the key issues to address, and you've explored how these change drivers and uncertainties could affect your business. Turbulence brings threats and opportunities that might require actions inside and outside your core. The next question is how to formulate appropriate responses to the turbulence. This is the strategizing phase where we make clear strategic choices that will impact your future performance.

In this chapter, we present four potential strategic responses to turbulence. We outline the key dimensions of this turbulence strategy model and then continue to explore the four strategies in greater detail. We finish this chapter by outlining when to use each strategy.

# A shaving powerhouse is challenged

On 6 March 2012, Michael Dubin, CEO of Dollar Shave Club, uploaded a YouTube video titled 'Our Blades Are F***ing Great'. This video immediately drew massive attention from the American public because of the sarcastic yet humorous way Dubin promoted his new business concept—a shaving club where you could order your razors online. The Californian startup had been founded one year earlier. The company's website immediately crashed, and the video prompted 12,000 orders in a two-day time span after it was released.

The year 2012 was the same year in which Gillette reported another top line record—revenues amounted to $8.339 billion with an EBIT margin of 21.7%. Gillette had dominated the grooming industry for decades and had a market share of over 70%. The secret behind the company's success was a dedication to a continuous stream of innovation, supported by huge above-the-line spend on television, print media and billboards. At the same time, Gillette considered its retail channels—department stores, general stores, supermarkets and drugstores—as partners in crime and rewarded them well.

Now, what do you do when a small startup challenges you with a funny 2-minute video? Probably nothing. You're the indisputable market leader and the financial results have never been better. So, what is there to worry about? It's very likely that Gillette's sensing team declared Dollar Shave Club as an issue that was 'out of scope', meaning an issue that is 'very uncertain' but with a 'low impact.'

Fast forward to 2017. Dollar Shave Club's YouTube video has 24.7 million views and the company has about $200 million in revenues. Dollar Shave Club is everywhere. Business schools are writing cases about how David is beating Goliath. But there is more: Gillette gets challenged by a bunch of new kids on the block—Bevel, Harry's, OUI the people, and billie—all new ventures that try out variations on the Dollar Shave Club business model. By this time, the arrival of all these new disruptors will probably have become a 'key issue' in Gillette's boardroom—a trend still classified as 'highly uncertain' but definitely 'great impact'. Highly uncertain because none of them is making a profit yet, but definitely high impact: Gillette's revenues have decreased from $8.3 billion to $6.6 billion. Those new players affect Gillette's core badly. Action is needed. But what action?

# Many options available

How do you deal with the arrival of new disruptors? Or with a long-lasting health crisis? Or with any other form of turbulence?

The typical advice that managers get today is to respond quickly and boldly. Many academic writers and consultants advise you to 'lead and disrupt', 'seize the white space', shift towards 'blue oceans', 'creatively construct', engage in 'big bang disruption', or build 'the corporate startup'. These are titles of great books written over several years to help managers deal with turbulence, and the message is clear: turn your organization into an innovation and entrepreneurial super-champion. Engage in business model innovation and try to change the rules of the game in your industry. Don't be afraid to disrupt yourself—even to burn your company to the ground to rebuild it later.[80]

Our review of the literature and many case studies revealed that companies have a wide spectrum of strategies at their disposal. But not all strategies call for a radical renewal, and some are even very *unambitious*:
- Do nothing.
- Sue the newcomer.
- Throw the towel into the ring and sell the business.
- Retreat into a niche segment where the turbulence is hitting less hard.
- Fight back and aggressively defend your turf.
- Embrace the turbulence and fundamentally transform your core business.
- Disrupt the disruptor and launch a new business model innovation to fight the disruptors.
- Buy a company with a new business model.
- Or team up with competitors and build an entire ecosystem to reinvent your own industry.

Research from IMD's Global Center for Digital Business Transformation indicates that, despite all management advice, many companies still resist engaging in radical innovation. Although disruption and turbulence have made it to the agendas of most top management teams, companies struggle to handle the turbulence challenge appropriately.[81] As Figure 18 shows, the share of companies struggling with disruption—the focus of IMD's research was on the digital disruption—is increasing over time, from 25% in 2015 to 36% in 2021.

The main point we would like to make is that, despite the abundance of books and articles and consulting advice telling us how to transform and reinvent ourselves, many companies have not taken (appropriate) action. And, in some circumstances, this is even the right choice.

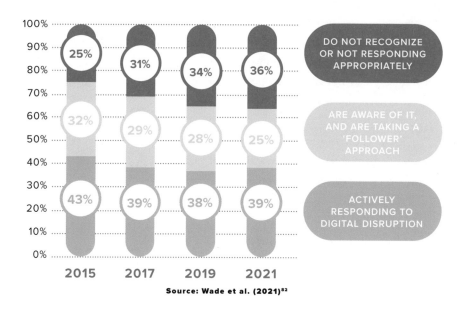

Source: Wade et al. (2021)[82]

**Figure 18** • Reactions to (digital) disruption

# Playing offense or defense?

What is the appropriate answer to turbulence? Is radical innovation always needed? Or can companies play defense successfully? How ambitious should your strategic response to turbulence be? In our opinion, the fundamental strategic question is not whether to play offense or defense—instead managers should answer two strategic questions:

- How should you react in the core business? Can you remain competitive with your current business model? Or do you have to fundamentally change your business model in the core and start a *transformation journey*?
- Turbulence also brings opportunities that are situated outside your core. Should you jump on those opportunities and engage in business model innovation outside your core? You can neglect the opportunity or you can embrace it and start an *innovation journey*.

Bringing these two dimensions together generates the Turbulence Strategy Matrix, which shows that firms can choose between four strategies to respond to turbulence (see Figure 19). They can choose the '*core resilience*' strategy, by which they focus on their core with their current business model. They feel confident that they can achieve their business targets without fundamental change. A second strategy, called '*corporate innovation*', involves building a new business model next to your existing core. This is the strategic innovation approach described in most turbulence books. With the third strategy, '*core transformation*', an organization focuses entirely on its core business and adapts to turbulence by integrating fundamentally new elements in its existing business model. The last strategy, '*corporate transformation*', consists of playing both offense and defense. Companies launch both a transformation journey (core transformation) and an innovation journey (corporate innovation) simultaneously, which affects the entire organization deeply.

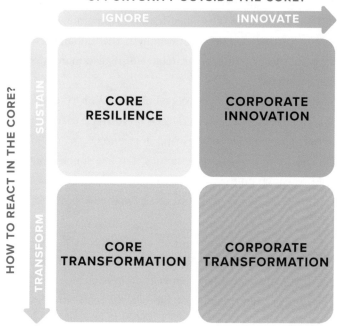

**Figure 19** • The turbulence strategy matrix

To select the appropriate strategy for your organization, it's important to understand two key concepts. The first one is the concept of the core business, the second is business model innovation.

# Reacting to turbulence inside versus outside the core

**THE IMPORTANCE OF A STRONG CORE.** In their book *Profit from the Core*, Chris Zook and James Allen from Bain & Company convincingly showed that the most successful growth companies have very few, highly focused, and well-defined core businesses.[83] You define your core (business) by specifying your competitive arena and competitive theme (see Figure 20).

Source: Verweire (2014)[84]

**Figure 20** • Defining your core

A well-defined *competitive arena* provides a clear answer to the question: Where do you play? When asked this question, most firms refer to the industry in which they compete: "We are an airline company," "We are a construction company," "We are a financial services organization." But such a definition is too broad and not useful in practice. For example, easyJet is not an airline company but a short-haul airline company targeting price-sensitive, European customers. easyJet does not compete with Singapore Airlines or Southwest Airlines. Ducati and Harley-Davidson are both motorcycle companies, but they are hardly competitors because they compete in different competitive arenas. Ducati competes in the sport bike arena, while Harley competes in the cruiser motorcycle arena. As a consequence, the customers of Ducati and Harley are also very different and they expect different things from a motorcycle.

When you define your competitive arena, you need to specify who your core customers are, but also who you will *not* serve. This is an important strategic choice. At the same time, you need to specify clearly what products and services you will offer, but also what you will not offer. Here people often refer to the job-to-be-done.[85]

A well-defined *competitive theme* provides a clear answer to the question: How will you win? Firms not only need to specify the arena within the industry in which they want to compete, they also need a strong value proposition and a clear operating model. The value proposition specifies how you will win relative to your competitors. Companies need to choose whether they will be the best at price, access, product, service, or connectivity.[86] The main idea is that you can't be the best at everything—again, strategy is making choices. And that choice corresponds with a particular operating model—a way of delivering the value proposition that you have promised to your customers. More than 25 years ago, Michael Treacy and Fred Wiersema identified three successful operating models: operational excellence, customer intimacy, and product leadership. Companies with a strong core have made a clear choice for one of those three operating models.[87]

In reality, however, many companies don't have a clear definition of their core business and forget to make it explicit. They underestimate the power of a strong core and stretch their core too far. They offer too many products and services to too many different customer segments with too many different operating models, raising the complexity in the organization, which in turn leads to lower profitability. Strategy is about focus and making choices about who not to serve, what not to provide, and what not to promise. This is not just theoretical advice. In our consulting practice, we've seen it time and time again: performance increases significantly after companies decide to say goodbye to a particular customer segment and stop producing a line of products and services that require a different operating model.[88]

Multi-business firms need to do this exercise for every business unit. But you can also adopt this thinking at the corporate level. Some divisions are financially and strategically stronger than others and have more growth potential. These divisions can then be considered as the 'core divisions' of your group.

STRATEGY IN TURBULENT TIMES

**REACTING TO TURBULENCE.** Companies react to turbulence by taking initiatives *inside their core business*. Here we mainly refer to the company's competitive arena—i.e., core customers and core products. Some firms optimize their supply chains or build cash buffers to withstand tough times. Other companies change their business model but continue to focus on the same competitive arena. For example, The New York Times transformed itself from a print newspaper company into a digital-centric news brand. A huge change indeed but focusing on existing customers and fulfilling the same need: providing news. However, the news was no longer provided on a printed platform only but offered on a digital platform as well. That required massive changes in the organization's business model. You can observe the same trend in the financial services industry, where many banks and insurance companies are adapting their business model to the digital revolution. Once again, that is a fundamental change but nevertheless focused on the traditional core: the company addresses the same target customers and fulfills the same banking and insurance needs—payments, credits, deposits, investments, and insurance.

Some companies react to turbulence by launching new entrepreneurial ventures *outside their core*. Norwegian media group Schibsted expanded into online marketplaces in addition to its print and digital news core business. For a long time, media companies have offered classified advertising. But the digital disruption moved this business to the big online giants, such as Amazon, eBay and specialized online classifieds companies, such as AutoTrader and Cars.com. Schibsted first built an online marketplace in Norway, and then started buying online marketplaces in the whole of Europe. The company has become a global online classified specialist, operating digital online classifieds in more than 20 countries. In 2019, Schibsted spun off the international marketplaces into a new company, Adevinta, which has nothing to do with journalistic content and news provision—thus, it has defined a very different core than its parent company Schibsted.

The idea of launching new business models outside your core is not new. For example, think about Nestlé, who launched Nespresso, and ING, who set up ING Direct. When Nespresso was launched in 1986, Nestlé focused on the retailers and the mass market and sold cheap, reliable products: coffee, chocolate, and baby food. Nespresso was clearly a unit that operated outside Nestlé's traditional core: it positioned itself as a luxury brand to individual customers through the new Club Nespresso. The company focused more on innovation, branding, and building a customer experience, supported by strong marketing campaigns and Nespresso boutiques.

ING was a Dutch bank-insurance group when it founded ING Direct. It launched ING Direct outside its home markets in different countries where it had only minor operations. In its home market, ING offered a full range of banking, insurance and investment products through branches close to its customers. ING Direct was a banking group positioned outside the core: it was a specialized bank, with a more limited product range, focusing on savings and mortgages, and with an operational excellence operating model, focusing on simplicity, speed, and convenience.

What is new is that many companies now consider moving outside their core as the way to deal with turbulence.

## Business model innovation

A second key concept in the Turbulence Strategy Matrix is business model innovation. Figure 19 shows that firms can decide to engage in business model innovation or not. And they can do that in and/or outside the core business. But what exactly is a business model? And is it a good idea to pursue business model innovation as a reaction to turbulence?

**WHAT IS A BUSINESS MODEL?** This seems like a trivial question since everybody talks about business models these days. Yet there's a lot of confusion about what a business model is and what its main building blocks are. Here is our pragmatic and easy-to-understand definition of this important concept: in essence, a business model describes how a company delivers value to customers, how it organizes to do so, and how it captures a portion of the value that it delivers.[89] Authors use the terms value creation, value delivery, and value capturing to describe these three key activities. One of the most popular business model frameworks was designed by Alexander Osterwalder and his colleagues: he built the famous 9-block 'Business Model Canvas'.[90] In this book, we will use a simplified version that consists of four building blocks, as defined by Mark Johnson, Clayton Christensen and Henning Kagermann.

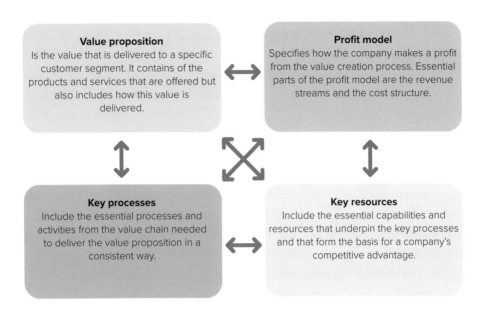

Source: Adapted from Johnson, Christensen and Kagermann (2008)[91]

**Figure 21** • Business model framework

- The **value proposition** specifies how a company creates value for a given set of customers at a given price. The value proposition covers more than just the product or the service, also incorporating how the product or service is brought to the customer. It also includes other aspects, such as the service and the sustainability level associated with the offering.
- The **profit model** describes how the company makes a profit from the value creation process. It specifies the company's revenue model and cost structure. The difference between revenues and costs is profit, and this block tells you about the value capturing capabilities of a firm.
- **Key resources** (and capabilities) are the unique people, technology, products, data, facilities, equipment, partnerships, funding and brand required to deliver the value proposition to the customer.

- **Key processes** are those activities of your value chain that are essential in the delivery of the customer value proposition. They consist of operational and managerial processes like research and development, sales, operations and logistics on the one hand, and planning, control, and leadership development on the other.

**BUSINESS MODEL INNOVATION.** Now that you understand what a business model is, we can turn to the concept of business model innovation. In quite a few cases, turbulence is caused by disruptors entering a market with business models that are fundamentally different from the business models of the incumbent players. Netflix, Ping An Good Doctor, Uber, and Airbnb are all great examples of disruptors that have successfully entered an industry with a new business model. Or take our example of Dollar Shave Club (DSC). This disruptor challenged the all-time market leader Gillette not with a new shaving technology innovation but with a business model innovation, turning the existing industry rules on their head.

Huge research and development costs? No issue: Dollar Shave Club outsourced the design and manufacturing of razors and blades to Dorco, a leading manufacturer of razors and blades in Asia. Dorco was also the outsource manufacturer for some large US and European hypermarket and supermarket chains, such as Walmart, Aldi and Lidl.

Huge above-the-line advertising spending on television, print media and bill-boards? No issue: DSC used YouTube as the main marketing and promotion channel. The company created more than 60 videos that were viewed more than 40 million times. On top of that, the company's Facebook page was also a big hit with over 3 million likes.

Access to supermarkets and hypermarkets? No issue: DSC had its own website and used a subscription model where subscription fees were automatically debited at an agreed frequency. Customers could change the characteristics of the subscription at any moment in time. Amazon and other e-commerce players took care of the rest.

Competing with Gillette's high-quality razors and blades? No issue: DSC competed on price and access. Razors were significantly cheaper than Gillette's. DSC's tag line was: 'Shave Time. Shave Money'. And no need to visit the retail store; your product package was delivered right onto your doorstep.

The results? In 2016, the company had 3.5 million members and $200 million in revenue. Not too bad for a 190-person company that mainly consisted of stand-up comedians, a team of creative bloggers, and YouTube movie makers. And the story didn't end there. That same year, Unilever paid $1 billion for the company. For Gillette, a company of the P&G family, now the battle was really on.

**USING BUSINESS MODEL INNOVATION TO FIGHT TURBULENCE.** When the rules of the game are changing in your industry, or a significant disturbance affects your performance, you might consider business model innovation as an appropriate strategic answer. This means that you fundamentally transform your core or that you set up a new business model outside your core.

How do you know when you're engaging in business model innovation? Business model innovation starts with a fundamental change in the value proposition block of the Business Model Framework, presented in Figure 21. Business model innovation is about the creation of substantial or radical new value for customers. This means that the value proposition should improve significantly and be fundamentally different compared to what competitors offer. What is fundamentally different? The new value proposition must not only be new to the innovating company, but also new to its industry—which makes it quite an ambitious journey.[92]

This fundamental change in your value proposition inevitably causes changes in your key resources, key processes, and/or your profit model. That's what distinguishes business model innovation from other types of innovation, such as product or process innovation, where the change takes place in only one component of the Business Model Framework. The following test allows you to check whether your new idea or venture qualifies as a business model innovation.

| Value proposition | VERY SIMILAR TO COMPETITORS | SOMEWHAT SIMILAR TO COMPETITORS | | VERY SIMILAR FROM COMPETITORS | |
|---|---|---|---|---|---|
| Product performance | ○ | ○ | ○ | ○ | ○ |
| Price level of the offering | ○ | ○ | ○ | ○ | ○ |
| Accessibility of the offering | ○ | ○ | ○ | ○ | ○ |
| Service level associated with the offering | ○ | ○ | ○ | ○ | ○ |
| Sustainability of te offering | ○ | ○ | ○ | ○ | ○ |
| **Key process and activities** | VERY SIMILAR TO COMPETITORS | SOMEWHAT SIMILAR TO COMPETITORS | | VERY SIMILAR FROM COMPETITORS | |
| Front-end activities | ○ | ○ | ○ | ○ | ○ |
| Back-end activities | ○ | ○ | ○ | ○ | ○ |
| Support and management activities | ○ | ○ | ○ | ○ | ○ |
| **Key resources** | VERY SIMILAR TO COMPETITORS | SOMEWHAT SIMILAR TO COMPETITORS | | VERY SIMILAR FROM COMPETITORS | |
| Core resources and capabilities | ○ | ○ | ○ | ○ | ○ |
| Network of suppliers and partners | ○ | ○ | ○ | ○ | ○ |
| Role in the entire ecosystem | ○ | ○ | ○ | ○ | ○ |
| **Profit model** | VERY SIMILAR TO COMPETITORS | SOMEWHAT SIMILAR TO COMPETITORS | | VERY SIMILAR FROM COMPETITORS | |
| Revenue structure | ○ | ○ | ○ | ○ | ○ |
| Cost structure | ○ | ○ | ○ | ○ | ○ |

**Figure 22** • Business model innovation test

Business model innovation requires that you have at least one bullet in the colored zone for the value proposition block—the zone above the dotted line—and one in the colored zone in the key processes, key resources, or profit model blocks—below the dotted line. If that is not the case, you are innovating within the contours of an existing business model.

If we take the example of Dollar Shave Club (see Figure 23), you will note that Dollar Shave Club provided customers with a fundamentally cheaper and easier solution—Dollar Shave Club's tag line was to help you 'shave time and money'. That's the value proposition change it created. To deliver such a radically new value proposition to its customers, Dollar Shave Club also had to change the front-end activities (customer relationship management and distribution) and the back-end processes (outsourcing of production and logistics, no investments in R&D). The company's resources were very different from the traditional players—focused on attracting customers to its website and building strong relations with them. And finally, its profit model was also fundamentally different: it used a different revenue model—a subscription model (like Netflix)—and had a fundamentally different cost structure than a competitor like Gillette.

**Dollar Shave Club**

| Value proposition | VERY SIMILAR TO COMPETITORS | | SOMEWHAT SIMILAR TO COMPETITORS | | VERY SIMILAR FROM COMPETITORS |
|---|---|---|---|---|---|
| Product performance | ● | ○ | ○ | ○ | ○ |
| Price level of the offering | ○ | ○ | ○ | ○ | ● |
| Accessibility of the offering | ○ | ○ | ○ | ○ | ● |
| Service level associated with the offering | ● | ○ | ○ | ○ | ○ |
| Price level of the offering | ● | ○ | ○ | ○ | ○ |

| Key processe and activities | VERY SIMILAR TO COMPETITORS | | SOMEWHAT SIMILAR TO COMPETITORS | | VERY SIMILAR FROM COMPETITORS |
|---|---|---|---|---|---|
| Front-end activities | ○ | ○ | ○ | ○ | ● |
| Back-end activities | ○ | ○ | ○ | ○ | ● |
| Support and management activities | ● | ○ | ○ | ○ | ○ |

| Key resources | VERY SIMILAR TO COMPETITORS | | SOMEWHAT SIMILAR TO COMPETITORS | | VERY SIMILAR FROM COMPETITORS |
|---|---|---|---|---|---|
| Core resources and capabilities | ○ | ○ | ○ | ○ | ● |
| Network of suppliers and partners | ○ | ○ | ○ | ○ | ● |
| Role in the entire ecosystem | ○ | ○ | ○ | ○ | ● |

| Value proposition | VERY SIMILAR TO COMPETITORS | | SOMEWHAT SIMILAR TO COMPETITORS | | VERY SIMILAR FROM COMPETITORS |
|---|---|---|---|---|---|
| Revenue structure | ○ | ○ | ○ | ○ | ● |
| Cost structure | ○ | ○ | ○ | ○ | ● |

**Figure 23** • Business model innovation Dollar Shave Club

# How should you react to turbulence?

How should Gillette have reacted to Dollar Shave Club's move? Now that we've explained the axes of the Turbulence Strategy Matrix, let's investigate the four options for established firms to fight turbulence by linking each strategy to a particular animal (see Figure 24) and by providing some examples of each strategy. In the next chapters, we will then elaborate on each strategy in much more detail.

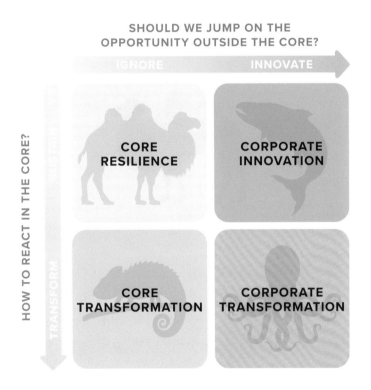

**Figure 24** • The turbulence strategy matrix (animal version)

## Camel strategy: Core resilience

Reacting to turbulence through core resilience is applying the *camel strategy*. With this strategy, companies stick to their current business model and improve and fortify it when necessary. We call this the camel strategy because camels are among the most resilient animals on earth: these animals are built for survival. When thinking about camels, we immediately think about the deserts of the Sahara and the Middle East. But the true master of resilience is the two-humped Bactrian camel that lives in Central Asia and is even better equipped to deal with extreme weather conditions—both extremely cold and hot temperatures.

Some firms are resilient and react to turbulence by sticking to their core business, exploiting their current business model, and ignoring the opportunities to build a new unit next to the core. This seems like the beginning of the end. We tend to associate turbulence with companies like Kodak, Nokia, RIM (Blackberry) and Thomas Cook—companies that have gone bankrupt because they didn't react (properly) to the threat of turbulence.

But in many cases, turbulence doesn't necessarily mean the end of your core business. You might still have a future—even when turbulence knocks on your door. In the case of *disturbance*—which means there is a temporary shock in your demand or supply—the market might go back to the pre-disturbance phase. That's what we are noticing today in many industries—festivals, restaurants, business schools—which are now picking up again to a level similar to that of pre-Covid-19. But even when you are facing *disruption*—i.e., when new competitors are entering your industry—we see that some parts of the industry remain relatively unaffected. Disruption often creates a new market in the periphery of the established market. Even when the new market grows at the expense of the established one, it never destroys the established market completely.[93]

Some companies have found a good defensive strategy against turbulence and still perform well. One of those companies is Handelsbanken, a Swedish financial institution. Handelsbanken has been a market leader and a profitable financial institution for decades. Following its motto—'The Branch is the Bank'—Handelsbanken gave a lot of authority and responsibility to branch managers, even for large accounts. This high level of decentralization enabled better service and deeper relationships for its customers, including more detailed customer information, which led to much fewer credit defaults. Handelsbanken's losses from non-performing loans have been among the lowest in the industry.

But what happens if disruptors enter your market with online and mobile banking applications that turn branches into expensive assets—maybe even liabilities? Despite these trends, Handelsbanken has continued with its strategy and has no plans to reduce the number of branches. Of course, Handelsbanken has adapted its branches to the modern world. For example, branches in High Street locations have moved from the ground floor to an upper storey. And some of the older branches have been assigned a new role as customer-service centers. The bank embraced digital solutions and developed banking apps—but it remained convinced of the importance of physical relationships with its customers.[94] As the next graph shows (see Figure 25), this strategy still proves to be successful. Every year since 1973, the bank has outperformed its competitors in terms of return on equity, customer satisfaction and credit losses. A trend that continues, even in current turbulent times.

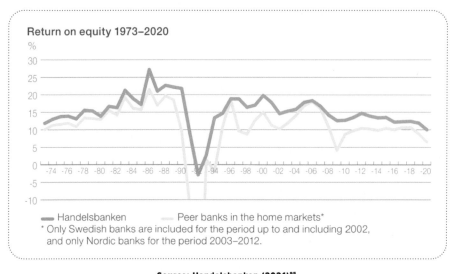

Return on equity 1973–2020

━━ Handelsbanken ━━ Peer banks in the home markets*
* Only Swedish banks are included for the period up to and including 2002,
and only Nordic banks for the period 2003–2012.

**Source: Handelsbanken (2021)[95]**

**Figure 25** • Return on equity of Handelsbanken versus competitors

## Salmon strategy: Corporate innovation

We call corporate innovation the *salmon strategy*: in this case, companies react to turbulence by adding a new business model to their existing core. Those firms explore new territories, just like salmon do. Salmon are born in freshwater where they spend a few months to a few years—depending on the species. Then they make the move to the ocean—a very different territory for fish, as freshwater clearly isn't saltwater. Salmon undergo significant behavioral and physiological adaptations to make this move, which is also what corporate innovators need to do if they engage in business model innovation outside their core.

Read any consulting document on turbulence and you will immediately find a recommendation for Big Bang innovation. Some academics and consultants suggest doing this quickly and boldly by making a clean break from the past and turning your firm into something entirely new. Their advice is to build 'speedboats' that will become the tankers of tomorrow. These new units are stand-alone units with the freedom to develop their own business model, strategy, and culture.[96]

Clearly, the need to engage in radical innovation has significantly increased: business boundaries are shifting ever more quickly and competition is increasingly coming from different corners. Market leaders have less time to profit from their market leadership status. And there are some interesting companies that show us how to do it: the management literature is full of stories of start-ups that have become market leaders by changing the rules of the game. Think Amazon, Google, Facebook, Airbnb, Uber, Tesla, Tencent, Netflix and all of the other usual suspects. Some of these players—like Apple, Google and Tencent—have turned into serial business innovators. But the list is not restricted to tech firms. Consider Ping An, the Chinese property and casualty insurer founded in 1988, which has expanded its business portfolio into finance, automotive, healthcare, and smart city services.

Despite all these inspiring examples—and the great advice to create blue oceans or white spaces—many incumbents have suffered from business model innovation. Nevertheless, corporate innovation can be a useful strategy for incumbents who want to fight back and build a new business with a different business model.

One great example is Next, the digital bank of Brazil's second largest private bank Bradesco. Like many other financial institutions, Bradesco had to deal with the digital transformation and the emergence of fintech's as new competitors. Nevertheless, the company took the bull by the horns and building on its nice track record in innovation, created an entirely separate digital bank for millennials This was a natural thing to do because "moving with the evolutionary cycle and using technology as an enabler for that was already part of the business culture," according to Jeferson Honorato, Next's 'Executive Superintendent'.[97] The company had been watching trends and analyzed the various business models of digital banks worldwide. Honorato's team concluded that focusing on a hyper-connected, young demographic was the most promising new business idea, and they started with the plans for the new venture in 2014. Next saw the light of day in 2017—and at the end of 2020, the company had already reached 5 million customers in the age 18 to 35 cohort.

"Some 86 percent of the digital bank's customers didn't do business with Bradesco, so the company is reaching out to a new market. When we created Next, the idea was not to cannibalize the relationships with the existing customer base at Bradesco but to address the expectations of this audience between 18 and 35 years old. We have the opportunity to deliver a different value proposition to this specific audience, in line with what they are consuming across other platforms and connect more effectively with them.

Engagement with our customers has been key. Growth has to be sustainable, not only from a numbers' perspective but also from a business standpoint: we don't simply want 5 million open accounts, we want those accounts to be active. Our churn is less than 2 percent.

Another key aspect of the digital bank is the ability to integrate external partners offering discounts of services that are appealing to its target audience, such as Uber, local food delivery app iFood, and cinema chains. We are working towards the open banking concept, by connecting our platform to several other non-financial partners."[98]

Bradesco was convinced early on to create an entirely separate digital bank. And this position remains unchanged: Next gets greater autonomy to keep up with the fintech's that are scaling up fast. Nevertheless, Next has benefited from the link with Bradesco—its credit and investment systems are bolted onto Bradesco's systems. But building new business models outside your core remains a challenge.

Managing an existing business—and investing in a new division at the same time—leads to a number of conflicts in the corporation. With regard to this challenge, Charles O'Reilly and Michael Tushman introduced the concept of 'ambidexterity', which is the ability to compete in mature businesses—where a company can exploit its existing strengths—as well as in new domains where it leverages existing resources to do something new. This remains one of the most difficult management challenges.

## Chameleon strategy: Core transformation

Core transformation adopts the *chameleon strategy*. Firms transform their core and change their existing business model, just like chameleons who can change colors rapidly. The chameleon's hue-shifting skills are some of nature's best and most multifaceted and help the animal blend into its surroundings. Chameleons also change color to defend territory against other males—the color then turns into red or bright green, blue, or yellow, and even white.[99]

Setting up speedboats is probably the most common advice for managing turbulence. But you can also react to turbulence by fundamentally transforming your core business. Then you apply business model innovation not outside but inside your core business. When turbulence strikes so hard that it affects your core significantly, it can pay off to fight back and invest in fixing and adapting your core. Some companies have emerged stronger after the turbulence: they have embraced the turbulence and built new capabilities that, combined with the traditional strengths, have created a new powerful combination. Many traditional banks have fully embarked on digital transformation journeys—and some have been very successful in adapting their banking products to the digital needs. Many have reduced the number of branches, but they've increased digital or mobile accessibility significantly, offering an even better service than before.

Newspaper companies have also had to find answers to the digital threats. They have transformed from printed newspaper organizations with some digital extras to digital content providers with some printed outputs. That transformation hasn't always been easy, but a large number of incumbent newspaper companies have survived well, and today they are reporting good performance figures.

Hilti—a specialist in professional tools—is another example of a company that has transformed its core. At the end of the 1990s—while profitability levels were still good—the company saw some dark clouds appearing on the horizon. The management team realized that its market was commoditizing and that the company was losing ground to Chinese competitors and players in the small-tool market segment. The company used the threat of commoditization to create a fundamentally new business model in its core business. Hilti saw that construction workers viewed the tools as virtually disposable, which led to lower productivity and increased repair costs. Hilti's answer was to offer a fleet management solution. The company still offered power tools to its traditional customer segment (the commercial segment rather than do-it-yourself customers) but its promise to its customer had changed radically: "Tool management is a pain. We take care of everything, and you always have the newest technology and the safest tools, well organized and readily available."[100] Customers no longer bought tools, but tool availability. This new value proposition required a new profit formula. Hilti proposed a leasing formula whereby the customer no longer paid upfront when buying the tools but instead paid a monthly fee.

This new business model posed significant challenges to the company. Nevertheless, the company persisted and, in 2016, went one step further with the launch of the ON!Track initiative. This was Hilti's professional solution for the management of a construction firm's assets—not restricted to the Hilti power tools, but encompassing all tools, even those of the competitors. With this strategic move, Hilti had stepped into the Software-as-a-Service business, further diversifying its revenue streams. All these moves enabled the company to grow both top and bottom line significantly while still concentrating on its core business.

## Octopus strategy: Corporate transformation

Finally, corporate transformation is reacting to turbulence with the *octopus strategy*. With this strategy, companies transform their core and simultaneously build a new unit to capture the opportunity that turbulence brings. We've made the association with the octopus, probably one of the most intriguing animals on earth. Octopuses are unique in many ways. They have three hearts, a doughnut-shaped brain and eight arms. Each arm contains its own mini-brain, allowing it to act independently.[101] Corporate transformation requires that organizations also build at least two independent organizations that can act independently. And just like the octopus, there is a centralized brain that manages the whole.

The last strategic option for dealing with turbulence is to transform the core and simultaneously add a new business to the corporate portfolio. This comes down to transforming the entire corporation: the corporate portfolio changes and there is also a fundamental change in your core business. This strategic move follows the ideas presented in the book, *Dual Transformation*, written by Scott Anthony, Clark Gilbert, and Mark Johnson.[102] According to the authors, this is probably the hardest management challenge facing leaders today. Creating a new business outside of your core is hard, and, at the same time, executives of incumbents need to stave off never-ending attacks on existing operations, because they provide vital cash flow and capabilities to invest in growth.

Apple chose this strategy in the late 1990s. It repositioned its struggling PC business, emphasizing functionality and design, and afterwards it launched the iPod and opened the iTunes store, which, as we all know, was the start of a remarkable growth journey.[103] Another example of such a dual transformation is Xerox, which had to react to low-cost Asian competitors. The company repositioned its core by offering a line of copiers that were simpler and more cost-effective to produce, but also more technically advanced and less expensive to operate. At the same time, it created Xerox Global Services, a unit that performed document management for larger organizations.[104]

Another intriguing story of corporate transformation has been written by Schibsted, a company that we introduced earlier this chapter. Schibsted is an international media group with 8,000 employees in 29 countries. The company started as a newspaper company in Norway in 1839 and evolved into one of the most agile media companies in the world. Starting in early 2000, the company expanded its newspaper business in Scandinavia and transformed its newspaper companies from print to digital—a transformation that many other newspaper and media companies were facing too. However, Schibsted transformed its core years before most of its competitors.

The business world took keen notice of the company when it aggressively entered the online classified ads market. Classified ads have always been a major source of revenue for newspaper companies. But with the arrival of the internet, companies like Google, Facebook, and YouTube grabbed a significant part of that market. Schibsted quickly understood that the internet would have many farther-reaching implications for its businesses, and so it turned the threat into an opportunity. It set up its own online classified advertising businesses and experimented with several business models. When it found the right model, the company scaled it up. Buying numerous classified ad companies in Europe, Schibsted became a global marketplace specialist. On 10 April 2019, Adevinta—Schibsted's international marketplaces company—was introduced on the Norwegian stock exchange as a separate company. The new company further strengthened its ambitions by acquiring eBay's Classifieds Group. Schibsted is a good example of how an organization can reorganize itself into two growth-oriented companies, thriving in turbulent circumstances.

# What strategy did Gillette choose?

**EARLY REACTION.** In 2012, Dollar Shave Club's Michael Dubin uploaded the company's first video on YouTube and attracted a lot of attention from potential customers and investors. In that year, Dollar Shave Club reported $4 million in revenues. 2012 was also the year in which Gillette reported its highest revenues ever—$8.339 billion, an increase of almost $100 million compared to the year before. That year the EBIT margin improved slightly from 21.5% in 2011 to 21.7%. Given these figures, we may assume that Gillette kept focusing on growing its core. There was no need to change its core—results had never been better—so the company could apply the camel strategy. We are not sure whether Dollar Shave Club was even mentioned in Gillette's executive and board meetings.

But from 2013, Gillette began to lose revenues (see Figure 26a). In 2015, revenues had almost decreased by $1 billion compared to 2012. And in 2016, revenues dropped further to under $7 billion. Despite the significant drop in revenues and market share, it's fair to notice that the company maintained its EBIT margin (see Figure 26b). But one can imagine that, given those figures, Gillette could no longer ignore the turbulence but had to find an appropriate response.

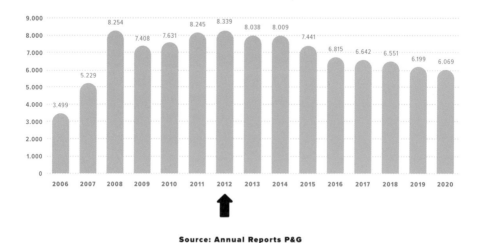

**Source: Annual Reports P&G**

**Figure 26a** · Gillette's revenues ($ million)

---

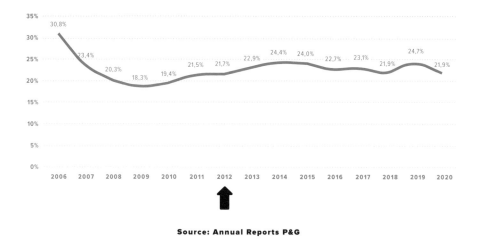

Source: Annual Reports P&G

**Figure 26b** • Gillette's EBIT margin

The company decided to stay focused on its core—thus continuing with a camel strategy—but reacted more aggressively to the threat of the new online players, such as Dollar Shave Club and Harry's. It filed a patent-infringement lawsuit against Dollar Shave Club—a strategy it had used before to fight new entrants. It also launched a 'welcome back' campaign, to lure customers back to the brand and featured a website and infographic that compared Gillette's razors to its competitors. The message was clear: Gillette offered the highest quality razors. But this marketing campaign backfired: independent testing suggested that Gillette's products were not superior at all—but even inferior, in some cases. In 2017, the company introduced price reductions of up to 20% in the US market and launched Gillette on Demand, a direct-to-consumer e-commerce site for the US market.[105] But the figures presented in Figure 26 show that these initiatives didn't really pay off: revenues continued to drop.

**THE GAME IS ON.** In 2016, Unilever acquired Dollar Shave Club and paid $1 billion for the company that had $200 million in revenues but had not yet made profits. This acquisition sent a shock to P&G's Grooming team. While the online players had remained mainly a US phenomenon, the acquisition of Dollar Shave Club by Unilever could be the start of a global disruption game in the grooming market. Gillette started to undertake more drastic action and decided to change its turbulence strategy. In 2018, it bought Walker & Company, the parent company of Bevel, a grooming line for men of color, and Form, a hair-care line for women of color. With this acquisition, Gillette shifted its strategy to a salmon strategy: it expanded its core with a new business model. In the press, founder and CEO Tristan Walker explained that the Walker & Company group would operate as a separate and wholly-owned subsidiary of P&G. Walker remained the CEO of this unit and was confident that he could continue to grow his business: "They [P&G] aren't tinkering with our formula. On the contrary, they are just giving us the resources and fuel needed to continue delivering on our promises, but on an even larger, global scale."[106] The jury is still out over whether this will lead to improved results for P&G's grooming business.

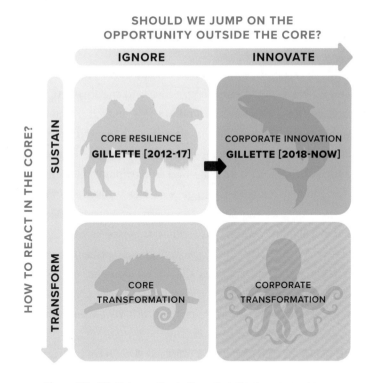

Figure 27 • Gillette's reaction to the online shaving companies

# Which strategy when?

In the previous section, we described the four strategies firms can adopt in order to deal with turbulence. To date, there is no conclusive evidence as to which strategy is the most popular and yields the best results. However, we can offer you some advice on which strategy to use when.

**WHEN TO JUMP ON A NEW OPPORTUNITY OUTSIDE THE CORE?** One of the key messages of this book is that turbulence not only brings threats but opportunities as well. The arrival of low-cost airline companies created a new market space for budget travel. The Covid-19 crisis also saw the creation of many new businesses in non-store retail, which includes e-commerce, truck transportation, accommodation, and food services. Taking our Gillette example, the arrival of the online disruptors created a new arena for the more price-sensitive customers.

You should take the following elements into account when you are considering jumping on the new opportunity that turbulence brings.

A first element is the *size of the new market* that is created. If the size of the new market is large and is expected to grow significantly, then it's worth considering entering the new market. But the market's size is not enough. You should also try to estimate the profit potential of the new market. Low-cost airlines are a large market, but the overall profitability in that market has been disappointingly low. Unfortunately, it's difficult to assess the future profitability of many new markets. As the turbulence unfolds, one can notice over time if there is a winning business model evolving and if the new players earn decent returns. But if that's not the case, it's wise to ignore the opportunity.

Whatever the profitability of the new business, if the new market is a significant *threat to the existing business*, then companies are more inclined to jump onto the new opportunity. In keeping with the old adage "If you can't beat them, join them", both Coca-Cola and Facebook have long traditions of strengthening positions in upcoming businesses that pose a significant threat: e.g., Coca-Cola with Aquarius in the sports drink market; Facebook with Instagram and WhatsApp in the social media landscape.

A third element to consider relates to your organization's *strengths and capabilities*. Businesses make money by being sustainably different and better, not just by pursuing growth. This is the cold truth of hot markets. In such markets, only a limited number of players are able to capture part of the profit pool. The rest of the players barely earn more than the cost of capital.[107] Therefore, our advice is that you should only enter a new business if you have a fair chance of winning. If you want to be a winner, you need resources and capabilities that help you win. These resources can be manifold: a strong brand, a specialist workforce, unused production capacity, R&D skills, and so on. And that's where an incumbent has an advantage over start-ups: Apple's iPod, iTunes and iPhone benefited from the Apple brand. The iPod was the fastest-selling MP3 player ever to hit the market—and part of that success can be attributed to the easy link with smart software developed at Apple's computer business. That was clearly an advantage for Apple, compared to the other players in the portable MP3 market. Deseret Digital Media, the new business unit created by Deseret News, an American newspaper group, used the brand and the journalistic content of the legacy business, which gave it a competitive advantage compared to other multimedia companies. One prerequisite is that those resources or competences help increase the attractiveness of your offer, either by lowering the cost relative to the newcomers or by increasing the differentiation potential.

Resources can also be financial. Companies with a war chest of cash have more opportunities to create new ventures. It's questionable whether Larry Page and Sergey Brin would have built the Alphabet corporation with ventures like Nest, Calico, Google X, Google Ventures and CapitalG (the former Google Capital) if the search engine business wasn't such a cash-generating machine. Larger corporations can explore new uncharted territory simply because they have the means.

But we must not consider financial resources alone—having the right management skills is equally important. Firms that engage in business model innovation outside their core need to master two businesses: the traditional one and the new one. This is a huge managerial challenge that shouldn't be underestimated. The more corporate managers can manage different business models in their portfolio, the more they will be able to deal properly with new businesses. If firms have a dominant business model that they roll out in every business, there's a big chance that adding a new business model will be a huge challenge.

Launching new business models outside your core requires a strong innovation ambition and innovation skills. An innovation ambition should be supported by a clear innovation strategy and a powerful corporate innovation infrastructure. The infrastructure allows the firm to devote sufficient resources—people, money, and time—to implement the strategy, set the right priorities, and check whether the innovation projects are on the right track.

Figure 28 brings all of these factors together and allows you to judge whether or not a particular turbulence is creating an opportunity outside your core.

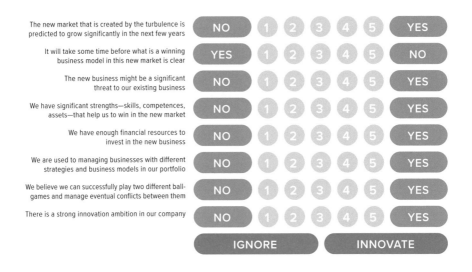

**Figure 28** • Jump on the new opportunity: Yes or no?

If you end up with a score higher than 32, our advice is clear: it's time to build a new speedboat and jump on the opportunity that turbulence brings. The opportunity is there and you have the skills and capabilities. If your score is lower than 16, the advice is equally clear: stick to your core and don't jump on the opportunity. Just because there is an opportunity in the market, it's not necessarily an opportunity for you. A score between 16 and 32 is a tricky score: there are elements that point to jumping and other elements that point in the direction of not jumping.

**WHEN SHOULD YOU TRANSFORM YOUR CORE?** Strategizing in turbulence is not only about deciding whether or not to build a new speedboat. It's equally about deciding to sustain the business model in your core or to fundamentally transform it. This decision is driven by the following factors.

The first one is the *nature of the change*. Recall that, previously, we distinguished between disturbance and disruption. Disturbance means that there's a shock in your demand or supply. This shock is usually temporary, but it causes a significant loss of revenue or increase in costs, leading to performance challenges. Think Covid-19 or supply chain problems. Disruption, on the other hand, means that there are new competitors entering your market with new business models. Disturbance doesn't force you to change your core, although it might force you to resize and rescale your business. Disruption, however, forces you make fundamental changes to your core, especially if the disruption threatens your core and if it makes your business model obsolete. If your value proposition is no longer attractive to your customers, and your capabilities and assets become obsolete, your profitability will drop soon. And the faster the disruption comes, the sooner you have to act.

The second major factor to consider is your own *transformation skills*. If you lack good change management capabilities, the transformation will be painful and tough. And there's a significant chance that you won't make it. This might be an indication that you should stick to your core and reduce it. However, if the disruption hits hard, this is not a viable option.

Figure 29 presents a list of variables to consider when choosing between sustaining or transforming.

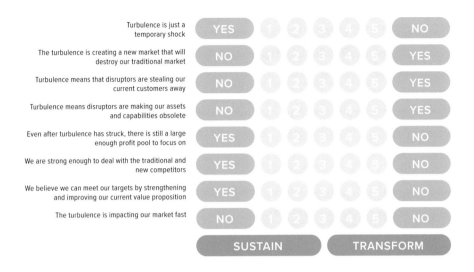

| | | 1 | 2 | 3 | 4 | 5 | | |
|---|---|---|---|---|---|---|---|---|
| Turbulence is just a temporary shock | YES | | | | | | NO | |
| The turbulence is creating a new market that will destroy our traditional market | NO | | | | | | YES | |
| Turbulence means that disruptors are stealing our current customers away | NO | | | | | | YES | |
| Turbulence means disruptors are making our assets and capabilities obsolete | NO | | | | | | YES | |
| Even after turbulence has struck, there is still a large enough profit pool to focus on | YES | | | | | | NO | |
| We are strong enough to deal with the traditional and new competitors | YES | | | | | | NO | |
| We believe we can meet our targets by strengthening and improving our current value proposition | YES | | | | | | NO | |
| The turbulence is impacting our market fast | NO | | | | | | NO | |
| | SUSTAIN | | | | TRANSFORM | | | |

**Figure 29** • Transform the core: yes or no?

The interpretation of the scores is similar to the previous decision. If you end up with a score higher than 32, we believe it's time to transform your core fundamentally. If your score is lower than 16, you can stick to your current business model. Again, a score between 16 and 32 is a tricky score, as it's not very clear what to do: sustain or transform. There are elements that point in the direction of the transformation alternative and others that point in the direction of sustaining.

**HOW MANY DIFFERENT STRATEGIES ARE POSSIBLE?** In most cases, firms can identify rather clearly the major sources of turbulence affecting their business, and they can develop an appropriate turbulence strategy. Then, once such a choice is made, it's important to review it regularly (once a year, for example). Just like the case of Gillette and Dollar Shave Club, as the world evolves trends become clearer, which sometimes forces you to re-interpret the impact of a source of turbulence on your core and the potential opportunity it could bring.

But some larger corporations might face multiple disruptive trends. Chapter 5 covers the Daimler Group, known primarily as a leading car manufacturing company. Few industries are facing as many disruptive upheavals as this industry. One source of turbulence is the pressure to comply with more ecological forms of transportation—which is why major automobile manufacturers are switching to electric vehicles. But there is more. There is also the trend towards automated vehicles and self-driving cars. If that were not enough, car makers see that the ideas of the sharing economy are also invading their industry: the car is losing its allure as a status symbol, and thus car ownership is losing its attraction. Customer demand is shifting from owning a car towards mobility as a service.[108]

Daimler had to react to these different sources of turbulence and adopted different strategies. For example, it tackled the challenge of electric vehicles by adopting a chameleon strategy and fundamentally integrating this change in its core businesses. On the other hand, it has tackled the mobility challenge with a salmon strategy: setting up a Daimler Mobility division, where it has built an entirely new business offering a broad range of mobility solutions (see Chapter 5 for more information on this move).

# KEY TAKEAWAYS

- Firms have several options for dealing with turbulence. Radical innovation is not always the appropriate answer. Sometimes, it's best to stick to your core and continue with your current business model.

- Firms should address two questions when dealing with turbulence. The first question is how to react in your core: do you sustain your traditional business model, or do you transform it to a new model? The second question is whether to jump on the opportunity that turbulence brings outside your core: neglect the opportunity or embrace it?

- We've identified four turbulence strategies: (1) core resilience, (2) corporate innovation, (3) core transformation, and (4) corporate transformation. We've linked those four strategies to four animals: (1) the camel, (2) the salmon, (3) the chameleon, and (4) the octopus.

- The main factors that direct you to corporate innovation and corporate transformation are: the size of the new market, the threat of the new market to your existing business, and the strengths and capabilities of your organization.

- The choice of whether to sustain or transform your business model in your core business is mainly driven by the nature of the change and your company's transformation skills.

# CHAPTER
# 4

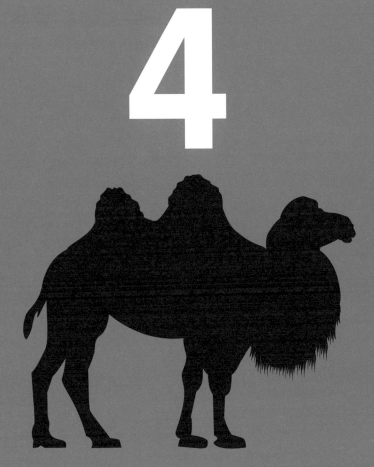

## chapter of the camel
—
Core resilience

# Key questions addressed in this chapter

What is a core
resilience strategy?

Can firms use such
a strategy to deal with
turbulence?
Or is core resilience a
sign of weakness
and laziness?

Which companies
have succesfully
used a core
resilience strategy
to fight turbulence?

A core reslience strategy
consists of different tactics:
what is the differcnce
between crisis management,
resilience, and agility?
And which tactic
to use when?

The core resilience strategy is the first of the four turbulence strategies. It looks like the least ambitious and 'sexy' answer to turbulence. But don't underestimate the challenges of implementing this strategy—it entails more than doing nothing and waiting for something to happen.

You use a core resilience strategy to deal with disturbance when you're facing the consequences of a natural disaster or a big accident, for example. This strategy can also be used when you're facing longer periods of turbulence. I've also seen firms use core resilience in the case of disruption when new companies enter their market with new business models. Handelsbanken, the Swedish bank that I introduced in the previous chapter, is a good example.

Firms implementing this strategy concentrate on their core business and don't see any added value in setting up new ventures outside their core. They feel that if they manage the turbulence well—either by avoiding potential turbulence, by reacting fast and decisively or by further strengthening their core—they can meet their performance goals. Core resilience encompasses an arsenal of tools from many different management disciplines such as risk management, crisis management and emergency planning, human resource management, operations and IT management, supply chain management, non-market strategy, stakeholder management, and innovation management. Management authors use different labels such as adaptability, strategic flexibility, resilience, robustness, corporate vitality for a set of management practices that help you win in times of drastic change.

In this chapter, I will integrate some of these ideas and group them in three broad tactics—crisis management, resilience, and agility (three different yet interrelated concepts)—that specify what firms can do to defend their core in turbulent times. I will illustrate those tactics with four camel stories from different industries and different time periods.[109] But let's first make a brief visit to the animal kingdom to find out about a master of core resilience.

**The camel:** A master of core resilience

Have you ever seen a camel in the snow? We associate camels with the Sahara desert, but the camel depicted on the first page of this chapter is the Bactrian camel that lives in Central Asia in the Gobi desert—an area that consists of rocky mountain massifs, flat arid desert, stony plains, and sand dunes. It's a very tough environment where vegetation is sparse, water sources limited and the climate extreme—brutally cold in the winter and immensely hot in the summer. The Bactrian camel has to withstand temperatures ranging from -40°C to +55°C.

The animal has adapted well to survive in such an unforgiving climate. It can go for impressive periods of time without drinking water—for months if necessary. When water and food are scarce, it survives from the fat that is stored in its two humps. The Bactrian camel is not a picky eater—it eats and drinks whatever crosses its path. Thanks to its resilient lips and mouth, it can ingest any plant—be it prickly, thorny, bitter, or salty. It can also drink salt water (which is even more salty than our seawater), rarely sweats and passes highly concentrated urine to retain the most liquid possible. There are other adaptations worth noting. To withstand sandstorms, it can close its nostrils and two rows of thick eyelashes shield the camel's eyes. Bactrian camels also benefit from a fur coat that grows thick in winter but is shed when summer arrives.

And if that was not enough, the wild Bactrian camels had to endure over 30 years of nuclear testing in the desolate area of Lop Nur in northwest China. They managed to breed normally despite the effects of radiation from more than 40 nuclear tests.

This animal will never win a beauty contest, but it can win a race —camel racing is quite a popular sport in numerous parts of the world. Although not as fast as the dromedary camel, the Bactrian camel is known for its endurance and strength here as well. They can maintain a steady pace for a longer period of time, making them ideal for long-distance races. So when there are prizes for resilience and agility, the Bactrian camel definitely deserves its place on the podium.

Let's now turn our attention to the business world to find the masters of core resilience there.

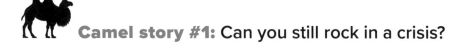 **Camel story #1:** Can you still rock in a crisis?

It probably comes as no surprise that the first turbulence story deals with the Covid-19 pandemic, undoubtedly one of the most impactful global crises of the last several decades. As with many other companies, business looked pretty grim for Fender Musical Instrument Corporation, the leading instrument company that produced iconic guitars for rock legends such as Jimi Hendrix, Kurt Cobain, George Harrison, and Keith Richards. When the Covid-19 virus reached American shores in March 2020, Fender's worldwide dealers' physical stores closed, as did many of its online seller's distribution centers. CEO Andy Mooney wondered what to do to survive this crisis.[110]

**NOT A GLAMOROUS INDUSTRY.** At first sight, the guitar industry seems like a cool industry given the fact that the guitar has been seen as a global symbol of youthful freedom and rebellion for more than 70 years.[111] Unfortunately, the business dynamics in that sector are less glamorous and cool. The truth is that electric guitar sales have skidded down by one third since 2007. The industry is characterized by intense competition and souring demand—two ingredients for a bad tasting musical cocktail. The number of guitar makers has increased steadily over the years, but demand hasn't. In today's music world, the guitar plays second fiddle to electronic music instruments. The main competitor, Gibson Guitars, started a diversification strategy to counter this trend, but failed miserably. The company filed for Chapter 11 bankruptcy protection in 2018. All of this was enough for *The Washington Post* to declare the slow death of the six-string electric.[112]

Despite this poor industry context, Fender was still doing relatively well. Although the company had acquired other musical instrument companies in the past, it had decided to refocus on electric guitars again, and that strategy paid off. Andy Mooney, who was appointed CEO in 2015 had set a clear strategic goal to work on the loyalty of novice musicians. The company used the internet to reach out to this target group. For example, in 2017 the company launched Fender Play, a digital platform, to help beginners learn to play. The guitar maker also developed an app to help beginners tune their guitars, and for more advanced players, it launched Fender Songs, an app that provided the chords for a million songs.[113] But then Covid-19 arrived.

**CRISIS MANAGEMENT.** The Covid-19 crisis hit the guitar industry—including Fender—extremely hard. The pandemic was a disaster for an already vulnerable industry. Mooney took swift action:

> "On 17 March 2020, 90% of our nearly 1,000 dealers worldwide closed. Our offices and factories closed. We were staring at the edge of a cataclysmic drop-off in sales, so our focus was on cash preservation. We did everything possible to mitigate cash flow. We canceled orders, everybody in the company took pay cuts from 5 to 50%, and we canceled bonuses.
>
> Early on, after I joined Fender, we had moved all our distribution centers to third-party providers, taking out our capital and lease costs. That proved to be a big blessing, because our third-party provider in the U.S., FedEx, was an essential business. It never closed down when the rest of California, our factories, and our dealers did. We provided a lifeline to the dealers for their online sales, shipping them inventory we had in our warehouse during the early parts of the pandemic."[114]

The company had planned to launch a line of updated electric guitars but had to cancel this strategic initiative—sales reps weren't able to physically show dealers the guitars. Fender postponed the introduction of the new product line to October and injected a massive amount of money in online marketing. With great results.[115]

**OPPORTUNITIES FROM A CRISIS.** But the crisis wasn't only doom and gloom. In the pandemic music became a source of relief for many people. During the first lockdown, many people started picking up the guitar as a quarantine companion, spurring a surge in sales for many guitar companies. And Fender was the luckiest one. Or the most visionary? In 2019, the company had commissioned a study that revealed that while 90% of first-time purchasers stopped playing within the first year, those who persevered would spend an average of $10,000 on equipment throughout their lifetime.[116] Hence, its focus on attracting new customers. In the lockdown, Fender offered Fender Play for free for 90 days just as a goodwill gesture. But in only four months, the app gained just short of 1 million new customers. Of all those customers, 99% were new to the Fender brand, which gave its top line a surprisingly significant boost and even led to a record year in sales in 2020.

**OPENING UP NEW AVENUES.** In the months after the lockdown, Fender did not just survive—it thrived during the pandemic because it could rely on the e-commerce infrastructure that it had built before the crisis. Mooney had adapted the company to the digital world by categorizing its dealers into pure-play online businesses, brick-and-mortar stores, and omnichannel dealers (who combined the two distribution models). Says Mooney:

> "There are very different growth rates in all three categories, and those growth rates have become even more profound among dealers during the pandemic. Some have adjusted really well, and others are struggling, but everybody understands the necessity now. Naturally, those with a pre-existing online presence were able to shift more quickly and adapt to the new demand."[117]

Fender also set up its own direct-to-consumer (D2C) e-commerce business as a complement to its dealer network. It invested significantly in digital marketing and digital presence. The pandemic accelerated existing trends by two or three years—working from home, having online meetings, and buying online all leapfrogged during the pandemic.[118] Edward 'Bud' Cole, president of Fender Asia Pacific, confirmed: "The biggest learning to come out of Covid-19 is the heightened increase in consumers gravitating to online purchasing and, specifically, for a brand like Fender, to fully embrace digital shopping."[119] The company noticed that so much information was consumed digitally so it increased its investments in online channels. The online platforms could not only be used to sell guitars but also to communicate the authenticity of the Fender brand. In September 2021, the company was the first major guitar brand with an official TikTok account. With over 160 million Fender video views towards the end of 2021, this turned out to be another great strategic move, engaging many new Generation Z music fans.

In 2020, Fender's business had gone from 50% online to about 70%—a trend that was even more pronounced in China. The sales from its flagship store on Tmall, Alibaba Group's B2C online marketplace, increased dramatically. According to Cole, Fender's Tmall store doubled its sales year-on-year and was on track to represent over 10% of the company's overall business in China.[120] This trend to more online business also meant changing customer habits. Fender discovered that the Chinese customers had no reservations about buying a guitar online without touching, trying and testing the instrument, even when it came to its most expensive models.

Fender looks confidently to the future; it keeps rocking in a turbulent world. And why worry? The company has proven it can master tough environments through differentiation and continuous adaptation.[121]

## Camel story #2: Is a crisis period the right time for innovation?

It is said that the best time to repair the roof is when the sun is shining. In a business context, this translates as: The best time to innovate is when things are going well. Paradoxically, most businesses don't do that. Their motto is: why bother if your business model is working fine? They innovate when they're forced to—for example, when there is a crisis. Starbucks, the popular American coffee chain, is an exception to this rule. It innovates when the sun is shining but also when it's raining.

**HIT BY THE PANDEMIC.** The Covid-19 virus created a huge shock in the food and beverage industry. Starbucks was hurt as well: 15,000 stores in the U.S. and 4,000 stores in China had to close down, resulting in reduced customer traffic and a significant drop in sales. The management team of Starbucks wondered how it could survive in a world under quarantine. But its 2020 financial results showed that the company had survived the crisis rather well. Total revenues dropped just a little more than 10%—from $26.5 billion in 2019 to $23.5 billion in 2020—but it reported a positive operating and net income. And in 2021 and 2022, the company announced record sales again. What did Starbucks do to survive and eventually embark on a growth path immediately after the Covid-19 crisis?

**QUICK ADJUSTMENTS.** Starbucks reacted quickly to the pandemic. Like all major competitors, it had to close stores everywhere. But while many restaurants and retailers waited long to reopen, Starbucks was prescient in its pandemic approach. It announced quickly that it would make its stores 'to-go only' in response to the virus outbreak. The company re-opened stores as of early May but used a slightly different format: over 60% of its U.S. stores provided limited seating.[122] The company instituted a mobile order pick-up system, allowing customers to drive up and collect coffee from an associate outdoors, solving the problem of queuing in an overcrowded store. Starbucks swiftly incorporated the service in its app, attracting more customers.[123]

**BENEFITING FROM EARLIER INNOVATION EFFORTS.** People need their daily dose of caffeine, which certainly helped keep Starbucks afloat. But another element of Starbucks' strong survival was its innovation attitude. Starbucks had always run experiments in the background and was among the first to introduce concepts like electronic payments, third-party delivery networks (including partners such as Deliveroo or Uber Eats), and mobile apps.[124] For example, Starbucks invested a lot in its loyalty program, called Starbucks Rewards which was introduced in 2008. With this loyalty program, customers could order and pay ahead and get access to many extra benefits—such as free coffee and tasty rewards. The more you spent, the more credits you earned, and the more Starbucks knew about you. Starbucks digitized this program and used the app to make the omnichannel retail experience even more convenient and personalized.

The company was also challenging its traditional business model of being the cozy third place—after home and the workplace. Starbucks had noticed that before the Covid crisis 80% of its business was grab-and-go. Customers didn't want to spend more time in the stores but preferred buying their coffee conveniently. The coffee chain giant experimented with the introduction of pickup-only stores and digital ordering and paying tools to increase convenience for the customer.

**THE PANDEMIC AS THE ULTIMATE TESTING GROUND.** During the pandemic, these innovation initiatives paid off. As mentioned earlier, Starbucks quickly operated its stores as 'to-go only stores' in response to the virus outbreak. Those grab-and-go stores consisted of little more than a line and a place to get your drink. The company also shifted one gear higher in launching drive-through stores: before Covid-19, about one-third of the Starbucks locations had drive-through, a figure that rose to 60% in October 2020. Customers could use their mobile phones to order safely. As part of the convenience strategy, Starbucks launched the 'Stars-for-Everyone' concept whereby all customers—not only the registered users—could earn stars for rewards. It also removed some annoying payment barriers for its clients—users no longer had to preload money into the app to purchase a coffee. The results were spectacular. The loyalty program exploded during the pandemic and, at the end of 2022, about 29 million people were enrolled—up from about 16 million in 2019.[125]

Starbucks decided to double down on its convenience strategy which was slated for rollout between 2023 and 2025. The pandemic offered the company the ideal excuse for further experimentation. Starbucks expanded its drive-through and curbside pickup activities so that customers no longer had to leave their car. They continued these investments even when the lockdowns were gradually lifted. The company also bet heavily on increasing its investments in automation. It introduced a new labeling system that automatically imported orders from its third-party delivery networks, the drive-through or the Starbucks app, funneling them into one queue to streamline the entire process. The company also invested in new equipment, making it easier and faster for baristas to produce a good cup of coffee or tea.[126]

All these initiatives demonstrate Starbucks' belief in experimentation, a major factor that helped the company survive the pandemic. Starbucks even challenged the essence of its business model—to be a person's third home—although it redefined it within the constraints of its current model. That's why this story is a great example of core resilience. Former COO Rosalind Brewer agrees: "We're learning that our customers really feel that experience isn't just sitting in the store. It's when you hand off that beverage, and the interaction between the barista and customer... That can happen at the drive-through, or the entryway pickup. We feel like we're creating a third place, just in a different venue."[127]

# Camel story #3: Can camel endurance help you become a market leader during a crisis period?

Turbulence is not always caused by a single event, like a pandemic or a natural catastrophe. Some industries face turbulence for years. The technology industry is a great example. Turbulence, however, not only impacts specific industries but also particular geographical markets. Brazil was such a market—in the country's economic history, the period 1981–90 is called the 'lost decade'. It was an extremely volatile and difficult operating environment for most companies.

And here we can turn to our camel example once again. In the introduction, I already referred to the Bactrian camel's strength and endurance in camel racing. Sometimes, in order to survive longer periods of turbulence, strength, endurance, speed and agility can be useful trumps for companies too. Brahma exhibited some of those characteristics and became a winner in the Brazilian beer market. Despite the adverse conditions, Brahma grew from the eternal-second to the dominant player in the Brazilian brewing industry. Let's see how they did all this.

**TURBULENCE IN THE BRAZILIAN ECONOMY.** After 15 years of growth and prosperity—a period that is referred to as the 'Economic Miracle'—the Brazilian economy entered stormy waters from 1980 onwards. Economists attribute this lost decade to a constant series of shocks that hit the Brazilian economy. One main driver for this turbulence was Brazil's dependence on the import of energy, primarily oil. High oil prices in the 1970s and higher interest rates rendered Brazil the largest debtor in the developing world. Another driver was Brazil's dependence on foreign capital, which left it vulnerable to sudden withdrawals from foreign investors—and that happened regularly, given all the macro-economic volatility in the region. Interest rates and exchange rates changed dramatically while inflation skyrocketed—inflation averaged 700% in the period 1981–1994. Meanwhile, Brazil's GDP grew only marginally, which put the country in a period of stagflation—stagnation of growth combined with high inflation. On top of that, the country defaulted twice on its sovereign debt.[128]

Brazilian companies also faced a lot of turbulence in their industries. When Fernando Collor de Mello was elected president in 1989, he initiated some dramatic economic reforms, including the privatization of state-owned enterprises in several industries. In the early 1990s, the government abruptly reduced protective tariffs, which exposed Brazilian companies to an inflow of foreign competitors. And the Brazilian brewers faced some extra challenges: they were confronted with price controls that prevented them from increasing their prices, which led to reduced margins.[129]

And the turbulence didn't stop there. In 1994, as part of a major macroeconomic reform, the Brazilian government introduced a new currency—the real—and pegged it to the US dollar. The 'real plan' ended hyperinflation overnight—from 40% per month to 4 to 10% per year by the late 1990s—which forced the brewers into cost-control mode. Add to that the Asian financial crisis of 1997 and Russia defaulting on its foreign debt in 1998, and then you understand what economic turbulence is all about.

**CAN YOU THRIVE IN TURBULENCE?** The answer is yes. During its entire corporate life (which started in 1888), Brahma had been the eternal-second beer company after the undisputed market leader Antarctica. For about a century, Antarctica had a higher market share, higher margins, and a better reputation. But in 1989, Brahma's fortunes began to turn around. That year, Brahma was acquired by Garantia Partners Investimentos (GP), a private equity firm owned by Banco Garantia. Marcel Telles, a partner at GP, was asked to take the lead of the brewing company. Telles had no brewing experience and had never run a company before, but he had been a trader at Banco Garantia for 20 years. Then, in 1999, the unimaginable happened: Brahma acquired Antarctica and created a new company, called AmBev. Don Sull described what happened in his book *The Upside of Turbulence*.[130]

**THE IMPORTANCE OF OPERATIONAL AGILITY.** Operational agility is a company's ability to find and seize opportunities to improve operations and processes.[131] Telles and his management team injected a huge dose of operational agility in every function of Brahma—an organization that in 1989 was synonymous with a government bureaucracy that happened to make beer.

Telles introduced a new information system to get daily profit-and-loss reports by product line for each of Brahma's million sales points. This provided the company with an information advantage compared to its competitors. Brahma executives spent a lot of time visiting local operations, customers, and suppliers and identified best brewing and management practices. That information brought better market insights, which were openly discussed in the management team. To promote better discussions, Telles created an open office that allowed managers to facilitate the sharing of ideas on how to improve the business.[132]

Brahma's managers then moved quickly from insight to action and selected three organizational priorities each year. Examples of such priorities were professionalizing and improving the distribution network, improving the product quality, increasing labor productivity, etc. It's not that Antarctica didn't pursue any of these opportunities, but Brahma consistently started earlier and was more efficient and effective in implementation. How did Brahma do that?

Brahma had built a powerful cascading system to translate the corporate objectives into clear performance objectives for each unit and each individual manager. Brahma's information systems tracked performance against objectives at the corporate, unit, and individual level, and the company posted the results publicly.[133] By providing very high bonuses to the top performers—up to 18 months of the base pay—Brahma tried to make its managers 'business owners', stimulating them to go the extra mile and to do whatever was needed to improve the business results.

**A VIKING CULTURE.** Agility requires courage, focus, and determination—qualities that, with a little imagination, you also associate with the Nordic Vikings. Vikings were conquerors; they took their ships and sailed to search for new opportunities. After they conquered a land, they settled down to cultivate the terrain they had acquired, growing comfortable with their plot of land and losing their edge. In other words, Vikings became farmers. In 1989, when Telles took the helm, the company was farmer-rich and Viking-poor. But that changed over time. Exhibiting some Viking blood became a key element when recruiting or promoting people.[134] The company also installed a partnership to keep the best performers on board—i.e., to have more Vikings on the war ships.

The company also cherished a rather strong, maybe even aggressive, culture: Brahma was about winning, being competitive, breaking the rules, receiving challenging targets, and so on. In short, a very performance-driven culture—a big difference from the company Telles inherited. Part of that culture was an ambition to become the number one. In 1999, Brahma had become the number one brewer in Brazil; now the ambition was to become the global number one. The merger with Antarctica created AmBev, which then merged with Belgian beer brewer Interbrew. After the acquisition of Anheuser Busch, this company became AB InBev—now the largest brewer in the world. It is still run on the principles that made Brahma a winner in turbulence in the 1990s.

## Camel story #4: How to get ready for the extreme and unexpected?[135]

Turbulence can be caused by a pandemic or a volatile and difficult macroeconomic environment—but one of the most common sources of disruptions is a natural catastrophe. Apart from all the human suffering that they cause, such catastrophes often have a huge impact on businesses as well. In the U.S., companies prepare for the annual hurricane season and build resilience for such adverse events. But how can you prepare for such high-impact, low-likelihood risks?

**THE GREAT EAST JAPAN EARTHQUAKE.** The final camel story covers one of the most impactful natural disasters of the last two decades, the 2011 earthquake in Japan—the most powerful one ever recorded in that country—followed by a tsunami and a nuclear disaster. Over 19,000 people died, about 50,000 were injured, and 400,000 lost their homes. This natural disaster also caused one of the heaviest business turbulences for Japanese companies and corporations from all around the globe, including Intel, the American technology giant. Intel had two facilities in Japan with about 600 employees, equally spread over Tokyo and Tsukuba, a city one hour northeast of Tokyo. Intel's office in Tokyo survived the earthquake well, but the quake badly damaged the Tsukuba office (though no employees were injured). Yossi Sheffi describes how Intel dealt with this catastrophe in his book *The Power of Resilience*.[136]

**FIRST REACTIONS.** Intel wanted to evacuate all of its Japanese employees, but the personnel vetoed the idea. When the quake occurred on the afternoon of 11 March 2011, Intel's well-honed and extensively practiced crisis management processes sprang into action. Business unit crisis management teams had kickoff meetings that same Friday. One day later, Intel activated its Corporate Emergency Operation Center (CEOC) to help coordinate the response at the highest level. Intel split its response to the Japanese disaster into two parallel streams of activities, which is Intel's standard approach for such incidents.

First, Intel's Emergency Management team ensured the safety of its people and facilities in the disaster zone. The company deployed predesignated local Emergency Response Teams and local Emergency Operations Center (EOC) personnel to stabilize the situation and prevent further casualties. This meant finding a temporary location for the 300 Tsukuba workers—not easy to do given that 1.2 million buildings were damaged by the quake. With support from the corporate real estate department, Intel found two sites for its people. Meanwhile, the company used its large global construction arm—which builds Intel's fabrication plants (called 'fabs')—to accelerate the repair of the Tsukuba office.

**ENSURING CONTINUITY.** The second stream of Intel's crisis response—Business Continuity (BC)—focused on Intel's products and processes. BC had to make sure that all of the raw materials flows, chip making, and customer-related activities didn't stop or that they were restarted as soon as possible. Whereas the Intel's Emergency Management team took care of the safety issues within a couple of weeks of the quake, the BC side took six months.

Intel's first step in BC was to determine the impact of the disaster on the operations of the company and its suppliers. Intel had no factories in Japan, so the BC team focused on the supplier issues. Intel assessed the status of 365 materials. By 15 March—4 days after the quake—Intel knew it had no major problems with its Tier 1 suppliers. By 20 March, Intel knew that Tier 2 suppliers had only minor issues. However, Tier 3, Tier 4 and deeper tiers had more substantive problems. Intel identified 60 suppliers who had issues. Many of them were single-source specialty chemical manufacturers with unique capabilities. After several more days, Intel realized that 75% of the assembly and test materials were at risk. One of the more significant challenges was getting enough silicon, the base material used for almost all of Intel's chips. One of Intel's top managers was charged with checking the status of the company's silicon suppliers.

Where possible, Intel sought to maintain business continuity using existing suppliers and prequalified materials. These efforts were focused on three work streams. The first was to quickly acquire materials from its normal portfolio of prequalified suppliers. Unfortunately, despite the suppliers' best efforts, they didn't have the spare production capacity to replace what was lost in the quake. Intel's second work stream was to search and secure the supply chain's inventories of critical materials. All supply chains have inventories at every level, which creates some buffer that you can use to resolve issues. The last stream focused on prolonging the life of constrained supplies by minimizing the quantity consumed at each step of the chip-making process. For example, in one case, Intel diluted a key chemical, qualified it for use, and used the alternative formulation for eight weeks. With these initiatives, Intel hoped to fill the gap until the affected suppliers could resume normal production.

In some cases, Intel couldn't find enough prequalified suppliers with inventory or capacity to meet Intel's demands while its Japanese suppliers recovered. The threat of a production disruption led Intel to look for alternative suppliers and alternative products. Under normal circumstances, Intel's fab managers would resist quick qualification of alternative chemicals and materials. But these were not normal circumstances. Intel would need to buy previously unqualified materials and quickly qualify them to ensure they met Intel's high-quality standards. Engineers sought alternatives to constrained materials and used fast-track qualification processes to get the replacement materials into use. Intel gave purchasing managers wide freedom to buy large quantities of materials 'just in case' and accelerate the usual materials and purchasing approval processes.

**COLLABORATING WITH 'UNUSUAL PARTNERS'.** Intel wasn't the only chip maker affected by the quake and other chip makers started calling Intel for help in locating silicon. Intel assisted some of them in locating additional supplies. Intel also helped in other ways. It joined a group of Japanese companies in asking METI—Japan's Ministry of Economy, Trade, and Industry—to expedite the repair of the electrical grid around key suppliers and to exempt certain key facilities from the mandatory daily blackouts—Japan's electricity supply suffered for months after the earthquake, and daily blackouts were a solution to give everybody access to some energy.

Some aspects of Intel's response were settled relatively soon. As the BC efforts progressed, the frequency of meetings declined. During the first two weeks of the crisis, the crisis management teams of the Worldwide Materials Group had daily meetings over the status of issues such as silicon, chemicals, and back-end supplies. Then, they reduced the frequency to three times a week during April and May. In June, they further reduced the frequency to just once a week. At no time were factories down for lack of silicon.

Once the recovery effort was under control, the CEOC closed on 6 April. The logistics crisis management center wound down one day later. Other business unit crisis management teams kept working until 30 June. In total, the business continuity effort took 6 months. Complete rehabilitation of the Tsukuba office took 10 months. Throughout the entire crisis, Intel never had to halt production at any of its fabs.

## Core resilience: A combination of different tactics

**BUSINESS MODEL INNOVATION IS NOT ALWAYS THE ANSWER.** The companies described in the 4 camel stories faced different sorts of turbulence: Fender and Starbucks had to deal with the pandemic, Brahma had to find an answer to economic turbulence and an extremely volatile economic environment, and Intel faced the consequences of a natural disaster. Handelsbanken, the short case that was described in Chapter 3, had to respond to the challenges of digital disruption.

What do all these companies have in common? They all handled turbulence by sticking to their original business model—they all used the core resilience strategy to respond to turbulence. Recall from the previous chapter that a business model can be defined along 4 dimensions:

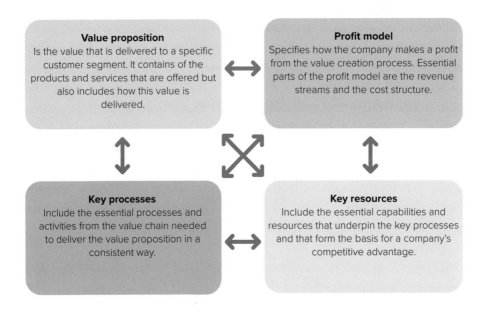

Figure 30 • Business model framework

None of the four companies—or five including Handelsbanken—changed any part of its business model. Fender, Starbucks, Brahma, Intel, and Handelsbanken kept on targeting the same set of customers with the same value proposition. They didn't change their profit model and didn't build new key processes nor new resources. (Fender and Starbucks had engaged in digital transformation, but that was before the Covid-19 crisis began.) And they were quite successful. The conclusion then is that you can survive—and even thrive—in turbulent times with an unchanged business model.

**DIFFERENT CORE RESILIENCE TACTICS.** The case studies also show that all companies have been quite active in tackling the turbulence they were facing. Core resilience is not a synonym for doing nothing and passive waiting. The stories, however, show that you can choose between different core resilience tactics and that choice depends on the nature of the turbulence that you are facing. In Chapter 1, I drew a distinction between disruption and disturbance. Core resilience is mainly used when you need to handle disturbance. Disturbance is often caused by a crisis, an event that managers and stakeholders perceive to be highly salient, unexpected, and potentially disruptive for the organization.[138]

Figure 31 distinguishes between three sorts of crises: immediate crises, emerging crises, and sustained crises.[139] The main difference between these crises is their detection lead time—the time between knowing that a disruptive event will take place and the event's first impact on the company. It is the amount of warning time during which a company can prepare for the disturbance and mitigate its effects.[140] When firms face an immediate crisis—like Intel—there is little or no warning and the detection lead time is (almost) zero. Emerging crises—such as hurricanes—develop more slowly than immediate crises and firms have some days to prepare and react. Sustained crises—such as the climate change and the economic crisis in Brazil—may last for months or years or even decades. The arrival of disruptors in your market is an example of an emergent or even a sustained crisis, where firms need to adapt to a 'new normal' or even to a 'never normal'.[141]

The different resilience tactics not only differ in terms of their detection lead time but also in their approach towards the turbulence—centered either on minimizing or avoiding the threats versus pursuing new opportunities.

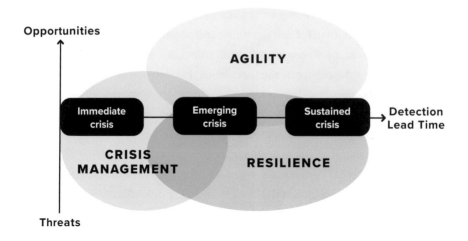

**Figure 31** • Core resilience: different tactics

The three core resilience tactics are: crisis management, resilience, and agility—three different concepts that are somehow related and sometimes even overlapping.[142] Crisis management is about readjusting an organization back into equilibrium as soon as possible.[143] Crisis management helps you to cope with an adverse event. But it's more than avoiding or minimizing threats: sometimes you're forced into embracing new opportunities, which is what many restaurant owners did when they had to close their venues. Many found opportunities to flex their well-developed off-premises muscles to stay afloat.

Resilience is the ability to maintain reliable functioning despite adversity—much like how a Bactrian camel survives in the tough environment of Central Asia. It's about how an organization anticipates, responds to, recovers and learns from adversity, especially adversity that threatens your long-term goals and survival.[144] Learning from adversity means that organizations do not just bounce back but emerge stronger. In this way, adversity is not simply a threat—it brings opportunities to improve and strengthen your company.

Which brings us to the concept of (strategic) agility—an organization's ability to continuously adapt to a complex, turbulent, and uncertain environment.[145] The literature doesn't link agility to a particular shock or adverse event but sees it as a capability that is needed in continuously turbulent and chaotic environments—so it's more useful when you are facing emerging or especially sustained crises.

Firms can choose several core resilience tactics over a relatively short period of time. When your company faces an immediate crisis, you typically apply crisis management tactics. But when the crisis mode continues—as was the case with the Covid-19 virus—and the situation stabilizes, you can start employing resilience and/or agility tactics. Fender and Starbucks both started with crisis management— they had to react quickly to the lockdowns and had to go into survival mode. But they both moved quickly in demonstrating their agility capabilities: they found new ways to create value for their existing (and new) customers.

The story of Intel is a story of crisis management. However, Intel was able to survive quite well because it had built up resilience capabilities after previous crises. The Brahma case is a nice example of how agility helped a company to become number one in its industry. There was not one particular adverse event: Brahma was confronted with a sustained state of volatility and unexpected shocks. Under the leadership of new CEO Marcel Telles, Brahma built agility capabilities to handle the sustained turbulence—capabilities that its main rival Antarctica didn't have. That's how the company grew from the eternal second into a local and, later, a global market leader.

Let's explore what each of these three tactics entail and let's then find out what your camel strategy capabilities are.

# Crisis management: The art of bouncing back[146]

When disaster strikes, organizations need to move into crisis mode and formulate a powerful response to the crisis. We're not talking about disruption—this is all about reacting to an immediate threat, an immediate crisis with a very short detection lead time, or none at all. A crisis mode is characterized by short decision times and a highly complex and ambiguous environment. It is often a stressful and difficult situation for the management team because the organization faces the risk of immediate damage. So, the goal of crisis management is to reduce the harmful impact of the event as soon as possible.

**ASSESS.** The first step in the crisis response phase is to assess the situation by collecting as much information as possible. The Intel case showed that this is not always obvious, especially when you're confronted with a large crisis. It took Intel six full days to realize that 75% of its assembly and test materials were at risk. Accept that you'll have to deal with a lot of imperfect information but try to collect as much of it as possible to make better-informed decisions so you're not flying blind.[147]

The goal of this assessment is to understand the scope of the crisis: Is this a global, regional or local crisis? Which organizational units are involved? Which stakeholders are involved? How severe is the damage? It's important to get an accurate view on your team's health and safety, your business strength—your relationships with your customers and your organization's top line, the status of your supply chain and other key resources and capabilities—and your financial situation. When trying to get a clear picture of the status of the crisis, dive back into your corporate memory and look for patterns. It is rare that crises are completely new. That was also the case with the Covid-19 pandemic. Taiwan immediately made the link to the 2003 SARS epidemic and put a public health emergency response mechanism in place that enabled experienced officials to quickly detect the crisis and to respond to it effectively.[148]

Many consultants have crisis response checklists that help you to get a clearer picture of the disturbance. Rule number one in all of the checklists is to express empathy and compassion for the human side of the upheaval.[149]

**CRISIS MANAGEMENT TEAM IN CHARGE.** At the onset of the crisis, it's important to activate a crisis management team (CMT) as soon as possible. The earlier managers realize they are in crisis mode, the faster and more effectively organizations can respond.[150] The CMT can start with implementing the crisis management plan—assuming, of course, you have one. The composition of the CMT depends on the nature of the disturbance. In the case of Intel, the CMT mainly included supply chain managers. If you are facing a cyberattack, then your CMT will be mainly composed of IT people. In the case of the Covid-19 pandemic, many organizational functions were represented because that crisis affected almost every part of the organization—from sales to operations to HR and finance. Intel had 2 such CMTs— the Emergency Management team took care of the safety of the people and facilities, while the Business Continuity team focused on the company's products and processes. These teams were predesignated—a sign that Intel was well prepared for such low-probability yet high-impact events.

The CMT is an 'integrated nerve center' that oversees the holistic crisis response. It consists of a core team that assembles a network of action teams around it. These action teams—e.g., the financial team, the supply team, the HR team, etc.—are empowered to take actions and develop policies in their respective fields. Crisis situations are characterized by high levels of uncertainty and unfamiliarity. A typical command-and-control structure is inappropriate as it is unable to deal with the complexity that disturbance brings. The CMT and the action teams are best composed of people from different parts of the organization.

These teams should work together to diagnose the current situation and design appropriate actions and interventions and then ensure that these actions are implemented properly. It's important to evaluate the impact of the implementation quickly, and then engage in another 'discover-design-execute' cycle. The operating cadence in which managers meet, discuss, and take action needs to match the evolution of the crisis.[151] When the crisis is erupting, it's important to meet frequently— daily or at least 2 to 4 times per week. When the crisis stabilizes, you can reduce the frequency of the cadence. This is what happened at Intel. During the first 2 weeks of the crisis, the CMTs met daily, but they then reduced the frequency when the crisis was more or less under control.

A final remark is to have an expert team that systematically challenges the proposed solutions. This expert team should pressure the team managers' decisions and identify potential weaknesses or overly optimistic assumptions. Many governments used a Council of Expert Advisors to support them during the pandemic.

**CRISIS COMMUNICATION.** It's a no-brainer that communication in times of crisis is of utmost importance. Nevertheless, some of the biggest corporate crises were partially attributable to big communication mistakes. The Deepwater Horizon accident in 2010 in the Gulf of Mexico is a painful example. BP's oil rig exploded in a massive blowout that killed 11 persons and injured 17 others. Two days later, the oil rig sank, setting off the largest offshore oil spill in U.S. history. This isn't a nice message to bring across, but BP's ambiguous public communication—underestimating the volume of the spill while overestimating its capability to plug the well—created an image of incompetence, at best, if not fraudulence.[152] This communication was even more painful because BP had invested massively in an identity campaign, called 'Beyond Petroleum', presenting BP's commitment to transform into a more environmentally friendly organization.

It's clear what good communication entails: effective communication happens when information is disseminated quickly, accurately, directly, and candidly to critical stakeholders, including the media.[153] Here is some advice on what *not* to do. (1) Play ostrich. Head in the ground and hope that the fuss blows over. Or the arrogant 'No comment'. This defensive attitude is still used in many cases. Unforgivable. (2) Wait until you have all of the relevant information. Crises are, by definition, uncertain and unpredictable. So, be honest about what you know and don't know. (3) Good news show. Honesty always pays off. (4) Impress with technical jargon. Or just stick to the facts but ignore feelings. Don't do this. Being precise is less important than showing the necessary emotional intelligence. Crises evoke strong emotions. Emails, texts and tweets don't address these emotions. Make use of videos: simply adding human elements, like tone of voice and body language, can turn an impersonal statement in a heartfelt message. (5) Inconsistent communication. Fatal. Make sure that you coordinate your communication well. Mixed messages coming from different parts of a disrupted organization just add to the confusion. Quite a challenge with the ever-present social media.

As already mentioned, these recommendations sound so obvious, yet organizations make these mistakes over and over again—like the Malaysian government after the disappearance of Malaysia Flight 370 from Kuala Lumpur to Beijing in the Gulf of Thailand. Malaysian officials only started communicating 6 hours after the plane was missing. They were also hesitant to reveal information because the information was "too sensitive". And when news was published, there were many inconsistencies in the reports by the Malaysian authorities on the event. There are many more examples—from public and from commercial organizations. Communicate to your employees, your customers and your key stakeholders. And it's better to define key stakeholders too broadly than too narrowly.

## Building resilience: How to react proactively

Resilience is the second major core resilience tactic. It's a very popular yet ill-defined concept in the management literature. Management consultants and business schools publish rankings of the most resilient companies, but they use a very broad set of criteria that I also associate with agility and adaptability. For example, in 2022 Swiss business school IMD published a report on the most resilient financial institutions and auto companies. The winners in the financial services industry—JP Morgan and DBS—were more conservative in their lending and managed costs through digitization. Having strong balance sheets is a prerequisite for survival in tough times. In the automotive industry, the winners were Tesla, Toyota, Volkswagen and BYD, a Chinese producer of electric vehicles. These companies continued their strategic move into electric vehicles—for me more an element of agility—but were able to navigate well through the chip shortage and supply chain threats that occurred during and after the Covid pandemic. Building extra stock and creating operational flexibility were key drivers of their success.[154]

Resilience is closely linked to risk management.[155] Recall that crisis management is about readjusting an organization back into equilibrium as soon as possible after an adverse event. Resilience is the ability to react to and recover from duress or disturbances with minimal effects on stability and functioning.[156] So, what's the difference? I define resilience more broadly than crisis management. While crisis management focuses on minimizing the impact of an immediate crisis, resilience management addresses not only the crisis but also the pre- and postcrisis phase (see Figure 32). To a large extent, Intel's success in dealing with the Japanese supply chain crisis could be attributed to the fact that the chip maker was well prepared for potential catastrophes and adverse events—i.e., thanks to how it managed the precrisis phase.

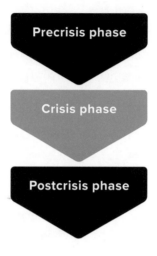

**Figure 32** • Stages of crisis management

**PRECRISIS PREPARATION.** Benjamin Franklin, one of the founding fathers of the US, once said: "An ounce of prevention is worth a pound of cure." That statement captures the essence of precrisis preparation. Precrisis interventions aim to either reduce the likelihood and/or the impact of disturbances. MIT professor Yossi Sheffi distinguishes between three precrisis interventions: prevention, crisis response, and detection. Prevention reduces the likelihood of adverse events. An appropriate crisis response diminishes the impact of an event. And it's best to use the two approaches in combination. A key element for lowering both the impact and the likelihood is early detection.[157] All this is captured in Figure 33.

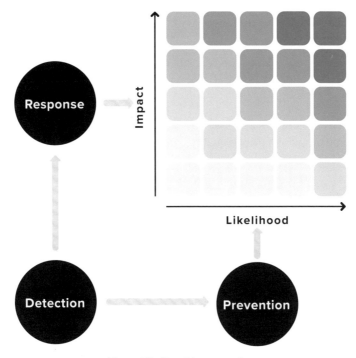

**Figure 33** • Precrisis preparation

Risk managers know that *detecting* potential risks before they occur helps reduce their negative impact. Risk managers typically plot risks on the risk assessment matrix as shown in Figure 33.[158] Risks that are plotted in the lighter zone (lower left) are 'low risks', mainly because their impact is negligible. Risks that are plotted in the darker zone (up right) are 'high risks' that deserve sufficient management attention.

Those risk managers have also become increasingly aware that they need to pay more attention to the unpredictable and unforeseen, yet highly impactful, events—the so-called black swans. That's why they complement the traditional risk management models with corporate foresight tools. Detection makes you more vigilant and there is general agreement that your warning systems should incorporate more than your traditional monitoring systems focused on your financials and operations—they need to integrate a strategic sensing system that gathers information on the most important strategic uncertainties and potential shocks. In Chapter 2, I described the key steps of such a strategic sensing process, but I also talked about what was needed to build foresight and vigilance capabilities.

A second element of good precrisis preparation is **prevention**. Prevention initiatives aim to reduce the likelihood of an adverse event. Prevention can take many forms: a company can reduce the likelihood of disturbances by being compliant with the rules, by building good relationships with its employees, customers, and suppliers, and by installing good quality management and security practices.[159]

Building a resilient organization is also about building redundancy and flexibility in your organization.[160] Redundancy is the intentional duplication of assets—this creates value from adding that little bit extra. You can build redundancy in your value chain by creating extra inventory, having several suppliers with different risk profiles, or having dual manufacturing sites or multiple warehouses. Redundancy increases your absorption capacity and applies to many business functions. For example, creating an extra capital or liquidity buffer increases your financial resilience. Be aware that the notion of redundancy goes against lean thinking and the notion of just-in-time. Many organizations have learned that striving for efficiency comes at a price, especially in turbulent times.

Flexibility is another crucial instrument for increasing resilience. Flexibility increases the number of potential uses for a given asset. A production line that you can configure to manufacture several products increases flexibility, having a diversified product portfolio increases your flexibility, and a diverse and multifunctional workforce all help you to become more resilient.[161]

Management authors have not only stressed the importance of organizational preparedness as a driver of resilience, but they've also highlighted the importance of good relations with stakeholders and partners. Stakeholders can have a huge impact on your firm—companies suffer a lot if their distribution partners or employees go on strike. Opinion groups and influencers play an increasingly important role in our society and shape the public debate on a wide range of topics such as child labor, animal rights, and many other sustainability issues. Firms can apply 'issue management' to get out in front of a potentially contentious subject. My Vlerick Business School colleague Leonardo Meeus, has identified key decisions in issue management.[162] This entails that you first identify potential issues and then make a choice on how to frame the issue: How are you trying to connect with the feelings of the audience that you are trying to persuade? The second step is building alliances and relationships with powerful actors in that field or involving NGOs and influencers. And finally, it's about deciding in which government and media arenas to make a move. Is it a good idea to take your case to court? Or can you use media campaigns to reach out to the public? And how can you connect with government officials to advance your interests on an issue? Issue management is an increasingly popular domain in strategic management that offers relevant insights on how to manage emerging crises.

Precrisis interventions can be oriented towards preparing an adequate **crisis response.** When firms build crisis management plans or set up crisis management teams with clear responsibilities and roles, they increase resilience. You can also improve crisis preparedness by creating crisis manuals or setting up a crisis management infrastructure, like Intel's Emergency Operations Center (EOC) and Business Continuity (BC) teams. The more that your people know what to do in a crisis, the more effective your response will be. Invest in training and documentation, and conduct exercises regularly to test your crisis management plan and teams.

**CRISIS PHASE.** When your firm is facing a crisis, I refer to the section on crisis management described earlier in this chapter. Try to get a good assessment of the situation to understand the scope of the crisis. This seems simple and obvious, but the reality is far different: "You should accept it as an almost universal truth that, when a crisis strikes, it will be accompanied by a host of diversionary problems. As a manager, your task is to identify the real crisis."[163]

Put your crisis management team in charge and activate the crisis response systems as soon as possible. Take action where needed and don't be afraid to deviate from your planning. Crises are always uncertain events with a considerable dose of surprise—so discover, design, and execute, and check the effectiveness of your actions. Finally, don't forget to communicate appropriately and try to avoid the many communication mistakes that so many firms have made in the past.

**POSTCRISIS PHASE.** Resilient organizations don't just pay attention to the precrisis phase and to the actual crisis management—they are aware of the importance of the postcrisis phase too. In the aftermath of a crisis, there is always the desire to resume business as usual. For that purpose, organizations have created extensive business recovery programs. But implementing these plans is not always the end of a crisis. The reality is that the postcrisis risks to an organization can be even larger than those during the crisis itself. The experiences of BP (with the Deepwater Horizon incident), Union Carbide (with the Bhopal crisis), and Exxon (with Exxon Valdez) show that postcrises issues can persist for years or even decades.[164] In those cases, operational recovery is just one element of the recovery process. Managing your reputation and winning back confidence from customers, employees, investors, and other stakeholders might be even more challenging endeavors.

Recovery is not just getting back to work but is also asking: What have we learned from this crisis? How can we prevent this from happening again and what could/ should we have done differently? Resilient firms also add an evaluation and learning module to their crisis management repertoire. They take the time to do profound analyses on multiple aspects of the crisis—operational, human, financial, stakeholder management, etc.—and they don't forget to communicate the lessons learned to the crisis management team and those most involved in and impacted by the crisis. And the communication suggestions remain relevant in this phase too. One author concluded: "The end of every crisis should be the beginning of the preparation step for the next one."[165]

## Agility management: Surfing the waves of volatility and uncertainty

Some organizations don't just bounce back from turbulence but bounce forward applying the proverb: "What doesn't kill you makes you stronger." Recall the examples of Starbucks and Fender. Both were struck by the consequences of the lockdown. The two companies first engaged in crisis management to stabilize the situation—but then, through searching and experimentation, they found a way to sustain the business in Covid-19 times. They doubled down on some strategic moves that they had initiated earlier and that forced them in a slightly different direction (but not a business model innovation)—Fender on conquering the e-commerce universe—and Starbucks with a new model focusing on increasing the convenience with a grab-and-go concept.

Brahma is another great example of surfing the waves of volatility and uncertainty. The company was able to detect opportunities for operational improvements and implemented them consistently before any other player in the market. This approach gave it a competitive edge, and Brahma became the market leader in the Brazilian brewing industry and later in the global beer market.

There are many more examples of companies who have benefited from turbulence by being agile, innovative and adaptive. Agility is a hot topic today and consultants compile various rankings of the most agile or adaptive companies—LEGO, Netflix, Cisco Systems, and Airbnb are just a few of the companies who often make it to these lists.

All these companies have embraced agility to fight the consequences of turbulence. Turbulence—whatever its form—brings threats *and* opportunities. Agility is about managing the opportunity part of the equation: it's the capacity to identify and capture opportunities more quickly than your rivals do.[166] There is sufficient evidence that links agility to success and survival in turbulent and unpredictable environments.[167] So let's figure out what you can do to improve your agility skills. That's easier said than done, because agility is a concept that is used in many different contexts. Most of us are familiar with 'agile' project management. But we're interested in the concept of *strategic agility*—sometimes referred to as organizational agility. When defining strategic agility, Donald Sull and Charles Sull, both faculty members at MIT, distinguish between operational agility and portfolio agility.[168] The first concept is more relevant for individual business units, the second for multi-business firms.

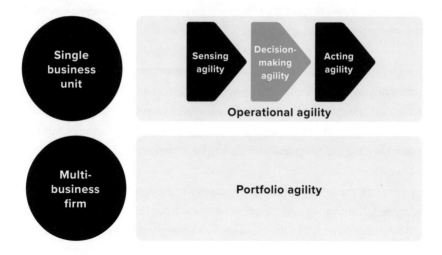

**Figure 34** • Building blocks of strategic agility

**AGILITY FOR A SINGLE BUSINESS UNIT.** Business units can win with operational agility, which is a combination of sensing faster, deciding faster, and acting faster. This speed factor gives you a competitive advantage relative to your competitors, leading to higher growth and better margins.

*SENSING AGILITY.* I've stressed it several times throughout this book: turbulence requires building sensing and foresight capabilities. While resilient companies focus more on the potential risks, it's important to consider the opportunities that turbulence brings. Sensing agility means scanning the environment continuously and making sense of the changes that are taking place. This is not just a top management responsibility—agile companies involve many people from many different departments in this scanning and futuring process, and they organize a rich and open internal dialogue.

Sensing agility is not restricted to examining macrotrends but also involves screening market information. Agile companies always try to understand what the competitors are doing and how customer expectations are changing. Recall that, in Brahma's case, sensing really started after the company introduced a new information system that provided detailed information per product line.

***DECISION-MAKING AGILITY.*** Turbulent environments require you to make decisions fast, often based on incomplete information. Don't wait until you have all the facts and figures to make up your mind—make assumptions based on the information you have and define the most logical action plan that will help you move forward. Regularly check whether those actions lead to satisfying results—and if that's not the case, revise your assumptions and renew the action plan. Companies like Zara and Airbnb are famous for their decision-making agility. Although Airbnb was hit hard by the Covid-19 crisis, it bounced back in 2020 and came up with more than 150 updates to improve the end-to-end experience for hosts and guests, focusing on a single priority to prepare for the travel rebound in 2021.[169]

You can increase decision-making agility by decentralizing decision-making to your local teams as much as you can. This is a common practice at Handelsbanken, the Swedish banking group and it helped the company beat its competitors during the Covid-19 crisis (and long before). Researchers have found a positive correlation between decentralization and success.[170] Decentralization increases the speed of decision-making and empowers middle managers, giving them the feeling that they make a difference. But decentralization only works if the managers and middle managers understand the broader strategic context. Companies like Brahma (and later AB InBev) identified a limited number of top priorities every year and cascaded them down through the rest of the organization. So, it's the combination of decentralization and strategic awareness that leads to higher levels of decision-making agility.

***ACTING AGILITY.*** Agility goes hand in hand with innovation. Even if your company decides not to engage in business model innovation, pursuing incremental innovation helps you withstand tough times better. A study by McKinsey revealed that rapid iteration and experimentation and continuous learning differentiate most between agile and non-agile companies. Agile companies innovated iteratively through fast cycles of field testing and learning from mistakes. They also worked a lot with concepts such as minimum viable products (MVP), trying to bring new products and services to the market fast. Agile companies embraced continuous learning and give their employees time to look for ways to improve business processes and new ways of working or integrating new technologies.[171]

Acting agility also involves the capability to work together both internally and externally. Agile firms use cross-functional teams to reduce response times for the customer or to improve products and services. But they actively collaborate with external partners as well. In Chapter 1, we saw that firms increasingly think in terms of ecosystems, in which you team up with partners to bring new products to the market.

A final element of acting agility is change capacity. Continuously moving the organization into new directions is easier said than done. People get tired of too much change, so don't underestimate the time and conviction that you need to get the organization in motion. This can only happen with dedicated top and middle managers. The story of Brahma showed that if the effort can be sustained, it can lead to a fundamentally different culture—in Brahma's case: very performance-driven, with an organization full of Vikings instead of farmers.

**AGILITY FOR A MULTI-BUSINESS FIRM.** Most of the agility practices apply to a business unit. Don Sull showed that agility can also be applied to a corporate business portfolio and he introduced the concept of portfolio agility. Portfolio agility allows you to quickly and effectively shift resources across different business units. Resources can be financial but they also include talented managers and employees and management attention.[172] Sull's research indicated that portfolio agility represented the biggest difference between the most agile and the less agile companies.[173]

Applying portfolio agility is also quite difficult. A large empirical study found that less than 20% of the managers said their organization quickly and effectively reallocated money or people when circumstances changed or cut their losses quickly enough when innovation initiatives failed.[174] The study indicated that managers often avoid reallocating resources to maintain a sense of fairness and to minimize conflict across units. However, in a downturn, the last thing you should do is keep everybody happy and apply flat, across-the-board cuts for every unit. Corporate managers need to deploy resources quickly towards new opportunities and shouldn't take historical allocations as a given for the present situation.

**CORE RESILIENCE = RESILIENCE + AGILITY.** Agility and resilience (including crisis management) seem like different management concepts. Resilience is more focused on protecting the core business against adversity, while agility allows a company to jump on opportunities inside (and outside) the core. And while both are effective in isolation, the combination of the two is what constitutes true core resilience. Resilient companies can weather a storm better, and their absorption capacity provides them with the resources to fund emerging opportunities. This only works if your company is agile enough to seize the opportunities.

Don Sull calls this combination 'agile absorption' and he makes a nice analogy with boxing.[175] He referred to one of the most legendary boxing matches between Muhammad Ali and George Foreman—called the Rumble in the Jungle, held in Kinshasa, Zaire (now the Democratic Republic of the Congo), in 1974. George Foreman was the absolute favorite—Ali came in as a 4–1 underdog against the heavy-hitting Foreman, who had an enormous absorption capability—Foreman was a master of resilience. Muhammad Ali, on the other hand, was a dancer—the equivalent of agility—he would 'float like a butterfly and sting like a bee'. What Foreman didn't know was that Muhammad Ali had changed his training regimen and fought with the hardest-hitting sparring partners he could find, improving his resilience skills. And during the Rumble in the Jungle, he deployed the 'rope-a-dope' strategy by deliberately placing himself on the ropes so that he could better absorb Foreman's massive blows. Although Foreman kept throwing punches, after the fifth round, he was worn out. In the eighth round, the unimaginable happened: Ali launched a five-punch combination, forcing Foreman to stumble on the canvas.[176] In this legendary fight, Ali was performing a master class of core resilience—combining the power of resilience and agility.

# What about your camel capabilities?

Managing turbulence requires that you defend your core business well. This chapter has shown that a company with agility and resilience/crisis management capabilities can survive longer and better in tough times—whether the challenge comes from shifting customer demands, changing legislation, technological developments, or sudden shocks. The following checklist tells you whether you have both the resilience and agility capabilities to become a true core-resilient company. If you score high on the resilience part of the questionnaire—this means at least a score of 30 out of 50—you're ready to counter the turbulence threats. If you score high on the agility part of the questionnaire—again a score of 30 or more out of 50—you're well-equipped to jump on opportunities that turbulence brings inside your core business.

| RESILIENCE AND CRISIS MANAGEMENT CAPABILITIES | STRONGLY DISAGREE | NEITHER AGREE NOR DISAGREE | STRONGLY AGREE |
|---|---|---|---|
| 1. We have early warning signals in place that help us to identify and anticipate emerging threats. | 1 ○ ○ ○ ○ ○ | | 5 |
| 2. We extensively communicate with a wide range of stakeholders to identify emerging trends, potential concerns or issues. | 1 ○ ○ ○ ○ ○ | | 5 |
| 3. We have built redundancy and flexibility into our operations (such as extra suppliers, extra stock, dual manufacturing sites, or a broad product portfolio) to deal with unexpected events and circumstances. | 1 ○ ○ ○ ○ ○ | | 5 |
| 4. Our organization has strong collaborative relationships with suppliers, distribution partners and other relevant stakeholders. | 1 ○ ○ ○ ○ ○ | | 5 |
| 5. Our organization has the capacity to respond to and recover from disruptions quickly. | 1 ○ ○ ○ ○ ○ | | 5 |
| 6. Our organization has a crisis management plan that is updated regularly. | 1 ○ ○ ○ ○ ○ | | 5 |
| 7. We have a designated crisis management team in place that is well-trained. | 1 ○ ○ ○ ○ ○ | | 5 |
| 8. We have an empowered and supportive workforce that is committed to going the extra mile even in tough times. | 1 ○ ○ ○ ○ ○ | | 5 |
| 9. Our leadership team is able to make critical decisions on how to run the business in times of crisis. | 1 ○ ○ ○ ○ ○ | | 5 |
| 10. We have a strong balance sheet including a large capital buffer to withstand periods of turbulence. | 1 ○ ○ ○ ○ ○ | | 5 |

| AGILITY CAPABILITIES | STRONGLY DISAGREE | NEITHER AGREE NOR DISAGREE | STRONGLY AGREE |
|---|---|---|---|
| 11. We scan and examine the environment to anticipate change and look for new opportunities to grow or improve the business. | 1 ○ ○ ○ ○ ○ | | 5 |
| 12. Our information systems provide us with detailed and reliable market data in real time. | 1 ○ ○ ○ ○ ○ | | 5 |
| 13. Every year, our company defines a limited set of corporate objectives that are translated further down in the organization. | 1 ○ ○ ○ ○ ○ | | 5 |
| 14. The teams in our organization take and implement decisions very quickly. | 1 ○ ○ ○ ○ ○ | | 5 |
| 15. Employees in our company have the power to influence decisions taken by the management. | 1 ○ ○ ○ ○ ○ | | 5 |
| 16. Top executives have the courage to invest in major opportunities when they arise. | 1 ○ ○ ○ ○ ○ | | 5 |
| 17. Team members regularly engage in innovation projects that develop through fast cycles of field testing and learning. | 1 ○ ○ ○ ○ ○ | | 5 |
| 18. Our employees are encouraged to take initiatives to learn new things. | 1 ○ ○ ○ ○ ○ | | 5 |
| 19. We set up partnerships with competitors or external partners to exploit short-term opportunities. | 1 ○ ○ ○ ○ ○ | | 5 |
| 20. Top executives are not afraid to reallocate cash and top management talent across business units. | 1 ○ ○ ○ ○ ○ | | 5 |

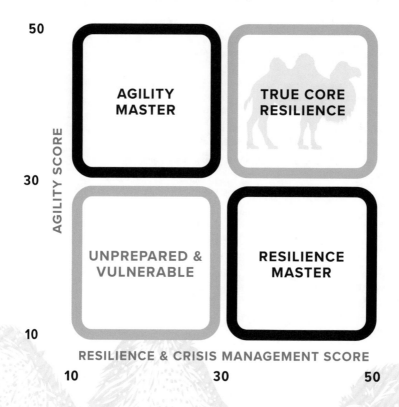

**Figure 35** • How well are you equipped for a camel strategy?

# KEY TAKEAWAYS

- Firms don't have to engage in business model innovation to counter turbulence successfully. A core resilience strategy—reacting to turbulence within the confines of your business model—can yield great results.
- Core resilience is not a synonym for just waiting and doing nothing.
- The stories of Fender, Starbucks, Brahma, and Intel show that core resilience can take different forms, depending on the nature of the turbulence that your organization is facing.
- One core resilience tactic is crisis management, which is needed to handle the consequences of an immediate crisis.
- But firms who embrace core resilience are not just reacting to a crisis or adverse event—they try to react proactively by developing resilience capabilities.
- Adding agility capabilities to your resilience skills yields a powerful combination to help you win your rumble in the jungle.
- Don't underestimate the challenges of building core resilience capabilities.

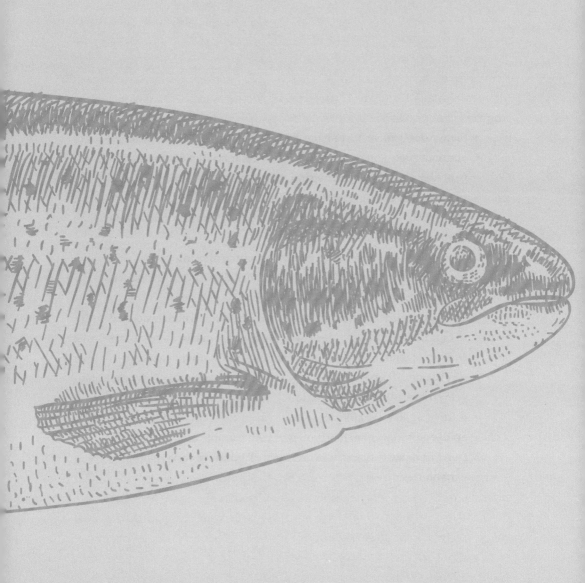

# CHAPTER
# 5

## chapter of the salmon
—
## Corporate innovation

# Key questions addressed in this chapter

What is a corporate innovation strategy?

Where do companies get their inspiration to build new business models?

What are the organizational requirements needed for business model innovation outside the core?

Is any top management involvement needed when building new business models outside the core?

How do you move from idea to project? And how do you move from project to a new business?

The first strategy firms can adopt to tackle turbulence is core resilience. That is probably the most often adopted strategy. The most described turbulence strategy, however, is the salmon strategy—or the strategy of corporate innovation. Many management authors have recommended engaging in transformational innovation activities and building new business models outside the core. The advice to set up speedboats or build unicorns is not new. Researchers have found that long-term survival and success depends on the ability to renew yourself. The failure to do so can endanger the most successful organizations. Corporate history is full of examples of market leaders that lost it and went bankrupt or were taken over because they lacked corporate innovation—Kodak, Borders, Polaroid, Wang, RIM, Pan Am, TWA, Compaq, and Tower Records are just some names out of a long list.

At the same time, inspired by books such as *Competing for the Future* and *Blue Ocean Strategy*,[177] strategy authors have increasingly focused attention on new entrants that have grown to become market leaders through disrupting the market with new business recipes—the stories of Apple, Google, Alibaba, Meta, IKEA, and Southwest Airlines are familiar to most of us. So, on the one hand, you have companies that have emerged as winners through innovation and others that have lost because of a lack of adaptation and innovation.

No surprise that the concept of corporate innovation—and especially business model innovation—has emerged as one of the main strategy topics of the last few decades. But as usually happens when hype takes over, managers are just stuck with half-hearted truths and all-too-simplistic recipes and recommendations. Launching speedboats is everything but obvious. Recent research from McKinsey shows that innovation, including business model innovation, remains a challenging journey: while 86% of the executives surveyed said that innovation was a Top Three priority, fewer than 10% said that they were satisfied with their organization's innovation performance.[178]

This chapter elaborates on how a salmon strategy can help you deal with turbulence. The recommendations are based on several examples of successful corporate innovators, spanning different sectors and tackling different sources of turbulence—digital disruption, low-cost competition, and sustainability challenges.[179] I start this chapter by describing three of them. These case studies highlight the typical challenges that occur when you build a business model outside your core. It turns out that the biggest challenge with a salmon strategy is not how to build your new business model but rather how to manage the relationships with the traditional core business. Successfully expanding outside your core requires that you have an organization that can run two different business models at the same time.

## The salmon: A master of corporate innovation

Corporate innovation is about building new businesses in different—and often new—markets. Some animals face similar challenges and are forced to move and live in a new environment. The story of the salmon is a case in point.

Born as freshwater fish, salmon spend a few months to a few years (depending on the species) in rivers before moving out to the ocean. In preparation for their time at sea, salmon must adapt their biology to survive in salt water and then enter an ocean they've never seen. This move is quite remarkable. Most fish can only tolerate a narrow range of salinity and are highly sensitive to any changes in the level of salt in the water in which they dwell. That's why most freshwater fish can't survive in salt water—the water inside their bodies would flow out of their cells and they would die of dehydration.

Fortunately, the salmon has some remarkable adaptations, both behavioral and physiological, that allow it to thrive in both fresh and saltwater environments. To offset the dehydration effects of salt water, salmon drink copiously—several liters per day. You're probably thinking: it's a fish surrounded by water after all... But salmons do drink. However, in fresh water, salmon don't drink at all. But there is more. When salmon prepare for a life in the ocean their kidneys reduce urine production dramatically. At the same time, molecular pumps in the cells of the gills also shift into reverse, pumping sodium out instead of in. This process is called osmoregulation and is an important transition in the life of a salmon. At this point, salmon are ready for their stay at sea where they spend most of their life.

The amazing behavioral and physiological adaptations allow salmon to move from fresh to saltwater and then back when they return to spawn, after which they die. The critical changes in osmoregulation are not immediate, though. When a young salmon leaves its home stream, it must rest in brackish water for several days or weeks while it adjusts. And that process repeats itself when the salmon returns to make the opposite transition.

It's amazing to see how animals adjust to the demands of their environment. Salmon are masters of adaptation as they can survive in environments with very different physiological requirements. Companies that pursue a corporate innovation strategy also build innovation ventures with a business model that is different from their traditional core. Let's explore the three salmon stories in more detail.

## Salmon story #1: Can you build a successful platform business if you're not a leading technology firm?[180]

Our first salmon story brings us to House of HR, a European talent solutions and recruitment company with headquarters in Belgium. It's 2015 and technology revolutions are causing fundamental change in the temping industry. Both companies and candidates want more individualized end-to-end solutions in the job recruitment process. Is this an opportunity for digital-native entrants who can set up staffing operations without the traditional brick-and-mortar stores? Recruitment marketplaces like Monster.com and Stepstone, both founded in the mid 1990s, were aggressively taking market share from the traditional recruitment players. Then in 2003, recruitment companies saw another player enter their market: LinkedIn. That company also became a much more mature competitor a decade later.

**A PARTICULAR CHALLENGE FOR HOUSE OF HR.** This was the context for House of HR, one of the larger HR service providers and recruitment companies in Europe. The board appointed Jérôme Caille as CEO to build a new strategy to tackle these trends and evolutions. Caille had management experience in the industry but had also been active in the startup world. Together with Peter Ingelbrecht, an experienced online startup builder who became Chief Innovation Officer of the House of HR, he was determined to launch corporate innovation initiatives. The two often discussed the disruption of the staffing and recruitment industry and involved House of HR employees in their brainstorm sessions. They sent them to innovation courses, set up future strategy workshops and even created a Kill Accent Team in October 2015—Accent Jobs being the founding company of the House of HR Group. The team had to foster innovation in the company "to become the most digital and human player on earth".

Accent Jobs' core business was the temporary-to-permanent recruitment market, where the companies have the candidates first work on a temporary basis before offering permanent employment. For Accent Jobs, this was a healthy, high-margin business. Accent consultants were, however, spending significant time fulfilling student and similar flexible working requests. Typical examples include a restaurant looking for a waiter or a barman for four hours, or a retailer looking for a cashier or cleaning help. The company figured out that consultants were spending 20% of their time on those requests which generated only 3% of the revenues. Furthermore, this was low-margin business, which didn't really fit the core business of the company.

**THE SOLUTION.** Peter Ingelbrecht compiled a small team that proposed a new solution for the instant temporary market. An international survey had pointed out that youngsters—especially students and flexi-jobbers—were waiting for an application that was 'do-it-yourself,' very easy and instant, with direct feedback. The new unit was called NowJobs and the ambition was to capture the European flexible staffing market and be a leading international marketplace for matching instant temporary assignments using a fully automated process. The company built a digital platform that handled all communication between the candidates and companies and fully automated the contracting and the administrative processing—100% online via the payroll platform. The new solution was all about accessibility: instant match of offer and demand (like Uber), smooth communication (like Snapchat) and fun interactions (like Pokémon Go). The other dimensions of the value proposition did not fundamentally change: fees were similar, the product—matching supply and demand—was similar too and service levels were minimal, but that didn't matter because the application was so straightforward and easy-to-use.

However, providing this fully automated digital solution required a fundamental change in the other blocks of the business model. Key processes and activities significantly changed because of the fully digitized interface with the customer and the (almost) fully automated back-office operations. Compared with other temping companies, the number of developers at NowJobs was significantly higher. NowJobs didn't introduce a new revenue model but aimed at working more efficiently at lower cost. Figure 36 compares NowJobs' business model with the model of the traditional competitors.

**A LEAN STARTUP.** The NowJobs team was led by Peter Ingelbrecht, CIO of the House of HR group, who reported directly to the group CEO. He assembled a team with two bright, young employees—one for product management and one for sales and marketing—and an experienced software developer. In June 2016, the four-person team received approval, funding, and a separate spot to set up a unit to tackle the opportunity in the instant temporary jobs market. The team had complete freedom on almost all strategic, operational and organizational decisions. 27 April 2017 marked the official launch of the new company. The development process went quite fast: the team knew there was a market for their solution and knew how the concept should look—it was about creating a vacancy, finding jobseekers, and getting the contract and the payments out—but in a digital way.

**NowJobs**

| Value proposition | VERY SIMILAR TO COMPETITORS | | SOMEWHAT SIMILAR TO COMPETITORS | | VERY SIMILAR FROM COMPETITORS |
|---|:---:|:---:|:---:|:---:|:---:|
| Product performance | ● | ○ | ○ | ○ | ○ |
| Price level of the offering | ● | ○ | ○ | ○ | ○ |
| Accessibility of the offering | ○ | ○ | ○ | ○ | ● |
| Service level associated with the offering | ● | ○ | ○ | ○ | ○ |
| Sustainability of the offering | ● | ○ | ○ | ○ | ○ |
| **Key processes and activities** | VERY SIMILAR TO COMPETITORS | | SOMEWHAT SIMILAR TO COMPETITORS | | VERY SIMILAR FROM COMPETITORS |
| Front-end activities | ○ | ○ | ○ | ● | ○ |
| Back-end activities | ○ | ○ | ○ | ● | ○ |
| Support and management activities | ● | ○ | ○ | ○ | ○ |
| **Key resources** | VERY SIMILAR TO COMPETITORS | | SOMEWHAT SIMILAR TO COMPETITORS | | VERY SIMILAR FROM COMPETITORS |
| Core resources and capabilities | ○ | ○ | ○ | ● | ○ |
| Network of suppliers and partners | ● | ○ | ○ | ○ | ○ |
| Role in the entire ecosystem | ● | ○ | ○ | ○ | ○ |
| **Profit Model** | VERY SIMILAR TO COMPETITORS | | SOMEWHAT SIMILAR TO COMPETITORS | | VERY SIMILAR FROM COMPETITORS |
| Revenue structure | ● | ○ | ○ | ○ | ○ |
| Cost structure | ○ | ○ | ○ | ○ | ● |

**Figure 36** · NowJobs' business model innovation

At the end of 2016—some months before NowJobs' official launch—Randstad, a major temping competitor, had launched its own venture, Ploy, to address the temporary staffing market. There was no time to lose. The NowJobs team worked even harder to get its app on the market. It first built a local app for companies and students in the Ghent area—a large Belgian student city close to the Accent Jobs' Head Office. A news report on the Belgian national television helped the new venture to get national exposure: within 24 hours, 21,000 candidates registered on the app and customers all over Belgium joined.[181] Revenues in the pilot year amounted to 0.54 million EUR and increased to 6 million one year later (2018).

Unlike Ploy, which continued to focus on the catering market (hotels, restaurants, cafés), NowJobs entered new industries—from catering to retail and cleaning. The startup also forged an important partnership with Tomorrowland, one of the world's biggest dance festivals, giving it even more national exposure.

NowJobs continuously improved the app and grew fast partially because all technology development was done in-house. The company quickly supported multi-day contracts and added more features to the app. To support its national expansion, NowJobs relied on Accent Jobs' national branch network. It's important to have enough candidates *and* customers in this business, and that's where Accent Jobs' network was a crucial advantage. NowJobs shared part of the revenues with Accent Jobs and that paid off: in 2019, revenues amounted to 33 million EUR—while competitor Ploy was dropped from the app store, meaning that NowJobs now had a virtual monopoly in this new market. NowJobs believed it was time to expand geographically and started targeting the Netherlands.

The following year, 2020, started off well. Artificial intelligence was further integrated for better matching and NowJobs arranged a partnership with a leading bank to accommodate instant payments. Their targets were ambitious: 50 million EUR in revenues. But then the Covid-19 pandemic struck—and within days 95% of the NowJobs sales staff were put on the bench.[182] But the commercial team reacted swiftly and looked for new industries, such as logistics and medical, and also contributed to staffing the many vaccination centers. NowJobs also added new customers like food delivery company HelloFresh, and retailers Carrefour, MediaMarkt, and Albert Heijn.

The product management team and the development team, however, were working extra hours, because the company had planned to enter the French market through the acquisition of the startup StaffMe. In 2020, the company reached revenues of 29 million EUR and the Belgian unit of NowJobs was break-even. In 2021, the company continued its growth path and achieved 58 million EUR in revenues. In 2022, NowJobs decided to add Germany as their fourth home market. The company's ambition is to become the best staffing app in Europe and a digital leader in e-recruitment. At the moment of writing, the organization has about 100 employees focusing on fourth different markets. Its ambition is to grow to 250 million EUR in the next three years.

## Salmon story #2: Is it smart to copy a failure story?

Why would an iconic brand that stands out for its high standard in care and service enter the low-cost airline industry? Singapore Airlines (SIA) set up Scoot in 2011, but many industry observers wondered why. Fueled by the stories of British Airways, Continental, United Airlines, and KLM, there was the common perception that full-service airlines could not successfully run a low-cost airline.

In 2011, the newly appointed CEO Goh Choon Phong was tasked with charting SIA's long-term growth path. At that time, the airline group had about 20 subsidiaries and numerous associated companies ranging from airlines and cargo to engineering and terminal services. The Singapore Airlines Group owned Singapore Airlines and SilkAir, two premium airline companies operating in the long-haul and short-haul markets. The group also had a minority participation in Tiger Airways, a low-cost short-haul carrier from Singapore. In 2011, the group had revenues of almost S$15 billion—or $10.4 billion—with about 22,500 employees.

**CHALLENGES IN THE ASIAN AIRLINE INDUSTRY.** CEO Goh Choon Phong and his management team were aware that the Asian airline industry was undergoing fundamental structural change. The main change drivers were the growing competition from the Persian Gulf carriers—Emirates, Etihad, and Qatar Airways—

who were challenging SIA in its core premium segment. SIA was also confronted with increasing competition from low-cost carriers in the Asian market and from Chinese airline companies. The low-cost carrier market took off in the 1970s in the United States and then moved on to Europe in the 1980s. Low-cost carriers appeared on the Asian and Australian market in the early 2000s but it wasn't until 2004 that the model was introduced to Singapore in short-haul form. Eight years later, 30% of Singapore's airline passenger throughput was carried by budget airlines.[183]

Goh Choon Phong was determined to react and was willing to set up a new business model in his portfolio. Goh appointed Campbell Wilson (a longtime SIA employee who made it to the management team) as CEO of Scoot, and Ng Chin Hwee as Chairman of the new venture. Ng was SIA's Executive Vice President of Human Resources and Operations.

**THE ANSWER.** SIA was known for its innovation culture, but entering the low-cost arena was clearly a daring strategic move that evoked much reaction from both inside and outside the company. Scoot would cover the gap that was left in SIA's portfolio: the low-cost long-haul segment (see Figure 37), a quite unique model in the global airline industry. According to Goh Choon Phong, this portfolio strategy gave the group the flexibility and nimbleness needed to adjust to a highly dynamic market.[184]

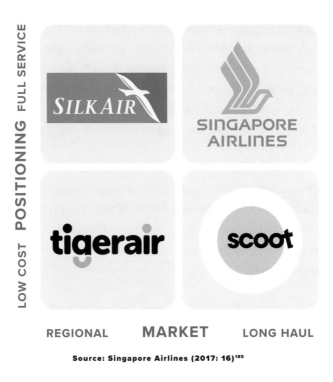

Source: Singapore Airlines (2017: 16)[185]

**Figure 37** • Singapore Airlines' Portfolio Strategy

Most low-cost carriers were targeting the price-sensitive passenger on the short-haul flights. The low-cost carriers saved costs on as many operational aspects as possible, thereby also reducing service levels for the customers. One key tactic to achieve lower costs was single-passenger class. Another was increasing aircraft utilization—i.e., having short turnaround times so that carriers could have as many flights per day as possible. This tactic was, however, less appropriate for long-haul flights. The long-haul's greater distance meant that more fuel was required, which slowed on-the-ground refueling. At the same time, greater distance also meant fewer trips per day. These factors brought low-cost long-haul utilization rates close to the rates of the full-service carriers.[186] Nevertheless, SIA believed that it could set up a low-cost airline company for the long-haul market. Wilson and Ng were given quite a bit of freedom to create the new carrier. Says Wilson:

'There was a spreadsheet with a pro-forma business case, which had been used to get Singapore Airlines' approval for the project. And there were two PowerPoint slides, one of which essentially said, "It's going to be a leisure-focused airline targeting the young, the young at heart, and the cost conscious." And then another slide with a list of potential names for the airline, names like Singapore Express and Fresh Air.'[187]

The new venture aimed at reducing prices by 40% compared to SIA and reducing the service level significantly. If the plane arrived late—which would only occur sporadically—passengers had to suffer the consequences themselves. Building a low-cost airline company was not rocket science—it was a matter of relentlessly focusing on reducing unit costs. Scoot went far. Employees didn't get laptops or other stationery.[188] The new company tried to save costs when recruiting cabin crew, pilots and flight attendants—and they succeeded because Singapore is a popular place to live and hence the new jobs attracted a lot of interest. Wilson commented,

'Our aircrafts are fully customized Boeing 777 with 402 seats—40% more than a full-service carrier would fit. Because of the simpler service model—no hot towels for everyone, for example—we can remove 1.5 galleys and fit an extra seat in each row by having narrower aisles. We can take out one and a half tons of equipment and cabling that feeds the seatback TV system because we give you a wireless streaming entertainment system instead, resulting in an aircraft that is 7% lighter. And because our schedules are not built around the corporate traveler, and our fares are so attractive, we can keep the aircraft in the air 40—50% more hours per day than a typical full-service airline. Added together, our unit cost is about 40% lower than even the most efficient legacy carriers.'[189]

But the company did not compromise on operational security and safety standards—there the bar was kept as high as with SIA. Later on, Scoot replaced its fleet of Boeing 777s with Boeing 787s, which resulted in further fuel cost savings. The company also saved costs on marketing and advertising and actively used social media. As with the traditional low-cost carriers, a significant part of the revenue was derived from ancillary sales. And early on, the company looked for synergies with the other low-cost airline of the SIA group, Tigerair. All this led to a very different business model than that of its parent company (see Figure 38).

Still, according to Wilson, simply being low-cost would not help the organization stand out in the crowd. Therefore, early on, Scoot's core team focused on creating a very specific culture, called 'Scootitude'. Wilson coined the term to describe the fuss-free, fun attitude he hoped the airline would portray.[190] In this way, Scoot got a personality, captured well by the color yellow—bright and loud—which was very much aligned with its young and young-at-heart target group.

**FROM 5 TO ALMOST 2,500.**[191] The Scoot project started in 2011. Before that, analysts in the SIA Group had investigated the success and failure stories of low-cost carriers over the years, especially those who tried to enter the long-haul market. In February 2011, Campbell Wilson was appointed CEO of Scoot and he assembled a team of 5 employees from SIA, covering flight operations, engineering, safety and security. The team was located in a terminal at Singapore's Changi Airport where SIA did not operate, signaling the autonomy the team had in building the new company.[192] Driven by a startup spirit, the team laid out the basics of what Scoot was all about and how it should operate—deciding about aircrafts, seating configurations, procurement, inflight entertainment systems, fixing hubs and slots at international airports, people issues, IT systems, sales approaches, and much more...

The team started hiring employees mainly from outside SIA. Wilson only recruited former SIA employees for flight operations, safety and maintenance to ensure the same standards as the parent company. He recruited an HR manager from outside SIA to bring in a fresh, original, and professional HR approach for Scoot and to build the Scootitude culture that helped the company differentiate from the competitors.

**Scoot**

| Value proposition | VERY SIMILAR TO COMPETITORS | | SOMEWHAT SIMILAR TO COMPETITORS | | VERY SIMILAR FROM COMPETITORS |
|---|:---:|:---:|:---:|:---:|:---:|
| Product performance | ● | ○ | ○ | ○ | ○ |
| Price level of the offering | ○ | ○ | ○ | ○ | ● |
| Accessibility of the offering | ● | ○ | ○ | ○ | ○ |
| Service level associated with the offering | ● | ○ | ○ | ○ | ○ |
| Sustainability of the offering | ● | ○ | ○ | ○ | ○ |
| **Key processe and activities** | VERY SIMILAR TO COMPETITORS | | SOMEWHAT SIMILAR TO COMPETITORS | | VERY SIMILAR FROM COMPETITORS |
| Front-end activities | ○ | ○ | ● | ○ | ○ |
| Back-end activities | ○ | ○ | ○ | ○ | ● |
| Support and management activities | ○ | ○ | ○ | ○ | ● |
| **Key resources** | VERY SIMILAR TO COMPETITORS | | SOMEWHAT SIMILAR TO COMPETITORS | | VERY SIMILAR FROM COMPETITORS |
| Core resources and capabilities | ○ | ○ | ○ | ○ | ● |
| Network of suppliers and partners | ○ | ○ | ● | ○ | ○ |
| Role in the entire ecosystem | ● | ○ | ○ | ○ | ○ |
| **Profit Model** | VERY SIMILAR TO COMPETITORS | | SOMEWHAT SIMILAR TO COMPETITORS | | VERY SIMILAR FROM COMPETITORS |
| Revenue structure | ○ | ● | ○ | ○ | ○ |
| Cost structure | ○ | ○ | ○ | ○ | ● |

**Figure 38** · Scoot's business model innovation

With a fresh young team, Scoot started flying two and later five wide-body aircraft, six flights a day out of Singapore to 11 destinations. According to Wilson: "There's no other example of an airline doing so much so quickly."[193] In 2017, Scoot completed the merger with the low-cost short-haul carrier Tigerair, which had become a fully-owned subsidiary of the SIA Group the year before. The new combination kept the name Scoot, meaning that Scoot now offered both long- and short-haul flights. The newly formed company embarked on an intense integration process to fully realize commercial and operational synergies. With the merger, Scoot more than doubled its number of staff from 895 to 1,847 and revenues almost tripled to S$1.350 billion—$944 million.[194]

In the years that followed, the company expanded its route network in an increasing number of countries. Scoot also started with a direct flight between Singapore and Europe—in June 2017 it flew to Athens four times per week. Athens was one of the 63 destinations in 17 countries that Scoot offered. Scoot's revenues accounted for almost 10% of the group's revenues and profits. That percentage dropped drastically during the Covid-19 years. Asian low-cost carriers suffered a lot from the pandemic and passenger numbers dropped significantly, leading to reduced revenues and huge losses. This was no different for Scoot—Singapore closed its borders due to Covid and Scoot cut all but two markets—Hong Kong and Australia. The company started working on its recovery in late 2021—by end of 2022, it announced that both SIA and Scoot were steadily moving towards pre-pandemic passenger levels.[195]

# Salmon story #3: How to move out of your 100-year old core business?

The last salmon story deals with corporate innovation in a very large organization. This story brings us back to 2012 to Stuttgart, hometown of Daimler, a leading car manufacturer with, at that time, almost 115 billion EUR in revenues and 275,000 employees. The Daimler Group was then structured as five divisions—Mercedes-Benz Cars, Daimler Trucks, Mercedes-Benz Vans, Daimler Buses, and Daimler Financial Services. The cars and trucks division accounted for more than 75% of the revenues. How do you build a new growth platform—large enough that it matters—in such a giant corporation?

**TURBULENCE IN THE AUTOMOBILE INDUSTRY.** Over the last few years, the automobile industry has been facing gigantic challenges. Long before Covid-19 and today's supply-chain issues, car manufacturers have been scrambling to deal with multiple disruptive trends. For Daimler, the most decisive change drivers were: networking among people and machines (connectivity), autonomous driving, flexible use (shared & services), and electric drive systems.[196] These four change drivers—commonly known as the 'CASE trends'—were linked to shifting consumer behaviors, increasing urbanization, and the rise of the Chinese automotive market. According to Daimler's Head of Product Group and Development Uwe Ernstberger, 'Combined, these innovations were considered much more impactful to the car business than all that had happened in the previous 50 years.'[197]

**THE RESPONSE.** While autonomous driving and electric cars were tackled within the different core divisions (cars, trucks, vans, and buses), Daimler created a Business Innovation Team in 2007 to develop and support the implementation of new mobility business models. One of the first key projects was the introduction of *car2go*, a car-sharing initiative. This new idea fitted in with Daimler's new vision that the organization needed to adjust to a future with fewer privately owned cars and more flexible transport options.

Car sharing was a cheaper alternative than car rental because customers were charged by the hour—sometimes even by the minute or mile. At the start of the project, Daimler provided a pool of 50 Smart cars as a vehicle pool that could be accessed at any time. Following a one-off registration process, customers could spontaneously hire a car or book it in advance and use it for as long as desired. The car2go business was a fundamentally different business than the traditional car manufacturing business—this was no longer about selling cars but about selling mobility. The new business unit required fundamentally different interactions with end customers—no longer via dealers—and many new technical solutions.

In 2012, the Business Innovation Team came up with another new project, called *Moovel*, which would become Daimler's mobility-as-a-service project. Daimler created an entirely new division—Daimler Mobility Services GmbH—which hosted the *car2go* and the Moovel units. Moovel helped travelers to go from A to B by searching for, booking, and paying for different mobility offers. Moovel's ambition was to become the 'Amazon of mobility' and this was another major business model innovation for Daimler in addition to the *car2go* project. The free Moovel app allowed users to compare the travel times and costs for various modes of transport and then select an optimal route for their trip—and, in many cases, also to pay for it using their smartphones. No more jumping around between various apps, but one app, one route, and one payment process.

With the gradual integration of online tickets for buses, trams and trains, Moovel was the first provider to offer a genuine one-stop-shop for urban mobility and in-termodal routing.[198] The Moovel app continuously expanded and included mobility services ranging from local public transport companies, car sharing (including *car2go*) and mytaxi (a German answer to Uber and Lyft taken over by Daimler in 2016) to rental bicycles and the Deutsche Bahn network. In 2017, *car2go* and Moovel each had more than 3 million registered users, making the two companies worldwide market leaders in mobility services. Daimler had discovered a new, huge field of customers—metropolitan areas—and became a pioneer of innovative urban mobility services.[199]

**Moovel**

| Value proposition | VERY SIMILAR TO COMPETITORS | | SOMEWHAT SIMILAR TO COMPETITORS | VERY SIMILAR FROM COMPETITORS | |
|---|---|---|---|---|---|
| Product performance | ○ | ○ | ○ | ● | ○ |
| Price level of the offering | ○ | ○ | ● | ○ | ○ |
| Accessibility of the offering | ○ | ○ | ○ | ○ | ● |
| Service level associated with the offering | ○ | ○ | ○ | ● | ○ |
| Sustainability of the offering | ○ | ○ | ○ | ● | ○ |
| **Key processe and activities** | VERY SIMILAR TO COMPETITORS | | SOMEWHAT SIMILAR TO COMPETITORS | VERY SIMILAR FROM COMPETITORS | |
| Front-end activities | ○ | ○ | ○ | ○ | ● |
| Back-end activities | ○ | ○ | ○ | ○ | ● |
| Support and management activities | ○ | ○ | ○ | ● | ○ |
| **Key resources** | VERY SIMILAR TO COMPETITORS | | SOMEWHAT SIMILAR TO COMPETITORS | VERY SIMILAR FROM COMPETITORS | |
| Core resources and capabilities | ○ | ○ | ○ | ○ | ● |
| Network of suppliers and partners | ○ | ○ | ○ | ○ | ● |
| Role in the entire ecosystem | ○ | ○ | ○ | ○ | ● |
| **Profit Model** | VERY SIMILAR TO COMPETITORS | | SOMEWHAT SIMILAR TO COMPETITORS | VERY SIMILAR FROM COMPETITORS | |
| Revenue structure | ○ | ○ | ○ | ○ | ● |
| Cost structure | ○ | ○ | ○ | ○ | ● |

**Figure 39** · Moovel's business model innovation

This new value proposition also implied huge changes in the organization's key processes, key resources, and profit model. Pioneering with an intermodal digital marketplace forced Daimler to think about the entire value chain. In the front office, the focus was on customer acquisition and retention by locking in customers. This was done by making the service as convenient as possible—one point of contact for booking and paying—but also through network effects. The app became more attractive the more options Moovel could offer. In the back end, the challenge was to manage a broad network of partner companies and convince them to join and contribute, even though there was no clear profit model yet in place.

The company also had to build new key resources—a new technology infrastructure and partnerships skills—taking many new employees on board. A senior Moovel manager explained,

> 'We have a marketing unit, which is particularly strong in online marketing. Our controlling department is highly engaged in developing new payment systems, and, last but not least, we have a large IT development backbone that takes care of app development and IT innovation. Altogether, we employ around 700 people, many of whom you would not expect to find in an automotive company such as Daimler. In recruiting, we do not follow the classical industry approach of defining a position and hiring someone from the job market. Instead, we rely on our strong network in the startup community and on the contacts of Daimler's IT development service providers. They suggest people to us, who start on one project, often still outside Daimler, and are eventually taken on board. It is more of a startup recruitment model.'[200]

Moovel's profit model was also quite different from the competitors' models, although several traditional car manufacturers and technological disruptors were expanding their mobility offering as well. The company received commissions from its partners once a mobility offer was successfully arranged. The cost model was different too from the traditional manufacturing business and from its partners who owned the assets. Moovel was an asset-light company, like Uber and Airbnb.

**FROM INNOVATION PROJECT TO CORPORATE DIVISION.** Daimler's urban mobility adventure started in 2007 when a bunch of young employees who had just formed the new Business Innovation unit decided to start shaping the future. In a poorly furnished office, the founding members put their heads together and discussed urban mobility in the next 10 to 20 years.[201] They introduced car sharing as a bold idea and wondered how car rental concepts could be turned into a potential mass market. The *car2go* idea was born and after an enthusiastic preparation phase, the first pilot was introduced in Ulm. After a positive assessment, Daimler created a new company—*car2go GmbH*—to push forward the concept and staffed it with a management team that combined entrepreneurial spirit with the ability to deal with the political particularities of a large corporation.[202]

The company expanded its efforts in 2012 by launching the company Daimler Mobility Services, which would become the umbrella company for the newly created Moovel team and the *car2go* unit. The new company was a subsidiary of the Financial Services division. In 2014, the mobility division was renamed Moovel Group. With this step, Daimler underscored the importance of the mobility platform for the future of the company. In the years that followed, Moovel Group started an ambitious growth strategy, expanding both the range of mobility services (for example, by acquiring hail-riding companies such as mytaxi and Hailo in 2016) and countries (from Germany to the rest of Europe, North America and China). Moovel received continuous support from Daimler's top management—in 2016 the Moovel Group received an independent budget of $10 billion and was allowed to operate separately from the core.

Although the Moovel Group kept on growing, there were indications that the new direction into mobility was not always a smooth ride. In the 10 years from 2012–22, the company never reported the financial figures of the mobility unit. Interviews also revealed that the Daimler Group had to deal with cultural and people issues. For example, the obsession with excellence, precision and success hindered Daimler's efforts to reinvent itself. The new unit also needed young people more attuned to the new trends. This was not the traditional workforce, so the Moovel Group had to recruit very different profiles. Recruiting and retaining talent turned out to be a challenging job.[203]

A groundbreaking step for Daimler's innovative mobility trio—*car2go*, Moovel, and mytaxi—was taken in February 2019 when Daimler and BMW sealed the merger of Daimler's and BMW's mobility services in a new joint venture that was structured as the following three main units:

- Car sharing services via the unit *Share Now*—a merger between *car2go* and BMW's Drive Now.
- Hail riding via the unit *Free Now*—the name for mytaxi—and the Mobility-as-a-Service app called *Reach Now*—which integrated Moovel and BMW's Reach Now.
- Mobile payment for paid parking and car parks via the *Park Now* unit and for a digital charging network for electric cars, called *Charge Now*. The Park Now unit was sold in March 2021.

In 2019, Daimler also renamed the financial services division Daimler Mobility AG, which became one of the three divisions of the Daimler Group one year later, alongside Mercedes-Benz Cars & Vans, and Daimler Trucks & Buses. In 2021, Daimler announced another restructuring—a more fundamental one this time—by splitting the car business from the truck business because of the lack of synergies between the two main divisions. The Mercedes-Benz Group now consisted of a car division and a mobility division, called Mercedes-Benz Mobility, indicating the importance of mobility for the newly formed Mercedes-Benz Group.

On 31 March 2022, however, Mercedes-Benz announced that it would discontinue its Reach Now app. The company notified its users in an email about the termination of the contract. Some months later, BMW and Mercedes-Benz surprised the business community by selling the car sharing business (Share Now) to international car manufacturing group Stellantis. According to industry observers, the venture struggled with profitability issues.[204] Mercedes-Benz emphasized that these decisions did not imply the end of its business model innovation journey. According to the company, "the sale of the car-sharing subsidiary contributes to the realignment of the mobility joint ventures. In the future, shareholders intend to concentrate on two central business areas with high growth potential: digital multi-mobility Free Now, and digital services related to the charging of electric vehicles Charge Now."[205]

After 15 years, the Mercedes-Benz group significantly reduced its mobility ambitions, demonstrating that building a new growth platform through business model innovation is anything but simple.

## Building a new business model outside the core

The three salmon stories show that business model innovation is more than launching a new product or service. It's about creating a new business—and we all know that most new businesses fail.[206] This is even more true if the new growth platform occurs via business model innovation. All this is captured well in a great article from Harvard innovation specialists Clayton Christensen, Thomas Bartman, and Derek van Bever called 'The Hard Truth About Business Model Innovation.'[207]

Starting a new business model outside your core is a strategic experiment—a highly uncertain endeavor—much like the salmon's move to the ocean. Unlike other forms of innovation, business model innovation implies facing many critical unknowns, regardless of the level of prior research you've done. There are many risks to be tackled: customers may not be interested in your offering or not willing to pay for the product or service; you might—no, you will—encounter technological or operational failures; or you may not have an appropriate answer to the reactions of your competitors. Fortunately, the topic of business model innovation has been covered extensively in the management literature. So, there's some help out there.

**SEARCH FOR THE RIGHT VALUE PROPOSITION.** The innovation and entrepreneurship researchers recommend starting your business model innovation journey with a sound search process—a search for unsolved problems. According to those authors, you'd best build a large innovation funnel. And large is really large: research has shown that if you invest in 250 projects of $100,000 each, 162 will fail, 87 will find some success, and only 1 will become a new growth engine (i.e., a return of 50 times or more on the invested capital).[208] That's why organizations set up innovation bootcamps and tournaments to hunt for new ideas—new problems that need a solution.

Looking at the 10 cases that I examined (including the three salmon stories), I've noticed a different pattern. From the outset, the new business concepts were quite clear: Singapore Airlines—just like the Australian competitor Qantas—wanted to set up a low-cost carrier business; the mobility solutions developed by Daimler and other competitors were relatively straightforward conceptually; and NowJobs' new business concept was a logical conclusion to some basic internal financial research. Search is rather straightforward if you built a sound corporate foresight capability and if you follow up on the business models of outliers in the periphery of your market (see Chapter 2). The following questions help you build a vision for the future and the contours of your new business model:

- Why are we losing customers in our traditional core business? For whom do they leave us?
- What do customers like in the offering of the new players?
- What is the value proposition of the disruptors? And where is it different from ours?
- Given these new insights, how can we make our value proposition more attractive?
- What are the new players' key processes and key resources? How do they differ from ours?
- What is their profit model? Should we change ours?

This seems like a rather straightforward exercise. Nevertheless, it's good to take the following recommendations into account in this journey.

**ADOPT AN OUTSIDER'S PERSPECTIVE.** Managers tend to look at turbulence and disruption with the eyes of an incumbent. But according to Costas Markides, strategic innovation expert from London Business School, it's important to approach disruption with eyes that are free of the biases of the core business. He suggests forgetting about the core and asking the following questions instead: 'If I was an entrepreneur entering the markets created by disruption, what strategy would I have adopted? The idea is to look at the new market without the constraints of the core business and come up with a strategy whose aim is to make you a winner in the new market as opposed to making you a winner in your core market. In too many cases, the needs and requirements of the core business cloud and constrain the thinking.'[209]

STRATEGY IN TURBULENT TIMES

**AVOID COPY/PASTE.** If there are some disruptors in the market, you can examine their value proposition in detail. But rather than copying the business model of your disruptor, it's better to come up with a unique value proposition yourself, ideally one that builds on some of your traditional strengths. One way to identify how different your value proposition is from the competitors' offering—including the new disruptors'—is to depict a value (proposition) curve. This tool was first presented in the book *Blue Ocean Strategy* and is now commonly used to identify the value attributes in which you want to differentiate from the competitors. Here is an example of Uber's value (proposition) curve compared to traditional city taxis.

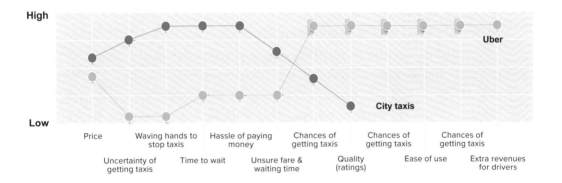

Figure 40 • Uber's value curve

When identifying the attributes of your new value proposition, first take a look at what the competitors/disruptors offer and list them one after the other. Then figure out on which value attributes they score high and low—a high score means the competitors or disruptors invest a lot in this particular attribute and customers get much value.

Then depict your own value curve. Check out the weaknesses in the disruptors' strategies. But also identify your company's current strengths. You may integrate them in your new value curve. For example, Daimler integrated some of its existing solutions in its mobility platform Moovel. Scoot could benefit from Singapore Airlines' reputation for operational security and safety, a valuable asset for any low-cost carrier. And NowJobs could offer national coverage because of its links with the branch network of its parent company.

Finally, come up with new ideas borrowed from other industries and integrate them in your offering. The goal of this exercise is to come up with a value curve that is different enough from the competitors/disruptors.

**ALIGN THE OTHER BUSINESS MODEL COMPONENTS.** Building a new business model starts with the value proposition component. After you've defined the new value proposition, it's time to consider the other blocks of the business model (see Figure 41). The second major block for a new business model is your profit model. Two of the salmon cases—House of HR and Singapore Airlines—developed a new business model with a fundamentally different cost structure. This is a common strategy if you build a low-cost model next to your existing business. Building a successful new business model requires a profound analysis of the major cost drivers of your new proposition. This is not always easy: building a new business model always entails a lot of experimentation and testing assumptions on the spot. Nevertheless, it's important to outline upfront what the major cost blocks are and how they evolve over time as you grow bigger.

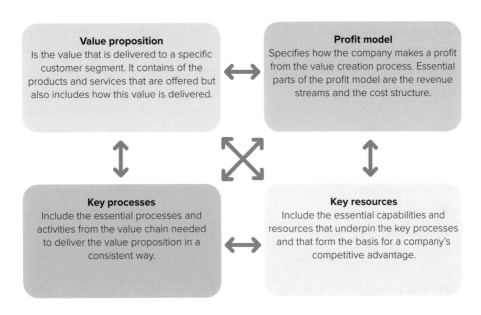

Source: Adapted from Johnson (2010)[210]

**Figure 41** · Business model framework

In the case of Moovel, Daimler decided not only to change the cost structure but also introduced a fundamentally new revenue model. Firms have several options for changing their revenue model. Most firms adopt a transactional revenue model: you charge for a product that you offer to the customer. But there are other revenue models as well. A common revenue model today is the subscription model, employed by firms like Netflix and Dollar Shave Club. An advertising model is commonly used by media companies who provide free or low-priced content. Revenues are, however, generated by charging advertisers. A freemium model is a revenue model in which a company offers free access to basic versions of its product or service. When customers want the more advanced version, they need to pay a fee. Other revenue models are pay-as-you-go (revenues are charged for actual use), razors/blades model (Gillette's revenue model), auction models, etc.

In the process of working out your profit formula, you will identify the key processes and key resources that are needed to generate the value proposition. How will you tackle sales? What about marketing? How will you organize operations and logistics? What about R&D? And how will you set up important support activities like HR, IT, or finance? What resources underpin these activities? Which resources are really unique and essential for your competitive advantage—these are the true core resources?

When building the blueprint for your new value chain and the underlying resources, identify points of compatibility and differentiation with your existing business. The goal is to figure out which of the key resources can be taken from— or must be shared with—the parent company. This exercise also helps you identify early on those potential points of conflict, where the expectations and habits of the core could interfere with the new unit.[211]

## Are you really ready to do this?

Building a new business is difficult and requires significant investment. On top of that, there's no guarantee of success as the Daimler story has illustrated. When setting up new ventures, managers should expect much skepticism and resistance from all parts of the organization. Be ready for some organizational inertia, internal politics, fights for resources, complacency, fear of cannibalization, fear of destroying competencies... The list of excuses for not engaging in corporate innovation is long.

Successful corporate innovators are aware of these issues but they persevere nevertheless. They don't wait for a crisis to start contemplating the future.[212] Corporate innovators believe that no strategy remains unique forever, and they actively try to get the organization in motion. They never stop challenging their existing strategy and their current business model. They are aware that, when markets change, traditional capabilities do not necessarily play out well—and that requires redefining the core business. This is a common characteristic of many salmon companies. For example, in 2014 Daimler CEO Dieter Zetsche said, 'We regard ourselves not only as a vehicle manufacturer, but also as a provider of mobility solutions.'[213] In 2009, CEO Anders Eldrup of the Danish energy company Ørsted had already formulated the compelling ambition to have 80% of heat and power come from renewable sources. He gave the company until 2040 to realize this ambition—and the target was already achieved in 2019. And House of HR/ Accent Jobs CEO Jérôme Caille launched 'Kill Accent' projects to solicit for ideas to build new business models.

You can convince managers to be more open to corporate innovation only when you shift from a focus on the core business dominating the agenda to making exploration equally important. There are many innovation books and websites that tell you how to build a case for change. For example, McKinsey's three Horizons model is a useful framework to convince the organization that it's important to experiment outside your core.

Explain well why this shift is needed. Sometimes this is an easy task: if your core business is declining, it's easier to create a burning platform than when your core is flourishing, as was the case with House of HR. Another great example here is Netflix, which built a new streaming unit even when the traditional core was still successful. In this latter case, what underpins such a shift in emphasis from exploitation to exploration is a strong drive to grow the company. If the core business does not allow for sufficient growth, you need to look for growth opportunities outside your core.

The more the innovation ambition is embedded in a strong culture of creativity and innovation, the better. This starts with an ambitious top team and high-profile senior managers who believe in and actively support innovation. Then the corporation can set up innovation initiatives to help employees to think outside of their traditional core activities. If you don't have the support of your top team, these activities don't make any sense at all. Ideally, innovation also has a prominent place in the organization's culture: Who are the heroes in the company? Do you celebrate successes? And how do you define success—is innovation part of it? Who gets rewarded? Who gets promoted? Do people have the freedom to develop new initiatives? And is there room for failure stories?

# Disciplined experimentation

Business model innovation is strategic experimentation. As already mentioned earlier, strategic experiments face many unknowns. They depart from the company's proven business definition: they often target new customers with a new value proposition, there is no clear profit formula, the company needs to build new processes or activities to deliver that new value proposition. And the results are quite ambiguous—it is difficult to know whether the new business will become the next growth platform.[214]

**START SMALL.** Most innovation projects are born out of some new and crazy ideas. An inventor creates a team and then builds a business plan, laying out all the assumptions. But the assumptions become assertions over time, and the innovation team ends up trying to prove that the assumptions are right. Unfortunately, building extensive business cases in uncertain environments is a waste of time.[215] Typically, entrepreneurs cope with this high uncertainty by 'just going for it and doing it'. They rely on their visionary capabilities and believe that they will make it because of their passion and persistence.

But this romantic view towards building new businesses is not what academics recommend. Instead, they prescribe a more scientific approach to business building, well described in the book *The Lean Startup*.[216] The goal of this methodology is to achieve product-market fit as soon as possible. Product-market fit means that the startup team has created a product that profitably meets the needs of the target market's customers.[217] This is best done through disciplined strategic experimentation. You no longer lock yourself up in your garage for 2 or 3 years working on the perfect product or service. No, you start small and build a prototype of your initial concept—called a 'minimum viable product' (MVP)—as soon as you can. Then you put it into the users' hands and assess their reactions and adapt the product or service. You repeat this process until you come up with an acceptable version of your solution.[218] The motto here is: always test before you invest.

Building a new business requires a fluid process of rapid experimentation, iteration, and learning.[219] Don't shy away from making mistakes—they're crucial in this process—they contribute to the learning and help improve the product-market fit. The startup team develops some initial hypotheses, which are tested relatively quickly with rigorous experiments. Should we focus on customer segment A or B? Just test it. Should we add feature C or D to the product? Test it. Should we use distribution channel E or F? ... That's how you fail fast and cheap.

But the need for speedy feedback is not an excuse for sloppiness—managers must think hard about the design of their experiments. First think about the outcome you want to achieve. Ultimately, you want your business model innovation project to have a substantial outcome—otherwise it will never become the growth platform that you have in mind. After you've specified the revenue and profit targets, ask yourself what would need to be true to meet your hurdle rate and get to the level that you would consider a success. Then you take those assumptions and rank them by level of uncertainty and potential impact. Testing starts with the most critical assumptions first. In other words, give priority to tests that can eliminate considerable risk at low cost. Then, based on the outcomes of the test, decide whether to persevere on the current path, or pivot and change some elements of the business model.[220] In the worst case, you have to abandon the project—you shut it down or you sell it to someone else.

**BUT THINK BIG.** When you've developed the building blocks for a new successful business model and the outlook is positive, it's time for scaling. That's the moment where you try to get the organization ready to realize its ambitions. This means you move from running a project to building a business. Scaling first means aggressively investing in customer acquisition and increasing revenues. Think about the following questions when you approach the scaling phase: How rapidly do you want to expand the business? Where do you want to expand the business: by enlarging the customer base, or by broadening the product range? Or do you want to go international? Do you have the financial and the human resources required to scale the business? If not, how will you get access to them?

Scaling is about structuring your processes, making them repeatable and scaling your operations. Improving efficiency is gradually becoming more important. If you want to grow your customer base rapidly, you need to amass the additional resources, which also means building more professional management systems. You start to establish business rules for standardizing processes and define metrics that track success.

The scaling phase is the phase where corporate innovators increasingly turn towards mergers and acquisitions (M&As) or to strategic partnerships to gain access to critical resources and to build critical scale. This is a risky activity—many mergers and acquisitions fail—but, if you get the financial and managerial support of the core, you may consider setting higher growth ambitions. Daimler is an example. It first established a strategic partnership with car rental company Europcar to set up the joint venture *car2go*. It also invested in technology companies to build the apps for *car2go* and Moovel. And, in order to become a global mobility player, it acquired companies such as Hailo (UK), RideScout (US), and GlobeSherpa (US). In 2019, Daimler even teamed up with archrival BMW and merged the companies' mobility solutions.

## Organizing for corporate innovation

**SEPARATION OR INTEGRATION?** Finally, building a new business requires carefully considering how to organize for corporate innovation. Can you launch a business model innovation out of your innovation department? Or is a separate unit necessary? And if you choose the latter option, to whom should the new venture report? In short, should you separate or integrate?

Building a new business inevitably creates conflicts between the traditional core business and the new business. Although the new business typically focuses on a different set of customers with a new value proposition, it's common that tensions arise between the managers from the core business and the new venture. One way to deal with these tensions is to separate the new venture from the rest of the organization—you deliberately build an organizational silo to protect the new unit from influences from the core. Separation ensures that every unit focuses on its own business model. Then you can prevent the existing processes and the culture of the core from suffocating the new business model.[221] So, it's clear that separation has its merits. But the story isn't finished yet.

Remember the story of Xerox PARC, the research and development unit of Xerox. It was the birthplace of some of the most leading-edge inventions that transformed the tech world—the graphical user interface, laser printing, the mouse, and many more. One author even called Xerox PARC the equivalent of porn for any IT nerd on the planet.[222] But it was not Xerox that benefited from all those innovations—it was Steve Jobs who hired many of the Xerox PARC researchers to help him make the Mac. What was the problem? Xerox had isolated PARC just too much from the core business—geographically, culturally and commercially.

So, separation is needed but not sufficient to ensure success. Companies that want to have a successful salmon strategy need to create linkages between the core and the new unit. These synergies help the new unit build a competitive advantage and give it a head start against the disruptors. In all three salmon cases, the new ventures could borrow something valuable from the core. For example, NowJobs could leverage the branch network of Accent Jobs to fuel its growth. Scoot benefited from shared resources—such as policies of operations management and insights on safety and security—that helped build credibility among customers. And Moovel could benefit from the brand, the financial support, and some of the mobility assets of the Daimler group.

**GIVE AUTONOMY.** So, the answer is not separation or integration but is a mix of both—call it 'autonomous but linked'. New ventures should get the autonomy to do their thing. In most cases, autonomy means creating some geographic distance from the head office or core business. But giving autonomy also means setting up an autonomous organization with its own general manager, who reports to a senior executive—at least one level above the manager of the core division. This structure ensures that the new unit is seen as more than an appendix to the core. The manager of the new unit can be an insider or outsider. But the new unit should be able to make its own financial and operational decisions.[223]

Autonomy also implies that the new unit has the freedom to hire sufficient managers and operational staff from outside the core. You cannot build something entirely new with the same old managers and staff. Scott Anthony and his colleagues at Innosight, a well-known innovation consulting company, recommend having a balance of 'aliens'—people who push you in a new direction—and 'diplomats'—innovative people from the traditional organization, who can speak core and alien, who know the right people and who understand the sensitivities in the core.[224]

Give the new venture the freedom to build an entirely new management infrastructure with new roles and new responsibilities to perform a new set of activities. A key element of that management infrastructure is a new budgetary system. At first, exploration is more about learning than earning. Don't apply the traditional performance measurement techniques to the new unit: these are more focused on profitability. With your new venture, it's more about conquering a market. Check first whether your solution gets traction in the market. Profit comes later. Give the new unit the time to build a profitable new business model. Be patient and don't interfere.

Finally, allow the innovation unit to build its own culture—one that will be quite different from the culture of the core business. There's nothing wrong with that. On the contrary, you need a new culture because your value proposition is fundamentally different from that of the core business. Think Singapore Airlines—a master of customer service and customer intimacy—and Scoot—a low-cost player. And, the new unit will be more entrepreneurial, more hands-on, and more innovative than the core business.

**BUILD LINKAGES.** Autonomy is important, but don't isolate—otherwise, you may end up with an unnourished orphan that has no advantage at all relative to the disruptors or that remains too small to become the company's new growth engine. The key is to borrow just enough from the core to create a competitive advantage without exposing the new unit too much. Otherwise, the new unit will become a lookalike of the core business, which is not what you want.

Carefully identify the resources that you want to borrow from the core. Borrowing opens the door to influences from the core, which will slow you down. Which capabilities does the new venture need to compete successfully with independent disruptive startups? These resources can be many things: a brand, access to a large customer base, production facilities, a distribution network. Resist the temptation to use whatever resource that comes to mind . Focus on two or three of the most influential resources. Don't go after shared services, like IT or HR. These synergies may seem convenient but are unlikely to be critical to the new venture's success. And think more about what the new venture needs from the core than the other way around.[225]

Establish favorable conditions for borrowing. This can be done by creating a formal exchange team with representatives from the traditional and the new company to discuss very specific synergy initiatives. These exchange teams have a clear mandate and a specific target benefit, which also means that these teams are designed to be temporary. It is a good idea to reward the core for borrowing through some form of transfer pricing. Be aware that the fee should not be too high. It's more of a symbolic fee that creates goodwill so that the core keeps on sharing and helping the new unit move forward.[226]

Finally, make sure key senior managers—including the CEO of the group—are closely involved. Implementing a salmon strategy means that you have 2 management teams pursuing different targets—some need to meet hard financial targets (exploitation), others need to build a new business with lots of uncertainty (exploration). These are different assignments whereby managers have to optimize different outcomes. This inevitably leads to tensions. At that moment, you need to have high-caliber leaders who are ready to intervene. Clark Gilbert, a former Harvard Business School professor and a successful corporate innovation manager himself, says, 'There are times when the CEO has to come down and be the tie breaker, and generally bias in favor of the new unit.'[227]

# Well-equipped for a salmon strategy?

Many academics and consultants advise you to set up a speedboat or unicorn but this chapter has shown that this is a challenging journey, full of uncertainties and surprises. You cannot just create a new venture out of the blue. The checklist below tells you whether or not your new venture has a high probability of success. The questionnaire first asks you to judge the quality of the new venture's business model. The second part asks you to analyze your company's innovation skills.

| BUSINESS MODEL INNOVATION | STRONGLY DISAGREE | | NEITHER AGREE NOR DISAGREE | | STRONGLY AGREE |
|---|---|---|---|---|---|
| 1. The value proposition of our new (set of) product(s) and service(s) is very different from the competitors' value proposition. | 1 | ○ | ○ | ○ | ○ 5 |
| 2. We have developed a very different profit model for our new (set of) product(s) and service(s). | 1 | ○ | ○ | ○ | ○ 5 |
| 3. The key processes needed to deliver our value proposition are fundamentally different from our competitors' key processes. | 1 | ○ | ○ | ○ | ○ 5 |
| 4. We have created a set of new capabilities and/or resources that help to differentiate ourselves from the competitors. | 1 | ○ | ○ | ○ | ○ 5 |
| 5. We have leveraged some of our traditional strengths in our new business model. | 1 | ○ | ○ | ○ | ○ 5 |

| INNOVATION CAPABILITIES | STRONGLY DISAGREE | | NEITHER AGREE NOR DISAGREE | | STRONGLY AGREE |
|---|---|---|---|---|---|
| 6. In our company, there is a willingness to experiment with new business models. | 1 | ○ | ○ | ○ | ○ 5 |
| 7. From time to time, we challenge our core business's existing strategy and business model. | 1 | ○ | ○ | ○ | ○ 5 |
| 8. The business model innovation activities have a prominent place in our corporate strategy presentations. | 1 | ○ | ○ | ○ | ○ 5 |
| 9. Our top management team believes in innovation as a crucial driver of future success. | 1 | ○ | ○ | ○ | ○ 5 |
| 10. Building a new business model happens through a process of rapid experimentation, constant evaluation, and continuous learning (see e.g., Lean startup methodology). | 1 | ○ | ○ | ○ | ○ 5 |
| 11. We work with 'minimum viable products' when building new business models. | 1 | ○ | ○ | ○ | ○ 5 |
| 12. When scaling the new business, we pay attention to structuring the operations and setting up repeatable processes. | 1 | ○ | ○ | ○ | ○ 5 |
| 13. We actively use mergers and acquisitions or partnerships to grow the new venture and/or to gain access to critical resources. | 1 | ○ | ○ | ○ | ○ 5 |
| 14. We have created an autonomous organization for the new venture, with its own general manager, who reports to a senior executive. | 1 | ○ | ○ | ○ | ○ 5 |
| 15. The new unit hires many outsiders, for either operational or management roles. | 1 | ○ | ○ | ○ | ○ 5 |
| 16. The new unit has the freedom to build an entirely new management infrastructure with new roles and responsibilities to perform new activities. | 1 | ○ | ○ | ○ | ○ 5 |
| 17. The new unit has built a culture that is significantly different from the culture of the core business. | 1 | ○ | ○ | ○ | ○ 5 |
| 18. The new unit can leverage some key resources from the core business. | 1 | ○ | ○ | ○ | ○ 5 |
| 19. Our corporation's top team actively arbitrates when there are conflicts between managers from the core business and the managers from the new venture. | 1 | ○ | ○ | ○ | ○ 5 |
| 20. The corporation applies different performance measures for the new unit than for the established businesses. | 1 | ○ | ○ | ○ | ○ 5 |

| Scores | Interpretation |
|---|---|
| 20 - 39 | **Problematic** – No prospect for successful corporate innovation |
| 40 - 59 | **Weak** – Corporate innovation will be a huge challenge |
| 60 - 79 | **Good** – Good chance that corporate innovation will be successful |
| 80 - 100 | **Strong** – You are equipped to manage the corporate innovation well |

**Figure 42** • How well are you equipped for a salmon strategy?

# KEY
# TAKEAWAYS

- The salmon strategy is appropriate when turbulence opens up a new market.
- The examples of House of HR (NowJobs), Singapore Airlines (Scoot), and Daimler (Mobility Services) show that incumbent firms can build a new business model outside the core. However, success is not always guaranteed.
- Building a new business model is in essence an innovation exercise. But it's more than creating a new product—it is about building a new business, and this is a far more challenging endeavor.
- The success of your salmon strategy depends on the quality of your business model innovation but also on some preconditions in your core business.
- The top team needs to be convinced about the importance of business model innovation. Exploration should be considered as equally important as exploitation.
- Business model innovation is best done through a process of rapid experimentation, iteration and learning.
- Pay attention to the organizational challenges of corporate innovation. Corporate innovation can only work if the new unit has sufficient autonomy. At the same time, allow the new unit to borrow some key resources from the core business. That will give it a head start compared to its competitors.

# CHAPTER
# 6

## chapter of the chameleon
---
Core transformation

# Key questions addressed in this chapter

What is a core transformation strategy?

Is this an easier strategy to implement than the corporate innovation strategy?

What are the typical challenges of implementing a core transformation strategy?

Is implementing a new business model a different change challenge than any other strategic change program?

This chapter elaborates on the third turbulence strategy: core transformation. While most attention in the management literature has gone to the salmon strategy, several companies have chosen a different approach to tackling turbulence. Rather than building a new unit next to the traditional core, they have decided to fundamentally change their existing business model. From Chapter 3, we learned that this strategy is appropriate when you are facing disruption—not disturbance—where new players with new business models threaten to make your core assets obsolete and reduce your profit pool. When your core is under threat, improving it may no longer suffice. What you need then is a fundamental transformation of your core business—a chameleon strategy.

That's what Michelin did when it launched its Fleet Solutions unit in 2000. This unit no longer sold tires but kilometers, which turned Michelin from a product into a services company. Rolls-Royce also offered a TotalCare® service to its aerospace customers, enabling airlines to pay for the use of Rolls-Royce jet engines, partly as a function of hours flown. Many firms dealing with digital transformation have adopted a chameleon strategy. Media companies such as the Financial Times (FT) and The New York Times (NYT) transformed from newspaper companies into digital-centric news brands. This change required a fundamental reconfiguration of their business model: given the huge drop in advertising revenues caused by digital disruption—advertising for print generates much more revenue than advertising for the web and for mobile—FT and NYT started focusing on digital subscriptions. Another example is John Deere, a market leader in agricultural equipment. This company took the lead in precision agriculture, offering its customers solutions for machine performance, field management and data analysis. Adding these precision agriculture tools forced the company to build radically new capabilities, quite a challenge for a traditional product-focused company.

This chapter tells you how to tackle such a core transformation. I start this chapter with three core transformation stories to show what a business model transformation in the core entails. Building a new business model in your core business poses challenges that are very different from building a business model outside your core. The salmon strategy essentially revolves around building a new innovative unit next to the core. The chameleon strategy is all about managing change in the existing organization.[228] Therefore, this chapter describes how to build a new business model in the core and provides some guidelines on how to manage the transformation journey. The learning lessons are based on several case studies that I examined in great detail.[229] At the end of this chapter, you can check the quality of your chameleon capabilities.

## The chameleon: A master of core transformation

Animals facing danger can move to new territories. Others stay where they are and adapt to survive. That's not uncommon in nature. For example, red foxes have fluffy fur that keeps them warm in winter. And bears hibernate, allowing their metabolism to slow down to burn fewer calories and survive with no food for months.

But one of the most intriguing adaptations can be noticed with chameleons. These solitary animals are very territorial and when attacked they fight. But fighting is dangerous, especially when you're hunted by a predator like a big bird or a snake. That's why they rely on camouflage as their primary defense. Chameleons can change color because they have multiple layers of special skin cells, called chromatophores. Some contain yellow, red or black pigments, while others contain transparent crystals that reflect light and can produce blue or white colors. Chameleons not only change color to blend into their environment, but also to attract mates. And the colors also say something about the chameleon's mood.

Chameleons also have other defense mechanisms: they can flatten out to appear bigger and they can also lash out with their feet and jaws. This unique animal also has an amazing attacking strength: its tongue. Chameleons can snap their tongue out to almost twice the length of their body to snatch their prey.

Yet, despite these defensive and offensive qualities, over a third of the world's chameleon species are threatened with extinction. Not only are the numbers for chameleons bleak, they are even bleaker than those for the reptile family as a whole.

In this chapter, I will present some companies that have pulled through better than the chameleons. What does core transformation mean in practice?

## Chameleon story #1: Does more customer intimacy help you out of the commoditization game?

Our first chameleon story brings us to Hilti Corporation in Liechtenstein, a manufacturer of high-end power tools for construction companies. Hilti stands for quality, innovation, and direct customer relationships. The company has a direct selling approach that allows it to be closer to construction companies, which it considers its prime customers, not the end customer (which is the focus of most of the competitors).

**HILTI FACING TURBULENCE.** During the late 1990s, Hilti was confronted with increasing commoditization, especially from suppliers in the small-tool market. The commoditization turned power tools into a disposable product, meaning that workers didn't care as much about them. They left them in the rain, they didn't maintain them properly, and even left them at the site at the end of the job.[230] Marco Meyrat, General Manager of Hilti Switzerland and later Executive Board Member, recalled, 'We found ourselves losing ground to competition in the small-tool market. We are a premium brand, and in that segment premium was of less value. Differentiation was harder for us to attain.'[231]

**THE SOLUTION.** In 2001, Hilti came up with a fleet management offering upon request of one of its major customers, Batigroup. This customer asked for a holistic tool management system that would cover the management of the tool fleet, including the administrative activities, maintenance, and financing.[232] Marco Meyrat and Pius Baschera, CEO of the Hilti Corporation, were personally involved in the discussions with Batigroup. Although the two realized this request would put high demands on the organization, they started a small pilot program. According to Baschera, 'We must put the initiative in a laboratory-like environment. It's important that we protect this initiative. It's a very small plant and we have big trees beside us.'[233]

The fleet management business model initiative started with eight customers in Switzerland, where the company had established the deepest relationships with its key accounts. After signing a fleet management contract, the client would be equipped with a fleet of new tools according to its needs in terms of quantity and assortment. The customer would pay a monthly fee on a subscription basis and then it would be entitled to a comprehensive service package for the tools under contract.[234]

This was a significant business model innovation for Hilti, as is illustrated in Figure 43. The company clearly evolved from a product company to a services company: it no longer sold power tools but committed to increasing the construction companies' on-site productivity. And that fundamental change in value proposition had a huge impact on the other dimensions of its business model (see Figure 43).

**Hilti Fleet Management**

| Value proposition | VERY SIMILAR TO COMPETITORS | SOMEWHAT SIMILAR TO COMPETITORS | | VERY SIMILAR FROM COMPETITORS | |
|---|---|---|---|---|---|
| Product performance | ○ | ● | ○ | ○ | ○ |
| Price level of the offering | ○ | ● | ○ | ○ | ○ |
| Accessibility of the offering | ○ | ● | ○ | ○ | ○ |
| Service level associated with the offering | ○ | ○ | ○ | ○ | ● |
| Sustainability of the offering | ● | ○ | ○ | ○ | ○ |
| **Key process and activities** | VERY SIMILAR TO COMPETITORS | SOMEWHAT SIMILAR TO COMPETITORS | | VERY SIMILAR FROM COMPETITORS | |
| Front-end activities | ○ | ○ | ○ | ○ | ● |
| Back-end activities | ○ | ○ | ○ | ● | ○ |
| Support and management activities | ○ | ○ | ○ | ○ | ● |
| **Key resources** | VERY SIMILAR TO COMPETITORS | SOMEWHAT SIMILAR TO COMPETITORS | | VERY SIMILAR FROM COMPETITORS | |
| Core resources and capabilities | ○ | ○ | ○ | ○ | ● |
| Network of suppliers and partners | ● | ○ | ○ | ○ | ○ |
| Role in the entire ecosystem | ● | ○ | ○ | ○ | ○ |
| **Profit Model** | VERY SIMILAR TO COMPETITORS | SOMEWHAT SIMILAR TO COMPETITORS | | VERY SIMILAR FROM COMPETITORS | |
| Revenue structure | ○ | ○ | ○ | ○ | ● |
| Cost structure | ○ | ○ | ○ | ● | ○ |

**Figure 43** • Hilti Fleet Management's business model innovation

**A BUMPY START.** Hilti had to overcome significant implementation challenges to bring the fleet management solution to the market. The first set of problems related to the sales department. Although the sales teams continued to focus on the same customers—i.e., the construction firms—they no longer talked to the managers of the construction sites, but were now sitting at the table with the CEO and CFO. The sales pitch was no longer about selling the quality of the construction tools, but increasingly involved administrative, financial, and legal matters.

The sales efforts were much larger too: fleet management was about selling a program instead of a product. There were many service options to choose from. Customers were not familiar with—and sometimes not even convinced about—the benefits of fleet management, since they had never been offered such a contract before. Furthermore, fleet management also required some change in the customer's behavior. Transparency became an issue, as there was constant fluctuation in the tool fleet due to theft and breakdown. Hilti had to educate its customers to report missing or stolen tools.[235]

The new offer also had repercussions for Hilti's back office and administration: the fleet management team had to develop novel IT systems to handle various components of fleet management, such as warehousing systems and a finance module. Furthermore, managing complex contracts posed far more challenges than anticipated.[236]

However, the pilot project with the eight Swiss customers showed promising results. Customers were buying into this new value proposition, and Baschera and Meyrat decided to roll out this new business model in the rest of the organization. By 2005, Hilti had introduced fleet management in Germany and Austria, and later it became a global program, with Meyrat becoming head of all sales and a member of the Executive Board. Hilti launched a fleet management training program for all of the sales teams and changed its incentive systems. In 2006, the company introduced the EasyFleet contract. This new contract was offered in all countries and was a major step forward: the new contracts were simplified—making them as easy as car rental agreements. The company also integrated the requirements for fleet management into its core R&D processes. These initiatives led to great sales successes—in 2009, the sales of fleet management services reached 27% of Hilti's tool sales.[237] Hilti's competitors also tried to set up a fleet management concept, but most failed because they lacked the direct sales force and had to work with dealers or were just too small in size.

In 2010, Hilti initiated the 'Customer Lifecycle' program, which further optimized the value delivery by enhancing customer support throughout the entire lifecycle of each contract.[238] Each new version brought its own challenges, but the continuous customer feedback helped Hilti move on and add new features that customers valued. For example, in 2016 Hilti introduced the ON!Track initiative, a professional solution for the management of all assets and tools used by a customer at a construction site, which included the assets of other manufacturers. Thanks to all these initiatives, Hilti remained a leader in the industrial and professional power tool industry.

## Chameleon story #2: What to do if the world's most powerful company enters your market?

**TURBULENCE IN THE SWISS WATCH INDUSTRY.** How do you react when one of the most successful and powerful global technology companies threatens to enter your market? This was the challenge for TAG Heuer—a Swiss watch company and part of LVMH, the French luxury goods conglomerate—at around 2013. LVMH's watch division had three brands: Hublot at the high end of the market, Zenith in the midrange, and TAG Heuer at the low end—still luxury, but watches selling for a few thousand (instead of 100,000) dollars.[239]

In 2011, there were rumors that Apple was developing a wearable device—a smart-watch—that could become a game changer in the market. The first smartwatches appeared on the market in 2013. And on 9 September 2014, Apple CEO Tim Cook announced the introduction of the Apple Watch as the next chapter in Apple's story. (The Apple Watch was effectively launched in April 2015).

Swiss watchmakers knew something was coming but had no clue about the impact of that new product on their market. There was, however, agreement that smartwatches would erode the lower end of the Swiss watch industry.[240] TAG Heuer realized that this new product category would be a formidable stretch for the company. When, in 2014, CEO Jean-Claude Biver asked his Technical Director and Head of Product Development Guy Sémon to develop a TAG Heuer Connected Watch, Sémon replied, 'Careful Mr Biver because this is not a watch. It's a computer.'[241] TAG Heuer knew how to make mechanical watches, but the smartwatch was definitely another ballgame.

**THE SOLUTION.** Nevertheless, the company announced the first Swiss luxury smartwatch in March 2015 and called it the Connected Watch. The Connected Watch incorporated newly developed technology from partners Intel and Google. Purchasers were able to exchange the Connected Watch for a TAG Heuer Carrera with a traditional mechanical movement. The Connected Modular series, which was introduced from 2017 onwards, allowed the wearer to switch the smartwatch module to an automatic watch module, using the same strap and lugs. This was a smart answer to a big challenge for TAG Heuer: how to guarantee 'eternity', an essential part of TAG Heuer's brand identity, when a smartwatch's technology changes every couple of years.[242] Consumers could easily switch between the mechanical module and the electronic Connected module. Says Biver, 'When you wake up in the morning and you feel young and tech-savvy, you insert the electronic module into your watch. In the evening, when you go to the opera and want to feel a bit more serious, you remove the electronic module and insert the mechanical module into your watch.'[243] This modularity was a unique feature in the smartwatch industry and helped TAG Heuer differentiate from both the new and the traditional competitors. It also allowed the company to keep charging premium prices—a TAG Heuer Connected Watch sold at three times the price of an Apple Watch. Furthermore, the product could also be bought online—quite unusual for luxury watch companies at that time. This resulted in the business model innovation shown in Figure 44.

**SOME SIGNIFICANT IMPLEMENTATION CHALLENGES.** The new product required significant changes in the company's business model. Biver realized this and assigned Guy Sémon as the project manager, with complete freedom to develop the Connected Watch. Sémon reasoned, 'To start a project like this one, you have to first have a commando attitude: light, fast, efficient.'[244]

Given the huge importance of electronics in smartwatches, TAG Heuer had to look for new partners to build the new watch. The company established partnerships with companies from Silicon Valley—Intel developed the microprocessor, and Google the software, for the watch. TAG Heuer also reached out to a Chinese touchscreen company, which was reluctant to collaborate at first, given the relatively small size of the orders for the Connected Watch. TAG Heuer was able to convince these new partners to collaborate, because the company could provide them with knowledge about the luxury market, a market that was new to all of them.

As said earlier, the company had brilliantly tackled the marketing challenge of linking luxury with smart capabilities. But other branding issues emerged. TAG Heuer's first Connected Watch could not be labeled 'Swiss Made', given that most of the development and manufacturing was done outside of Switzerland. So, the company invested substantially in its La Chaux-de-Fonds workshop and the second smartwatch, the TAG Heuer Connected Modular 45, could be labelled 'Swiss Made' again.[245]

## TAG Heuer Connected Watch

| **Value proposition** | VERY SIMILAR TO COMPETITORS | | SOMEWHAT SIMILAR TO COMPETITORS | | VERY SIMILAR FROM COMPETITORS |
|---|---|---|---|---|---|
| Product performance | ○ | ○ | ○ | ○ | ● |
| Price level of the offering | ○ | ○ | ○ | ● | ○ |
| Accessibility of the offering | ○ | ○ | ● | ○ | ○ |
| Service level associated with the offering | ● | ○ | ○ | ○ | ○ |
| Sustainability of the offering | ● | ○ | ○ | ○ | ○ |
| **Key processe and activities** | VERY SIMILAR TO COMPETITORS | | SOMEWHAT SIMILAR TO COMPETITORS | | VERY SIMILAR FROM COMPETITORS |
| Front-end activities | ○ | ○ | ○ | ○ | ● |
| Back-end activities | ○ | ○ | ○ | ○ | ● |
| Support and management activities | ○ | ○ | ● | ○ | ○ |
| **Key resources** | VERY SIMILAR TO COMPETITORS | | SOMEWHAT SIMILAR TO COMPETITORS | | VERY SIMILAR FROM COMPETITORS |
| Core resources and capabilities | ○ | ○ | ○ | ○ | ● |
| Network of suppliers and partners | ○ | ○ | ○ | ○ | ● |
| Role in the entire ecosystem | ○ | ● | ○ | ○ | ○ |
| **Profit Model** | VERY SIMILAR TO COMPETITORS | | SOMEWHAT SIMILAR TO COMPETITORS | | VERY SIMILAR FROM COMPETITORS |
| Revenue structure | ○ | ○ | ● | ○ | ○ |
| Cost structure | ○ | ○ | ○ | ● | ○ |

**Figure 44 •** TAG Heuer's Connected Watch business model innovation

The management team also had to reconsider its sales and distribution strategy. The Swiss watch brands had not been frontrunners in e-commerce and the digital revolution. Their belief was that the digital space could not recreate the in-store experience of the luxury showrooms. But Biver was determined to embrace digital all the way: "E-commerce is part of the behavior of the new generation. They will buy any product online. We won't be able to impose old distribution methods on them."[246] So Biver hired the former head of digital marketing of Red Bull, who started to build online communities around the new series of products. The product launch of the first Connected Watch, at the symbolic LVMH Tower in New York on 9 November 2015, was a great success. And the launches of the other models went according to expectations.

TAG Heuer has launched newer versions of the Connected Watch series, and the team responsible for this business line grew from four to 30 in five years. The company views the connected business as a new revenue stream, next to the traditional mechanical watches. But according to TAG Heuer's Chief Strategy Officer, Frédéric Arnault: 'The smartwatch market is really booming, with very high double-digit growth year over year [...] So we have strong ambitions and believe the volume can reach several hundreds of thousands of watches. We think this could reach 20 to 30% of the business in the years to come.'[247]

# Chameleon story #3: How to turn a traditional bank into a digital frontrunner?

Our last chameleon story covers KBC, a bank-insurance corporation operating in Belgium, the Czech Republic, Slovakia, Hungary, Bulgaria, and Ireland, and a leader in digital transformation. The company embarked on its digital transformation journey in 2013.

**THE CHALLENGE.** In that year, KBC felt the need to develop a comprehensive answer to the digital revolution in the financial services industry. It started a large sensing exercise with 75 colleagues from a variety of departments. The exercise showed significant acceleration of the drop in branch visits and a clear rise in online sales for financial products. New internet banks were slowly but steadily taking market share in many arenas of the financial services industry, including payments, deposits and savings. Fast-paced technological developments were changing the customers' behavior. The main conclusion was that the company was being attacked from multiple fronts by many different players.

**THE ANSWER.** KBC realized that it needed a fundamental strategic change to counter the challenges. The management team of the Belgian unit launched its 'Customer 2020' strategy in 2014. With this new strategy, KBC declared the front-end channels as the strategic battlefield for the coming years. Customer 2020 involved the transition from a traditional branch-based bank to a one-stop-shop financial institution. Customers chose the channel with which they wanted to interact with KBC—the branch, the agents, the contact center, the web or a smartphone. With this customer-centric omnichannel strategy, KBC wanted to provide a seamless, integrated and consistent customer experience across all channels.

KBC wanted to differentiate from the competitors by being the most solution-driven and accessible bank and insurance company. It wanted to be the reference by offering the most proactive and personal solutions to the customer and to be top notch in fast, reliable and easily accessible financial solutions. They translated this generic value proposition into ten specific customer promises for every business line in the bank—retail banking, corporate banking, private banking, insurance, asset management, etc. This was a huge change from the past: now, every business line had much more freedom to define its unique selling proposition. The company invested 500 million EUR and built a program management office to turn the value proposition into concrete propositions and to build digital capabilities.

The company's efforts paid off, and KBC grew in digital maturity while maintaining healthy profitability. In 2017, the company updated its strategy because fast-paced technological developments continued to change customer behavior. The new strategy was called 'More of the same, but differently'. The company revised its value proposition and introduced the '3 BEs', not only in Belgium but also in the other countries: (1) Be instant: fast was no longer enough. The new standard was 'instant'; (2) Be all-in-one: KBC's mobile banking app took center stage in growing the portfolio of banking and insurance products; (3) Be personal and proactive: by making smart use of data, the bank wanted to serve customers better and offer them personalized solutions at exactly the right moment.

KBC realized that data was taking a more prominent role in the financial services industry and understood that its customer database was becoming an increasingly valuable asset. Until 2019, the company had focused on creating its omnichannel business model for its own products and services. But it realized that this powerful distribution platform could be used to offer services from other partners as well. For example, the company started selling bus and train tickets via its app, which turned into a big success. To further boost traffic on the platform, the company started offering even more services from partner companies, which helped to diversify revenues. KBC worked on building five new business ecosystems—housing, mobility, healthcare, energy, and financial accounting (accountancy platforms). According to Erik Luts, KBC's Chief Innovation Officer, KBC's core did not fundamentally change: the company remained a trusted advisor for its customers and helped them with their most important financial decisions. But the product and service range had clearly expanded.[248]

In 2020, KBC announced another update of its strategy, now called 'Differently: the Next Level'. This new strategy was not a perfection of the strategy but an investment in a new future. The company had noted that the nature of the interactions with customers was changing fundamentally. KBC believed that future interactions with customers would be with fictional characters rather than with devices or apps. The key word for KBC was now 'proactivity'. The company introduced Kate, KBC's personal digital assistant, to fully tailor financial services to meet customer needs in a proactive digital-first manner. Customers could activate Kate on their mobile app with a promise of getting timely and personalized solutions and advice. For example, customers could ask Kate to make a bank transfer, book a bus ticket, or compare prices of energy contracts. But offering personalized and proactive advice required that KBC had data that was correct, up to date, and GDPR compliant. That's why KBC CEO Johan Thijs insisted that Kate be more than just a digital personal assistant, 'Kate is a core element of our disruptive strategy that has an impact on all products and processes, as well as on how we steer our organization and interact with our customers. Ultimately, all product and process development and updates will be driven by Kate.'[249] Kate would become the brain of the KBC organization. The company invested another 1.4 billion EUR in this new strategy. All this led to a very different value proposition (see Figure 45).

**CONTINUOUS BUSINESS MODEL INNOVATION.** The new value propositions presented huge challenges for the KBC organization. The Customer 2020 strategy implied rethinking and redesigning services from a customer's point of view in an increasingly digital world. KBC's management team realized this was more than delivering a set of new and fancy commercial applications. It meant building new capabilities for channel-customer interactions, hybrid customer journeys, and improving data analytics and marketing skills. A huge challenge for a traditional, product-oriented company. In this first phase of digital transformation, KBC concentrated on transforming its front-end operations.

The company set up a program management office to manage hundreds of different projects. Those Customer 2020 projects were managed in an agile way: project teams worked on a particular project for six months and were expected to come up with a clear delivery—a new service, a simplified process, or a new digital capability. Erik Luts, KBC's Chief Innovation Officer, explains, 'We work incrementally. We don't put the horizon on three years but focus on six-month deliveries. We expect very tangible results every six months. So, we focus on short-term delivery of solutions while always keeping an eye on the long-term vision.'[250]

**KBC's Digital Transformation**

| Value proposition | VERY SIMILAR TO COMPETITORS | | SOMEWHAT SIMILAR TO COMPETITORS | | VERY SIMILAR FROM COMPETITORS |
|---|---|---|---|---|---|
| Product performance | ○ | ● | ○ | ○ | ○ |
| Price level of the offering | ● | ○ | ○ | ○ | ○ |
| Accessibility of the offering | ○ | ○ | ○ | ○ | ● |
| Service level associated with the offering | ○ | ○ | ○ | ○ | ● |
| Sustainability of the offering | ● | ○ | ○ | ○ | ○ |
| **Key process and activities** | VERY SIMILAR TO COMPETITORS | | SOMEWHAT SIMILAR TO COMPETITORS | | VERY SIMILAR FROM COMPETITORS |
| Front-end activities | ○ | ○ | ○ | ○ | ● |
| Back-end activities | ○ | ○ | ○ | ○ | ● |
| Support and management activities | ○ | ○ | ○ | ● | ○ |
| **Key resources** | VERY SIMILAR TO COMPETITORS | | SOMEWHAT SIMILAR TO COMPETITORS | | VERY SIMILAR FROM COMPETITORS |
| Core resources and capabilities | ○ | ○ | ○ | ○ | ● |
| Network of suppliers and partners | ○ | ○ | ● | ○ | ○ |
| Role in the entire ecosystem | ○ | ○ | ● | ○ | ○ |
| **Profit Model** | VERY SIMILAR TO COMPETITORS | | SOMEWHAT SIMILAR TO COMPETITORS | | VERY SIMILAR FROM COMPETITORS |
| Revenue structure | ○ | ● | ○ | ○ | ○ |
| Cost structure | ○ | ○ | ● | ○ | ○ |

**Figure 45** • KBC's business model innovations

The strategic shift in 2017—when KBC introduced its 'More of the same, but differently' strategy—was another business model innovation in the core. The company changed its value proposition from fast to instant. And becoming more personal and proactive meant making smarter use of data. The strategic shift—which looked at first more like a small update of the Customer 2020 strategy—impacted not just the customer-facing activities, but also involved simplifying business processes, functions, applications and systems. The bank-insurance group also doubled down on its in-house data capabilities.

KBC also created an Open and Beyond Banking and Insurance (OBI) department to experiment with new ecosystems. The OBI team delivered several new initiatives, including an API-developer portal, allowing partner companies to integrate KBC's financial products and services into their own offerings.

The 'Differently: the Next Level' strategy was another fundamental business model innovation. The company upgraded its value proposition to the next level. Kate, KBC's new personal assistant, was the algorithm that guaranteed proactive advice. This new value proposition required KBC to embrace Artificial Intelligence to become a fully data-driven organization. The company realized it needed more and different data than what was available in its databases. The old data was used for reporting purposes. The company now needed richer data and deep data analytics in order to make personalized prognoses. Johan Thijs comments, 'The easy part of the job is the front-end. But proactive and customized solutions don't stop there. The difficult part is the back-end and especially the flawless connection between these two layers. Many banks had—and still have—analogue processes for which they made a digital front-end. This is like putting lipstick on a bulldog. To be successful in the 21st century, you must redesign the back- and front-end processes and be absolutely sure that they are seamlessly integrated. Only then can we be smart.'[251]

# Core transformation: It's not what you think

The three chameleon stories contain interesting lessons that challenge some conventional turbulence management wisdom. The first one is that turbulence should not always be countered by launching speedboats and moonshots outside the core. You can counter turbulence successfully in the core. The second major lesson is that the chameleon strategy is tough to implement. Core transformation is more than optimizing the efficiency of your operations—and it requires leadership skills at all levels across the organization. Let's explore each of these messages in somewhat more detail.

**MISCONCEPTION #1: "MANAGING THE CORE IS ALL ABOUT EXPLOITATION."** Many management authors suggest tackling turbulence by building a portfolio of radical or transformational innovation projects outside your core. These initiatives help the organization adapt to volatile markets, avoid complacency, and build new future businesses. Successful, invincible companies are not just nimble and innovative, they are well aligned to exploit the value of their existing businesses.[252] These organizations are called ambidextrous organizations, simultaneously mastering adaptability (exploration) and alignment (exploitation). Organizations often struggle to find the right balance between exploration and exploitation because these two activities require fundamentally different organizational capabilities, as is shown in Figure 46.

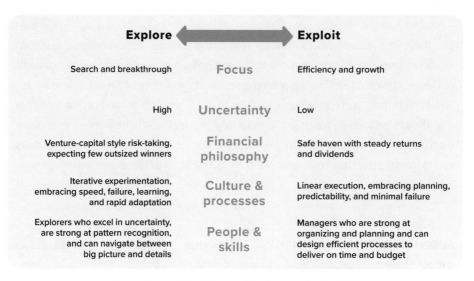

| Explore | Focus | Exploit |
|---|---|---|
| Search and breakthrough | **Focus** | Efficiency and growth |
| High | **Uncertainty** | Low |
| Venture-capital style risk-taking, expecting few outsized winners | **Financial philosophy** | Safe haven with steady returns and dividends |
| Iterative experimentation, embracing speed, failure, learning, and rapid adaptation | **Culture & processes** | Linear execution, embracing planning, predictability, and minimal failure |
| Explorers who excel in uncertainty, are strong at pattern recognition, and can navigate between big picture and details | **People & skills** | Managers who are strong at organizing and planning and can design efficient processes to deliver on time and budget |

Source: Osterwalder, Pigneur, Etiemble & Smith (2020)[253]

**Figure 46** • Explore vs exploit

One of the most common approaches for dealing with this dichotomy is to separate the exploration units from the exploitation units—an approach that we described in the previous chapter. The main idea is that the core business should focus on exploitation, while exploration activities should be done outside your core.

But our chameleon stories show that, in certain cases, this thinking is flawed. In some circumstances—especially when disruptors threaten your core aggressively—exploitation may not be enough. Efficiency improvements and incremental innovations are sometimes not sufficient to defend the core, even when you have built a powerful exploration engine. The management teams of Hilti, TAG Heuer, and KBC understood this well and engaged in nothing less than a fundamental transformation of their core business. They pursued business model innovation—a typical exploration activity—inside, not outside, their core.

**MISCONCEPTION #2: "MANAGING THE CORE IS ABOUT MANAGEMENT, INNOVATION OUTSIDE THE CORE IS ABOUT LEADERSHIP."** People associate exploitation with management and exploration with leadership. The idea behind this assumption is that exploiting the core is about 'making sure the trains run on time'. Many management authors consider building those transformational new units as the true management challenge. It's about growing the company by taking some risky and unpredictable bets on strategic moves where there are no statistics and references to tell you whether it's a good idea at all. That's where leadership is required. At least, that is the traditional thinking.

Again, our chameleon stories show a different picture. Managing the core is more than an exploitation exercise. It's not about managing a safe haven or about linear execution and managing predictability, as is suggested by Figure 46. It's about transforming an entire organization from within the core: it's about challenging traditional assumptions and about letting people know that the traditional core is no longer the future. And building that new future is a frustrating exercise. People find it difficult to learn something new. We tend to revert to what we are good at. And it's difficult to replace certain cash flows with uncertain ones. That's why core transformation is hard—we all know that many strategic change projects fail. And that's why core transformation requires as many leadership skills as building a new venture.

## Building a new business model inside the core

If you want to implement a chameleon strategy, your challenge is twofold. First you need to build a new business model that will complement or gradually replace your traditional solutions. Here, I can refer to the suggestions and recommendations that were described in the previous chapter. I will briefly repeat them and add some examples from the chameleon companies. The second challenge is managing the transformation journey.

**BUILDING A NEW BUSINESS MODEL.** How to start? Mostly you start building the future through a (yearly) sensing exercise (see Chapter 2) whereby you screen the business environment and look out for key change drivers. Based on that analysis, you build scenarios for the most uncertain drivers of change. Another typical exercise is that you systematically screen some of the new disruptors in your market and analyze their business models and performance. When you notice that these disruptors have started eating your business, it's time to react. In Chapter 5, I listed some questions that help you better analyze the consequences of these change drivers:

- Why are we losing customers in our traditional core business? For whom do they leave us?
- What do customers like in the offering of the new players?
- What is the value proposition of the disruptors? And where is it different from ours?
- Given these new insights, how can we make our value proposition more attractive?
- What are the key processes and key resources of the new players? How different are they from ours?
- What is their profit model? Should we change ours?

Even when you are early, and there are no immediate disruptors on the market as in the Hilti case, it's relatively easy to come up with the core elements of a new business model. There, one key customer came up with a rather concrete request for a holistic tool management solution. TAG Heuer had seen the first set of smart watches passing by in 2013. And KBC looked at what was happening in other industries. The financial services industry was not the first one to be disrupted—the travel industry, the hotel industry, the music industry, and the retail industry all fundamentally changed earlier in time. The pattern was clear: the customer wanted faster, easier, and cheaper solutions. Foresight capabilities help you scan, sense and imagine the new future.


**ADOPT AN OUTSIDER'S PERSPECTIVE.** Here too, it's good to adopt an outsider's perspective. Analyze the turbulence and try to imagine how your industry will evolve. Look at the turbulence and disruption with eyes that are free of the biases of the core business.[254] That's not easy and it takes guts to do it—but that's how you get the most honest and realistic view of where your industry is heading.

**AVOID COPY/PASTE.** Another piece of advice was to avoid copy/paste. Rather than copying the business model of your disruptor, it's important to come up with a unique value proposition yourself—ideally one that builds on your traditional strengths. All three chameleon cases have created a different value proposition—a significant upgrade of their former value proposition, and different enough from the offering of the competitors and disruptors. KBC leveraged its existing capabilities but built something on top of it. Says Chief Innovation Officer Erik Luts: "We've always been trusted advisors for our customers. People trust us. We know how to do this. And today we are digitizing that role. That's the essence of our transformation. The world is changing and the technology brings new opportunities to interact with our customers. Faster, easier, proactive, and more data-driven. We have the contact with the customer—that is the strength that we leverage—and we increase the interaction frequency. So, we expand our service offering and we are digitizing our value proposition. This is our new vision, but not a different vision. That's why we called our strategy 'Differently, the Next Level'."[255]

Here is another example. Mark Thompson saw a clear path forward for his company when he took the helm as CEO of The New York Times (NYT) in 2012. He believed that, in a world with a lot of free digital news, The NYT could be one of the tiny handful of trusted independent sources of news in the world. The key question was how to leverage the company's great newsroom—one of the best in the world—in a digital world and increase the digital subscribers' willingness to pay.[256] Thompson moved away from the notion that the NYT was a print newspaper with a little digital operation. Instead, he thought of the NYT as a news company with several platforms: a print platform, a web platform, and a smartphone platform. He didn't think about how digital could help the print newspaper but imagined what was needed to succeed with all three platforms. Obviously, that was easy for print: the company had the managerial strength for that part of the business. The challenge was to build the two other platforms.

Here is some more advice on how to adapt your value proposition. In identifying the dimensions of your new value proposition, first have a look at what the competitors/disruptors offer:

- Check out the weaknesses in the disruptors' strategies. Think about TAG Heuer's response to the Apple watch. TAG Heuer stressed eternity—a key element of Swiss watches. This was something that Apple couldn't deliver.[257]
- Check out where disruptors score well and complement that with your offering. Many incumbent firms have copied certain features of pure online players in their offering and survive with a hybrid offering, combining physical shops and online sales channels.
- Look critically at your current offering and figure out what attributes you can eliminate. Disruptors typically compete on value attributes that are different from those of the incumbents. They completely neglect some attributes. What dimensions of your offering can you leave out, without giving up too much value for your customer?
- Come up with new ideas borrowed from other industries and integrate them in your offering. See whether you can find solutions that address some of the pain points that customers experience when they use your product or service. Look out for what else has an impact on the customer experience. And look beyond just the product spectrum. Customers also appreciate better accessibility, more transparent pricing, extra service and connectivity elements, or a sustainability aspect in your offering.

# FINALLY, ALIGN THE OTHER COMPONENTS OF YOUR BUSINESS MODEL.

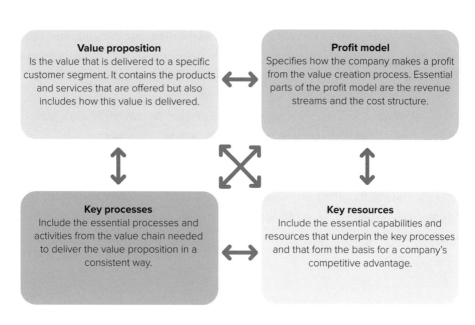

**Value proposition**
Is the value that is delivered to a specific customer segment. It contains the products and services that are offered but also includes how this value is delivered.

**Profit model**
Specifies how the company makes a profit from the value creation process. Essential parts of the profit model are the revenue streams and the cost structure.

**Key processes**
Include the essential processes and activities from the value chain needed to deliver the value proposition in a consistent way.

**Key resources**
Include the essential capabilities and resources that underpin the key processes and that form the basis for a company's competitive advantage.

Source: Adapted from Johnson (2010)[258]

**Figure 47** • Business model framework

Start working on your profit model. Look at your cost structure and see what can be changed by doing things fundamentally differently. Rethink your revenue model. The Hilti case shows that a new profit model can be a significant component and driver of business model innovation. Hilti introduced a 'subscription model' whereby it no longer charged for a particular product but for the use of a broad range of products for a certain time. Rather than selling the drills, the company offered its customers a leasing solution. This change helped the company move from a low-margins-and-high-inventory-turnover game into a higher-margins-and-asset-heavy profit model.

The cases of TAG Heuer and KBC showed some changes in the revenue model, but not to the level we saw with Hilti. TAG Heuer developed a new pricing model for its Connected Watch: the two modules—the mechanical and the electronic—were priced at $1,500 each. KBC also started thinking about new revenue models. When it opened up its customer base for other partners, it created a new revenue stream by taking commissions on those transactions. At the moment of writing, this is still a small revenue stream compared to the traditional business. But the management team believes that this new revenue stream can grow substantially in the future.

Finally, you have to rethink your key processes and key resources. The KBC case is a nice illustration of this. The bank first changed its front-office dramatically—from a traditional branch-based bank to a one-stop-shop financial institution. But then realized that being instant required a streamlining of the back office too. And when they figured out that their distribution power and their customer knowledge had become key resources, the company shifted another gear in their business model innovation.

# Managing the transformation journey

Core transformation is a challenging journey. Business model innovation is building something new that ultimately will be brought back into the business. For your people, this is change, something that many people don't like. So be prepared for a lot of resistance and a stormy journey. When firms are facing continuous turbulence, the transformation challenge becomes even more intense. Nevertheless, several companies have managed this change quite well.

In order to provide some structure for these change messages, I first would like to present a change model that helps managers see the key challenges in the core transformation journey more clearly.

**SIX BATTERIES OF CHANGE.** Some years ago, I co-authored a book with my colleagues Peter De Prins and Geert Letens, called *Six Batteries of Change*.[259] We developed this change model to help organizations deal with fast-paced change. Our approach to managing change was quite unique. While most academics and consultants use step models to deal with change, our main idea was that change is all about managing energy. Each organization has a certain level of energy, and when you generate enough energy, you can use it to make lasting change happen. If your energy reserves are running low, however, your change efforts will quickly fizzle out. The question then was to identify those key areas in an organization that must be energized for change. We identified six key areas—which we called the six batteries of change (see Figure 48). Here is a short description of those six batteries:

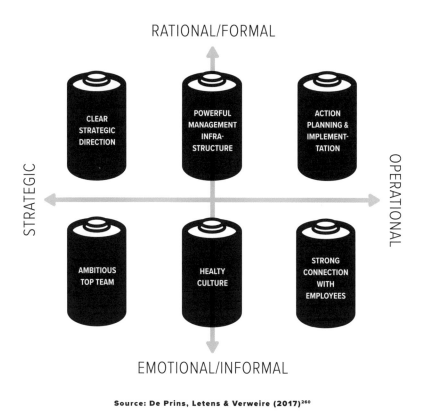

Source: De Prins, Letens & Verweire (2017)[260]

**Figure 48·** Six batteries of change

**Rational batteries**

**Clear strategic direction**: A robust strategy is crucial to make change happen and keep everyone in your organization working towards the same goals.

**Powerful management infrastructure**: This is the bridge between the strategy and the many projects that help implement it. It's made up of the structure and systems that help managers run your organization.

**Action planning and implementation**: Effective change demands sound process and project management. This is where your strategy is translated into clear customer benefits and improved organizational capabilities.

**Emotional batteries**

**Ambitious top team**: The most important source of energy is your leadership team. It drives change by setting ambitious aspirations and sponsoring the change efforts.

**Healthy culture**: Culture can enable change or be a barrier to it. In environments that are open, collaborative and receptive to new ideas, change is more successful than in unhealthy environments.

**Strong connection with employees**: To make change stick, everyone in your organization needs to commit to it. Your teams need to be willing to embrace change and the opportunities it brings.

The rational batteries cover the 'hardware of change'—strategy, management infrastructure (portfolio management), and action planning (project management). The emotional batteries affect the 'software of change', including the dynamics within your top team, culture, and the connection with your people. Our research revealed that successful change only happens when all six batteries are charged.[261] This means that change managers should manage both the rational and the emotional sides of change. Focusing solely on the rational batteries won't lead to sustainable success— launching project after project without tackling the emotional batteries will lead to resistance from your teams. Similarly, concentrating on the emotional batteries alone will not help address problems in strategy or project delivery.

To be effective, a change program needs to be holistic. Which is why the batteries cover all aspects of your organization—from the strategic to the operational level. Without a strategy and a committed top team, you will only achieve some local change success. It is, however, impossible to have some company-wide change success. But equally, without a solid implementation plan and motivated employees, your big ideas will never materialize.

STRATEGY IN TURBULENT TIMES

This batteries model can also be used to guide managers through the challenges of core transformation. In the pages that follow, I present six commandments, each one covering a change battery. I then add one extra commandment that focuses on the organizational setup that is needed to succeed with a chameleon strategy.

**COMMANDMENT #1: CREATE AN APOLLO UNIT FOR YOUR ENDEAVOR.** Building a new business model inside your core requires that you set up a separate structure for that new unit. This is similar to building a new unit outside your core. But the difference between a chameleon strategy and a salmon strategy is that, in the first case, the new unit impacts the core dramatically. It's like the Apollo space-flight mission, where the shuttle is launched into space but returns to earth after some time. In the salmon strategy, the new unit doesn't return to earth and follows its own path into space—just like the Voyager 1 and 2 missions that flew into the interstellar space never to come back (see Figure 49). (Recall that in the Voyager mission, the new unit is also somewhat linked to the core.)

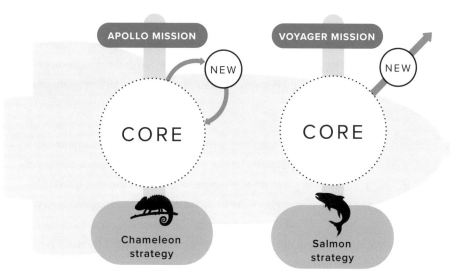

**Figure 49** • Apollo structure for core transformation

It's crucial to build a separate structure for the innovation team and keep it free from intervention from the core. This new team's task is to come up with a different business model that, by definition, doesn't match your organization's existing structure and systems—otherwise, you're in the core resilience quadrant of the turbulence framework. I've noted different formats of 'Apollo missions'.

TAG Heuer set up a small 'commando team', consisting of only a handful of people. Separation ensured that the team preserved an entrepreneurial spirit, needed in any business model innovation project. Guy Sémon, the Head of Product Development and program manager says, 'To start a project like this one, you have to first have a commando attitude: light, fast, efficient. For the next chapter, you need airfields, logistics, transport, airplanes, cavalry, infantry, a lot of people. It's not the same skills.'[262] The same philosophy was applied at Hilti, where the company created a small exploration team—'a very small plant surrounded by big trees.'[263]

Firms that face continuous change may adopt the approach followed by KBC. KBC launched a separate unit next to its traditional core to initiate the change and help change the big tanker's course. KBC called this organization 'the tugboat'—a very powerful but small vehicle that is better suited to the job than a fast speedboat. The company staffed this tugboat with 250 of its best employees from different departments. It consisted of a group of ambitious managers and employees who supported the vision and who were willing to shake things up a bit. With the visible support from the top team, this core team became—and still is—a major driver of internal change.

The tugboat was in charge of launching projects that generated commercial deliveries and built internal capabilities. After six months, some team members returned to the traditional organization while new people were recruited. This approach illustrates nicely how to implement ambidexterity in practice: one part is running the business, the other is rebuilding the business. The exploration team operates rather independently and has the power to bypass the traditional hierarchy. When people go back to their original job, they act as ambassadors, and that's how KBC increased the critical mass of transformers who ultimately change the course of the tanker.

**COMMANDMENT #2: BUILD A VISION SHARED AND SUPPORTED BY THE TOP TEAM.** According to Gary Hamel, a leading innovation guru, revolutions don't start at the top.[264] Our cases prove Hamel wrong: core transformation takes off only when the top team is involved early on. Otherwise, forget about it.

With top management, we mean the *entire* top team of the organization, not just 1 or 2 executives from the team. When disruption strikes, you need to take time to analyze, debate and hold tough discussions. Says CEO Mark Thompson from The New York Times: "We got into the habit of quite intense conversations. In 2015, we had nearly a year when the top five or six people met in a room. We'd meet Friday at noon, leave at 6:00 p.m. or 7:00 p.m. every Friday from early April to November. Ultimately, through lots of kicking and screaming and argument, we ended up with a genuinely shared vision that we eventually produced as a single page of bullet points."[265]

Having those discussions requires the top team to really be a team at the top, a team where top executives trust each other and dare to discuss and disagree. The strategic choices that are inevitably associated with business model innovation require tough decisions and sacrifices. There will be winners and losers in the top team and in the rest of the organization. You can only arrive at those tough choices if you have a top team where the collective goals are more important than the top managers' individual needs—first, you are a member of the top team, then you manage a department—not the other way around.

In successful chameleon companies, team members defend and back each other up. Cohesion is crucial. Obviously, some top team members will play a more prominent role in the transformation process. But that doesn't mean the other members can pull back. They should support their colleagues, help spread the message, and remove obstacles to change. It's important that the top team speaks with one voice.

The change narrative should contain both a positive and a negative story. Disruption should be framed both as a threat and an opportunity.[266] The negative part of the story is about challenging the status quo. 'The first step towards getting somewhere is to decide you're not going to stay where you are', is a famous quote from John Pierpont Morgan, founder of the well-known American investment bank. It's good to point to the threats out there—that gets the organization in motion. But only focusing on the threats leads to short-term reactions. As an organization, you want to build a story for the longer term. And that's why you need to focus on the opportunities that turbulence brings. When asked whether the top team was ready for the radical move of building a new connected watch, a TAG Heuer manager answered, 'The question is what are we doing here? Do we just look at what Apple and others are doing and just pray that it doesn't affect us? Or do we try to be a little bit more active? Since Apple is going there, there's probably a market... We don't know if we will be successful or not, but we know if we don't try, of course we won't be successful. Is it better to lose millions of euro in R&D than lose hundreds of millions in sales because we're not trying?'

Use outsiders to challenge your ideas. But don't forget: it's the top team's job to come up with the change vision and the broad contours of your new business model. As already said, building that new vision is usually not the most difficult part—assuming you take time to screen the industry and business environment. Also, check with your shareholders to see whether or not you have a license to operate. You wouldn't be the first one to find out that your great ideas about fundamental change are not supported by the shareholders or owners of the business. Therefore, have change conversations with your board members and shareholders too.

Finally, once you've identified your future model, be obsessed with it. Your transformation actions are needed to change the course of the tanker. This requires that you think big and that you spend a lot of time communicating that vision with fervor and passion.

**COMMANDMENT #3: BUILD A CLEAR STRATEGIC DIRECTION THROUGH DISCIPLINED EXPERIMENTATION.** The path towards a new value proposition and business model requires disciplined experimentation—a topic that I also addressed in the previous chapter. Don't expect everything to work out or unfold exactly like you had in mind. Business model innovation involves much experimentation. You will be confronted with failure. But experimentation is not about 'just trying'. Chaos is not the answer to big uncertainty. Disciplined experimentation is all about focused testing and validated learning. Formulate assumptions that are most critical to your future business success and then test them in a targeted manner to quickly prove or disprove their viability. That's how you assemble the bricks of your new business model.

Some organizations decide to invest in wild experimentation. For example, KBC invests about 4 or 5 million EUR per year in all kinds of weird initiatives. That's a very controversial decision within the company. These investments do not immediately pay off and they are not directly linked to the programs that are systematically rolled out in the tugboat. But these innovation experiments are done to provide an answer to some future trends and change drivers. Much of that wild experimentation leads to nothing—60 to 70% of those projects are killed. But the rest become part of later innovation solutions.

**COMMANDMENT #4: PLAN THE CHANGE AND DEVELOP A POWERFUL MANAGEMENT INFRASTRUCTURE.** Building an aspirational change vision is key but not sufficient for successful core transformation. Visions need to be translated into a portfolio of concrete projects. It's good to set up a program management office (PMO) to manage such a diversity of projects, with dedicated senior program managers, supported by visible corporate sponsors from the top team.

Organizations that go through fundamental core transformation need a well-functioning planning system—a powerful management infrastructure—in charge for managing priorities and capacity management in the exploration team. As Peter Drucker said, 'Time is the scarcest resource, and unless it is managed nothing else can be managed.' Organizations that can't find a solution to this problem create hotbeds of change fatigue and burnout. This involves setting up clear roadmaps for the most important projects, which are reviewed regularly—for example, once per year. The management infrastructure also ensures good resource planning. Prioritizing projects and giving them the right resources is essential. Otherwise, you become overwhelmed and 'management by decibels' decides what gets done and what goes on the back burner.

A powerful management infrastructure also allows you to measure the progress of the core transformation projects. Assessing where and how you are performing in your change programs is essential. Many companies, however, are swamped by reporting or drown in follow-up meetings. At that moment, your management infrastructure has turned into a bureaucratic reporting monster. Reporting is necessary, but do it efficiently and effectively. Good reports and meetings are more than activity reports; they describe whether results are achieved and what the next steps are. They evaluate good and bad performance to learn from it. Developing standardized reporting documents helps.

**COMMANDMENT #5: IMPLEMENT THROUGH EMPOWERMENT WITHIN CLEAR BOUNDARIES.** Many organizations today apply agile project management. So, this part of the core transformation challenge should be straightforward. The six batteries research project, however, showed that most companies struggle mainly with this battery and with the management infrastructure battery.[267] Action planning and implementation is anything but straightforward. How can you make it work?

Cut your roadmap into clear projects. For each project, work with a small team of four to eight people and time boxes of 3 to 6 months. Jeff Bezos, former CEO and Executive Chairman of Amazon, once said that if you can't feed a team with two pizzas, it's too large. Use multidisciplinary teams to work on concrete projects. Define clear assignments that solve a customer problem or that contribute to delivering a new capability. Explain what you want to achieve—not in big words— but in clear deliverables. And define an inspiring end-state to mobilize your teams for a journey of hope. The idea is that when a particular project is finished, your organization is a little better equipped to compete more effectively. Stay positive: there are no problems, just issues that need to be solved.

Companies that struggle with core transformation depend on heroes who excel in crisis management while smart transformers use the intelligence and energy of a well-trained team. In the fixed period of time that the team is together, provide sufficient training, organize bootcamps, and provide support to get fast, productive results. Work with a fixed rhythm and a fixed delivery and be hard on non-delivery. If that means dissolving teams, that's the price to pay. Be supportive as a management team, take time to listen to the teams and do what you can to help them, but be inexorable when it comes to results.

**COMMANDMENT #6: CONTINUOUSLY REACH OUT TO YOUR EMPLOYEES TO GET THEM ON BOARD.** When you launch your chameleon strategy, expect stickiness and resistance. Most employees and (middle) managers stick to the status quo, and they will resist any change that you propose. The reason is that you are trying to convince those people of something they don't see (yet) or that they consider impossible. A convincing top team and an aspirational vision definitely help but are not sufficient.

People aren't motivated to change just because their organization wants to. They need to understand their role in the change and what it means for them. Don't be afraid to disturb and embarrass the people in the tanker. Create a sense of urgency and trigger your people by launching some guerilla communication tactics: use the cafeteria to bring your change message, create inspiration sessions with speakers from inside or outside the company, change the hallways—in short, use the full spectrum of communication to fight for the mind of your employees. Humor is a good weapon for this—and try to figure out what messages and tactics do stick. At first, your people will still object—but if you continue disturbing and bombarding them, they will realize this is not a temporary gimmick and they will understand what you want to achieve.

Celebrate successes as much as you can—this a key step in every successful change journey. Put team members on the podium and reward them openly. Instill positive change. But also check the general change attitude in the rest of the organization. Many people resist change because they are afraid they won't be able to make the change because they lack the capabilities to jump on the boat. Offer training programs and webinars—force your people into a learning habit. Here too: reward them with diplomas and other tokens of appreciation. At the same time, keep on listening. Be responsive and willing to adjust where necessary.

Some management authors and consultants suggest bringing in a lot of new people and firing the people who are unable or unwilling to change—the equivalent of an organizational blood transfusion. But most managers of chameleon companies reject this idea. The change leaders at core transformers believe that most employees can be changed. They believe that those people have a lot of expertise that newcomers don't have. So, for a newspaper company (or any company faced with digital disruptors) the question could be phrased as follows: should we turn journalists into digital natives or should we turn digital natives into journalists? The first option clearly is the preferred one. Of course, people who are unwilling to change don't have a place in the new organization. And if you need capabilities you don't have, you need to recruit new employees.

**COMMANDMENT #7: CONTINUOUSLY WORK ON A HEALTHY ORGANIZA-TIONAL CULTURE.** The culture battery is the last but not the least one to consider in your core transformation. How does your culture generate energy for change, rather than drain it? In our six batteries book, we identified four aspects that point to a healthy versus an unhealthy culture.

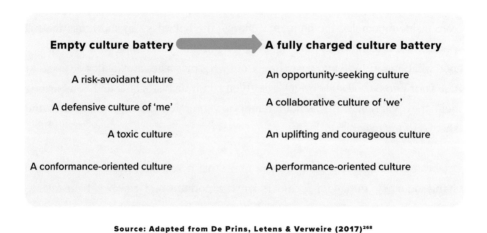

**Empty culture battery** ➜ **A fully charged culture battery**

| | |
|---|---|
| A risk-avoidant culture | An opportunity-seeking culture |
| A defensive culture of 'me' | A collaborative culture of 'we' |
| A toxic culture | An uplifting and courageous culture |
| A conformance-oriented culture | A performance-oriented culture |

Source: Adapted from De Prins, Letens & Verweire (2017)[268]

**Figure 50** • From an empty to a fully charged culture battery

Managing the culture battery in a core transformation process requires that you pay attention to all four dimensions of culture. It's absolutely essential that you in-still an opportunity-seeking, entrepreneurial culture in your company. Managing turbulence is a daunting task requiring the top team and the whole company to support and rally behind the idea that the firm needs to renew itself. This means that every few years something must happen to stir things up and destabilize the system all over again. If the current performance is good, create positive crises by setting new goals for the organization that makes current performance appear less than good. Set stretch targets for the company and force your people to think about how to achieve these targets.[269] Many organizations use 'Vision 20XX' documents to instill that ambition. But many fail to get people excited and committed to those targets.

Maintaining a startup mentality in an established organization is definitely difficult but not impossible. Jean-Claude Biver, CEO of TAG Heuer, replaced many of his top managers to establish a more entrepreneurial and participative culture, 'My concept was that I should never lose the speed and flexibility of a startup company. Speed depends on people and organization. If your organization is too heavy, too complicated, too much structure, too much responsibility at many levels, your speed cannot be fast. We have reorganized our internal chart, our responsibility hierarchical levels in order to enable the maximum possible speed, like a little startup.'[270]

A second element of cultural change is the shift from a defensive and silo-driven to a more collaborative organization. The new exploration unit should be composed of cross-functional teams. And that unit should have the power to deliver at any cost. This also requires an uplifting and courageous culture in the company. The people in the tugboat at KBC were told to accept no constraints at all from the traditional organization. In a bank dominated by risk and compliance managers, that was not always easy. But those managers were overruled when needed. And when members of the tugboat team wanted something from a department, they got priority treatment from other departments (which is only possible if you are supported by powerful and visible sponsors from the executive team).

Core transformation also works better if there is performance drive in your company. Teams have to deliver. They get the resources and the support, and sometimes priority treatment. Then there's no place for excuses and bad results.

## What about your chameleon capabilities?

Launching a business model innovation inside your core isn't a walk in the park. It's a daunting journey where you encounter many roadblocks. But it's a journey that you can tackle successfully if you plan the journey well. Check out how well you are prepared for a chameleon journey and discover the color of your chameleon. The questionnaire consists of two parts: the first part checks the quality of your new business model; the second part investigates the quality of your transformation skills.

| BUSINESS MODEL INNOVATION | STRONGLY DISAGREE | NEITHER AGREE NOR DISAGREE | STRONGLY AGREE |
|---|---|---|---|
| 1. The value proposition of our new (set of) product(s) and service(s) is very different from the competitors' (including the disruptors') value proposition. | 1 ○ ○ ○ ○ | | ○ 5 |
| 2. We have developed a very different profit model for our new (set of) product(s) and service(s). | 1 ○ ○ ○ ○ | | ○ 5 |
| 3. The key processes needed to deliver our value proposition are fundamentally different from our competitors' key processes. | 1 ○ ○ ○ ○ | | ○ 5 |
| 4. We have created a set of new capabilities and/or resources that help differentiate ourselves from the competitors. | 1 ○ ○ ○ ○ | | ○ 5 |
| 5. We have leveraged some of our traditional strengths in our new business model. | 1 ○ ○ ○ ○ | | ○ 5 |

| TRANSFORMATION CAPABILITIES | STRONGLY DISAGREE | NEITHER AGREE NOR DISAGREE | STRONGLY AGREE |
|---|---|---|---|
| 6. We have created a separate structure for our innovation unit that can operate freely and autonomously from our traditional business. | 1 ○ ○ ○ ○ | | ○ 5 |
| 7. The change story behind our new business model is framed both as a threat and as an opportunity. | 1 ○ ○ ○ ○ | | ○ 5 |
| 8. Our new change vision is shared and supported by the entire top team. | 1 ○ ○ ○ ○ | | ○ 5 |
| 9. We do regular screening and sensing exercises to check out how new disruptive offerings are affecting our current business model. | 1 ○ ○ ○ ○ | | ○ 5 |
| 10. Our organization allocates significant financial and human resources to experiment with and develop new concepts and products. | 1 ○ ○ ○ ○ | | ○ 5 |
| 11. We have set up a program management office with dedicated managers to run a portfolio of projects to renew our value proposition. | 1 ○ ○ ○ ○ | | ○ 5 |
| 12. We have developed clear roadmaps that help us in the prioritization and resource allocation of our projects. | 1 ○ ○ ○ ○ | | ○ 5 |
| 13. We systematically measure the progress of our transformation projects portfolio. | 1 ○ ○ ○ ○ | | ○ 5 |
| 14. We have developed a sound project methodology that helps us deliver our individual projects on time and within budget. | 1 ○ ○ ○ ○ | | ○ 5 |
| 15. Our employees receive sufficient training and support for dealing with a changing business environment. | 1 ○ ○ ○ ○ | | ○ 5 |
| 16. We employ a huge arsenal of communication tactics to get our organization moving in the right direction. | 1 ○ ○ ○ ○ | | ○ 5 |
| 17. We regularly celebrate change successes and appreciate our people for their change efforts. | 1 ○ ○ ○ ○ | | ○ 5 |
| 18. Our organization has an entrepreneurial culture that stimulates innovation and challenges the status quo. | 1 ○ ○ ○ ○ | | ○ 5 |
| 19. The culture of the exploration unit is characterized by a collaborative, performance-driven, and courageous culture. | 1 ○ ○ ○ ○ | | ○ 5 |
| 20. We know well how to bring projects from the exploration unit back into the organization. | 1 ○ ○ ○ ○ | | ○ 5 |

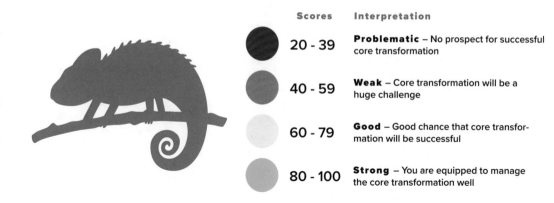

| Scores | Interpretation |
|---|---|
| 20 - 39 | **Problematic** – No prospect for successful core transformation |
| 40 - 59 | **Weak** – Core transformation will be a huge challenge |
| 60 - 79 | **Good** – Good chance that core transformation will be successful |
| 80 - 100 | **Strong** – You are equipped to manage the core transformation well |

**Figure 51 •** How well are you equipped for a chameleon strategy?

# KEY TAKEAWAYS

- The chameleon strategy is used to help companies change their original business model to cope with changing demands.
- The stories of Hilti, TAG Heuer and KBC have shown that incumbents can be successful in countering turbulence in their core business. The winners of turbulence are not only the challengers and disruptors but can be large, established incumbents as well.
- Core transformation is not an exploitation but a true transformation exercise: it's far more challenging and requires leadership skills to finish this exercise well.
- Core transformation requires you to build an exploration unit that is still separate from the traditional business, but nevertheless linked to it.
- The exploration unit is charged with building a new business model that is then gradually introduced in the core as a new product or service line (Hilti and TAG Heuer) or fully integrated in the existing business (KBC).
- Incumbents should not copy/paste the business model of the disruptors but should add their own flavor to it.
- Be prepared for a lot of resistance. You will need an extensive set of change skills to make core transformation a success.

# CHAPTER
# 7

## chapter of the octopus
---
Corporate transformation

# Key questions addressed in this chapter

What is a corporate transformation strategy?

Why is this the most challenging of the 4 turbulence strategies to implement?

What are the particular challenges of combining these 2 strategic moves?

How do you start? Do you start with changing the core or do you expand into new ventures first?

Which companies have succeeded with an octopus strategy?

The final turbulence strategy is the corporate transformation or octopus strategy. It's the most challenging of the four strategies as it requires a company to both transform its core business and at the same time add a new business model to the corporate portfolio. Corporate transformation is about playing offense and defense simultaneously.

You use this strategy when you realize that the change drivers that you identified in a sensing exercise—sustainability, a low-cost competitor entering your market, changing legislation, or any other disruptive threat—will have a significant and lasting impact on your core business and force you to take action there. For example, companies like Danone and Adobe faced turbulence in their core markets, and all engaged in drastic core transformation programs. Danone reshuffled its business portfolio to concentrate on its dairy business, divesting its beverage and biscuits divisions. Adobe, the company known for creating and designing documents and images, faced a shift to cloud-based business models and repositioned its core by bundling Photoshop and other programs into a Creative Cloud subscription service. Revenues went down, but Adobe realized good margins from this transformed core division.[271]

Danone and Adobe also expanded outside their core business. Danone started building a portfolio of health brands after it acquired Numico in 2007. In 2017, it went a step further and set up a business focusing on organic and plant-based products.[272] Adobe created a digital marketing unit that became the growth engine for the company, representing 45% of total sales in 2015.[273] Danone and Adobe prove that turbulence can also offer opportunities outside your core: you can set up a new business to capture new customers with new products and services. That's the offense part of the story.

The story of LEGO is another interesting example of corporate transformation. The company had engaged in a massive diversification as a reaction to a whole set of change drivers, including the threat of low-cost competitors and the arrival of video games in the toy industry. The company created new product lines, built computer games, expanded its distribution channels, and launched a platform for developing a virtual LEGO universe to accommodate LEGO fans of all ages. This was not about launching one corporate innovation initiative... the company had become one big innovation theme park. Unfortunately, most of these innovations failed, and the company was on the verge of bankruptcy in 2003.

LEGO repositioned its core, which in essence meant going back to its traditional core—construction-based play sold via the traditional retail partners. Revenues dropped by a third—but after two years of cost cutting and restructuring, the company wrote black figures again. The company had put some hit toys (back) on the market, such as LEGO Bionicle, Mindstorms NXT, and Ninjago—contemporary toys, but with a clear link to the original product lines. After the transformation of its core, LEGO took off on a growth path again. It targeted new customer groups—adults with LEGO Architecture, and girls with LEGO Friends—and engaged in new corporate innovation moves. LEGO explored board games and developed a massively multiplayer online (MMO) game, called LEGO Universe. Both the board games and the MMO game were business model innovations outside the core, yet they failed and were discontinued after a few years. Despite these failures, LEGO became one of the most successful toy companies for the period 2007–17 with astonishing yearly return-on-equity ratios ranging between 40% and 85%.

The strategy of corporate transformation looks like an immense challenge. It's about applying salmon and chameleon strategies simultaneously. That's why the octopus strategy is the least applied turbulence strategy. Nevertheless, this strategy has attracted significant attention from management scholars and consultants. Scott Anthony, Clark Gilbert, and Mark Johnson wrote a great book called *Dual Transformation*, where they offered recipes to tackle the octopus challenge. According to the authors, the octopus strategy is the corporate equivalent of highly invasive surgery.[274]

In this chapter, I present three octopus stories that shed light on how to perform this surgery in practice and illustrate how to combine a salmon strategy with a chameleon strategy. I will offer some recommendations on do's and don'ts for this turbulence strategy, and then I finish this chapter with a small questionnaire with which you can test your octopus capabilities.

# The octopus: A master of corporate transformation

Corporate transformation is about transforming the core business and simultaneously adding a new business model. It's called 'corporate' transformation because action is taking place on different fronts. The octopus is the 'corporate animal' par excellence: it has eight arms, three hearts, and a centralized brain. Each arm contains a mini brain and is capable of acting independently, like the business units in a corporation. The centralized brain processes visual information and keeps oversight, much like a company's headquarters.

When confronted with danger, octopuses react in surprising ways employing both transformational and innovation skills. Octopuses are among the most skilled camouflage artists in the animal kingdom—even more than chameleons, to which I referred in the previous chapter. Octopuses are really masters of disguise. They have specialized cells, called chromatophores, under their skin that help them change color. But they can also stretch, bend, and make their skin take on new shapes, making them masters of transformation.

Some octopus species do more than copy surrounding rocks and reefs; they disguise themselves as other animals that their predators tend to avoid. They even take on the appearance and behavior of venomous or bad-tasting creatures to foil would-be predators. The octopus is a true shapeshifter: while camouflaging yourself as a rock means you need to stay still while the predator is around, disguising yourself as an animal allows you to move out of the danger zone. The 'mimic octopus' deserves some extra attention: this octopus species is known to actively imitate several animals in order to elude predators and can switch rapidly between them. For example, when a mimic octopus is attacked by territorial damselfishes, it disguises itself as a banded sea snake, one of the fishes' predators.

That's not the only surprising fact about octopuses. These animals are also very innovative and creative. After years of surprising scientists with their cleverness, some octopuses appear to also use tools, a relatively rare phenomenon in the animal world, especially with invertebrates. Researchers have seen octopuses barricading their den openings with stones and shells. The octopuses flushed mud from buried coconut shells, stacked them for transport, and then carried them to a new location to assemble them as a shelter.

Octopuses are remarkable, smart animals. Their brain-to-body ratio—a rough measure for an animal's intelligence—is the largest of any invertebrate. As we will see throughout this chapter, intelligence and courage are crucial skills for making corporate transformation work.

## Octopus story #1: How can a centenarian become one of the hippest brands in the media industry?

The first octopus story covers one of the most intriguing players in the media industry. Together with the German Axel Springer Group, Norwegian Schibsted Media Group has been heralded as one of the most successful companies managing digital disruption. This company transformed from a local newspaper company into a global media company with more than 8,000 employees operating in 23 countries by taking advantage of the possibilities that turbulence brings. In 2005, the company's revenues amounted to 884 million EUR; by 2018 that amount had almost doubled to 1.6 billion EUR in revenue, despite an extremely turbulent business environment.

**A CHALLENGING ENVIRONMENT FOR NEWSPAPER COMPANIES.** For a long time, the business model of a newspaper company was simple and didn't fundamentally change: for a monthly fee, subscribers received a daily paper with articles on a wide range of topics. Advertisers paid to reach this audience through display ads and classifieds. Newspaper companies had subscription and advertising revenues and that proportion could substantially differ from company to company. For many, advertising revenues were larger than the subscription revenues.

With the arrival of the internet in 1994, readers gradually turned to online sites as the primary source for their news consumption, which put pressure on the newspaper companies' subscription revenues. They suffered even more in the advertising part of the business where they lost advertising income to social media companies like Google and Facebook who took the lion's share of global social media advertising. As a reaction, newspaper companies explored numerous online revenue streams, but with only moderate success: most of them reported only relatively small online revenues.[275]

In 1995, Norwegian publisher Schibsted owned the country's two largest newspapers, Aftenposten and VG, and had an investment in Norway's commercial television channel TV2. In that year, Schibsted's management team convened for a strategy session to discuss the impact of the internet. Kjell Aamot, the CEO at that time, recalls,

> 'The first thing we decided was that staying in the traditional newspaper business was putting ourselves on death row. As CEO of a listed company, I had to deliver growth. We acknowledged that the traditional newspaper was not going to deliver growth in the longer term. So we decided that we should utilize our strong position, our cash flow, and the strong competitive advantages of the two traditional newspapers, to take aggressive positions in the online market.'[276]

Schibsted was among the first publishers to formulate a strategic ambition and response to the digital transformation challenge.

**BUILDING THE ONLINE CLASSIFIED ADVERTISING BUSINESS.** Schibsted's managers were convinced that, 'Classifieds were made for the internet, and the internet was made for classifieds.'[277] The financial figures proved this assumption right: the daily Aftenposten saw its share of the auto classifieds drop from 100% of the market to 20% in just three years.[278] But formulating a strategic ambition was one thing, realizing it was another. In the first years, Schibsted made PDF copies of the newspaper ads and put them on the web. You could only buy those ads if you bought the newspaper ad, in which case you got the online ad for free. This was all done by one part-time employee from the newspaper business with some help from a consulting firm. This venture was not very successful.[279] Other publishing companies were struggling too. Building a new online classified advertising business was new territory for everybody—there was no clear formula for winning customers and no clear profit model yet. Schibsted's management team realized that the initial approach was not working. It was trial with a lot of error—mainly within the existing structures of the Schibsted organization. So, in 1999, the company changed its classified ad strategy. Sverre Munck, an Executive Vice President at Schibsted explains,

> 'We had to do something if we didn't want to fall behind, so we split the classifieds from the newspaper, and allowed them to compete with their own parent brand. And—what in hindsight was a necessary and logical decision—we gave the classifieds a new brand—FINN.no—which means 'to search and to find' in Norwegian. It was now 1998 or 1999. FINN.no had to start from zero, but we had a good influx of ads from our newspapers, and the good user interface and user experience gave them very rapid traction in the consumer market. Very quickly, we outpaced the competition to become dominant not only in cars, but also in jobs, real estate and, eventually, miscellaneous classifieds.'[280]

Offering classified advertising via the internet was a very different business from selling classifieds via newspapers. This was more of a tech business, something quite new for Schibsted. The company embarked on a corporate innovation strategy and introduced a new business model (see Figure 52).

**Schibsted's Online Classified Ads**

| Value proposition | VERY SIMILAR TO COMPETITORS | | SOMEWHAT SIMILAR TO COMPETITORS | | VERY SIMILAR FROM COMPETITORS |
|---|---|---|---|---|---|
| Product performance | ● | ○ | ○ | ○ | ○ |
| Price level of the offering | ○ | ○ | ○ | ○ | ● |
| Accessibility of the offering | ○ | ○ | ○ | ○ | ● |
| Service level associated with the offering | ● | ○ | ○ | ○ | ○ |
| Sustainability of the offering | ● | ○ | ○ | ○ | ○ |
| **Key process and activities** | VERY SIMILAR TO COMPETITORS | | SOMEWHAT SIMILAR TO COMPETITORS | | VERY SIMILAR FROM COMPETITORS |
| Front-end activities | ○ | ○ | ○ | ● | ○ |
| Back-end activities | ○ | ○ | ○ | ● | ○ |
| Support and management activities | ● | ○ | ○ | ○ | ○ |
| **Key resources** | VERY SIMILAR TO COMPETITORS | | SOMEWHAT SIMILAR TO COMPETITORS | | VERY SIMILAR FROM COMPETITORS |
| Core resources and capabilities | ○ | ○ | ○ | ○ | ● |
| Network of suppliers and partners | ○ | ○ | ● | ○ | ○ |
| Role in the entire ecosystem | ● | ○ | ○ | ○ | ○ |
| **Profit Model** | VERY SIMILAR TO COMPETITORS | | SOMEWHAT SIMILAR TO COMPETITORS | | VERY SIMILAR FROM COMPETITORS |
| Revenue structure | ○ | ○ | ○ | ○ | ● |
| Cost structure | ○ | ○ | ○ | ○ | ● |

**Figure 52** • Schibsted's business model innovation in the online classifieds business

For its new venture, Schibsted hired a number of employees from outside the print newspaper business.[281] It also ensured that FINN.no developed its own culture— much more entrepreneurial, focused on building a better product than the competition, with the sales team integrated with product development, which is quite a controversial decision for traditional newspaper companies. The new unit could also set its own prices and was no longer dependent for that on the print operations.[282]

Given the success in its home market, Schibsted decided to roll out FINN.no to Sweden, where it had bought a major newspaper some years earlier. But there it was competing with Blocket, a Swedish online classifieds company. This company was more successful and remained market leader even after Schibsted's entry. Schibsted bought Blocket for 18 million EUR when the company had only 4 million EUR in revenue and was barely breaking even. Looking back, Munck admits this was a crazy deal, but he believes it was Schibsted's best acquisition ever. For example, in 2013, Blocket had revenues of 70 million EUR, with a 50–55% gross margin.[283] Schibsted would later use the Blocket model as motor for its international growth.

**NO EASY ENDEAVOR.** Schibsted's classifieds business also faced serious challenges. There were many discussions with the sales managers of the printed newspapers who also wanted to go after the online classifieds—they also had budget targets to reach. FINN's managing director explained, 'When we started growing, the ad sales department in Aftenposten wasn't happy at all. The CEO of Aftenposten played a very important role, taking our fight to his own people, arguing that we will fight back but we can't stop them from doing it.'[284] Former CEO Kjell Aamot continues,

> 'When we launched our online classified initiative, it was defensive—our goal was to try and keep the classified ads in the print newspaper. We ran the venture this way for two years, and it didn't work at all. It started to work when we said to the people in FINN that, from now on, you can attack your mother, get as many ads as you can. That was challenging, and particularly so for Aftenposten—but if we hadn't done it, a competitor would have. This led us to believe, and we continue to do so today, that if you are going to take a position online, you must not be afraid of losing your main business.'[285]

In 2001, the dot.com collapse affected the results of media firms significantly. Despite the losses, the board of Schibsted—after huge discussions—decided to continue to invest, and even increase, its focus on their online investments—quite the opposite of what most other newspaper companies were doing, who scaled back, or even abandoned, their new business.[286]

In the period 2000–2005, Schibsted refined its online classifieds model and then used it to expand outside Scandinavia. The publisher acquired businesses in Spain and France in 2005 and 2006. When the firm acquired operations, it was not afraid to shut down print operations to concentrate on the online classified ads business. In 2006, Schibsted bought Trader Classified Media which helped to further increase the international scope of its classifieds business. And in 2008, the international classified ads operations were organized into a separate division, called Schibsted Classified Media, which then operated in 18 countries. Most of the businesses used the Swedish success model of Blocket.[287] In 2018, the company had operations in 23 countries. The classifieds division had an EBITDA percentage of around 30%. In 2021, the company announced it had completed the acquisition of eBay's Classifieds Group, further expanding its international scope.

Figure 53 shows the evolution of Schibsted's revenues and the proportion of classified ads—called Marketplaces—in total revenues. 2005 was the first year that Schibsted published figures on revenues from Marketplaces. Since then, the proportion of the classifieds business has steadily increased—from 9% in 2005 to 44% in 2017.

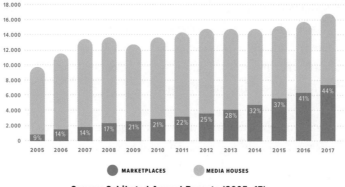

Source: Schibsted Annual Reports (2005–17)

**Figure 53** • Schibsted's revenue evolution: Media houses vs Marketplaces (NOK million)

**TRANSFORMING THE CORE.** Schibsted did not just build a new innovative growth engine as a reaction to the digital disruption but also transformed its core business. Although the financials had generally been good—for the period 1996–2000, the company reported an average return on equity of 16.2%—the management team realized that sticking to the old business model was not an option. Newspapers had been the core of Schibsted's activities since 1860 and Schibsted was not ready to give up its leadership position in that business. But the management team foresaw that circulation and advertising income would drop drastically in the internet age.

From 1995 onwards, the company launched online editions of its traditional newspapers. Here too, Schibsted was not shy about separating the new multimedia business from the print operations. The multimedia businesses relied on the content and the brand of the newspaper but could build its own operations and culture. Says Sverre Munck, 'We realized early on that our online news site should be developed on the premises of the online medium. For example, this meant that content had to be continuously updated. In addition to continuous updating, the front page was constantly reformatted, often in response to real-time feedback regarding the popularity of particular stories.'[288] This was a business model innovation inside the core: the competitive arena was the same—news provision for the traditional customers—readers and advertisers—but with a different value proposition, a different profit model, and different key resources and processes. Figure 54 shows the business model innovation framework for Schibsted's multimedia business.

**Schibsted's Multimedia**

| Value proposition | VERY SIMILAR TO COMPETITORS | | SOMEWHAT SIMILAR TO COMPETITORS | | VERY SIMILAR FROM COMPETITORS |
|---|---|---|---|---|---|
| Product performance | ○ | ○ | ○ | ● | ○ |
| Price level of the offering | ○ | ○ | ○ | ○ | ● |
| Accessibility of the offering | ○ | ○ | ○ | ○ | ● |
| Service level associated with the offering | ● | ○ | ○ | ○ | ○ |
| Sustainability of the offering | ● | ○ | ○ | ○ | ○ |

| Key processe and activities | VERY SIMILAR TO COMPETITORS | | SOMEWHAT SIMILAR TO COMPETITORS | | VERY SIMILAR FROM COMPETITORS |
|---|---|---|---|---|---|
| Front-end activities | ○ | ○ | ○ | ● | ○ |
| Back-end activities | ○ | ○ | ○ | ● | ○ |
| Support and management activities | ○ | ○ | ○ | ○ | ● |

| Key resources | VERY SIMILAR TO COMPETITORS | | SOMEWHAT SIMILAR TO COMPETITORS | | VERY SIMILAR FROM COMPETITORS |
|---|---|---|---|---|---|
| Core resources and capabilities | ○ | ○ | ○ | ● | ○ |
| Network of suppliers and partners | ○ | ○ | ○ | ● | ○ |
| Role in the entire ecosystem | ○ | ● | ○ | ○ | ○ |

| Profit Model | VERY SIMILAR TO COMPETITORS | | SOMEWHAT SIMILAR TO COMPETITORS | | VERY SIMILAR FROM COMPETITORS |
|---|---|---|---|---|---|
| Revenue structure | ○ | ○ | ○ | ○ | ● |
| Cost structure | ○ | ○ | ○ | ○ | ● |

**Figure 54** · Schibsted's business model innovation in its core business (media houses)

Schibsted learned that traditional news provision was a different ballgame than the new multimedia business. While traditional newspapers focused on bringing top journalistic content to readers, the new media was more about providing news fast and in a timely manner. This meant that the product was changing—less depth, but more focus on big news topics. Newspapers had to blend professional journalism with user-generated content. Accessibility and the price level also changed: it was about providing news 24/7, and all this often for free. Rolv Erik Ryssdal, Schibsted's CEO from 2009 to 2018, comments: "Whereas media houses and newspapers used to be a lot about classic core competences—of course, especially to have good journalism, to have good salespeople, and so on—there is a new core competence you need to master, and that is product and tech development."[289]

The separation from the traditional print business ensured that the multimedia unit could develop independently from the print format. The company hired people with a different mindset, not just determined to promote top-class journalism but able to tell great stories online. The goal was to attract as many people as possible to the news website—preferably several times a day. This strategy worked well. For example, VG.no, the online website and multimedia division of VG, one of Schibsted's main newspapers in Norway, was a huge success. In 1998, VG claimed a readership of 1,384,000. In 2012, VG had 830,000 print readers and 1,664,000 daily digital readers.

**CHALLENGES TOO.** The problem, however, was that despite the good reach numbers, Schibsted struggled to convert its online market leadership to great circulation and advertising revenues. Finding new revenues for the online services was crucial as print circulation and advertising sales continued to decline. In November 2013, all of Schibsted's media houses had implemented digital payment solutions for accessing premium online content. The company also reported that in that same year, two thirds of the EBITDA of the media houses had come from online platforms, a figure that was expected to increase.[290] This in turn created another problem: the print newspaper had to reduce its headcount, whereas the multimedia units were actively recruiting. Unfortunately, the redundancy in the print operations could not easily transfer into the online business.[291]

Despite these challenges, Schibsted continued to invest in its online media activities, built digital competence, and increased the proportion of digital revenues in the media core. In 2015, the company built a new, state-of-the-art media platform for the media houses and integrated the print and multimedia units. Figure 55 shows that the proportion of online revenues—online newspapers and classifieds—increased significantly over time: from 40% in 2012 to 69% five years later.

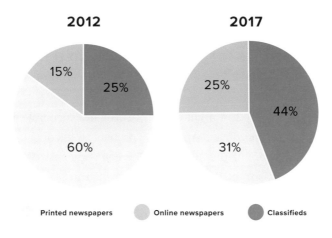

**Figure 55** • Schibsted's evolution of revenues

**OTHER EVOLUTIONS.** Like many publishers, Schibsted also experimented with free print dailies. In 1999, it had set up operations in Spain, France, and Switzerland to test and roll out the concept of quick-read newspapers, fully based on advertising revenues. But this venture—called *20 Minutes*—was sold in 2015. According to a Schibsted manager: "We don't do it half-heartedly. We do it to win. If we don't succeed, we sell it to someone else. We try a lot of things, and some work better than others."[292]

The company surprised the business world in 2018 when it announced that it would spin off its international marketplaces business into a separate, listed company, called Adevinta. At the moment of writing, Schibsted still maintains a majority ownership in this company, but it's not clear if this unit will ever be sold.

In the meantime, Schibsted built a new division, called Next, that groups Schibsted's new financial services and fintech acquisitions. Does Schibsted see more potential in a more geographically focused group but with a broader business portfolio, including publishing, Scandinavian classifieds and personal finance? Time will tell. But it confirms the image of Schibsted as one of the most innovative, forward-looking, and entrepreneurial media corporations in the world.

## Octopus story #2: How to win a fight against Amazon and Apple?

What company is involved in a battle with two of the corporate world's most powerful companies: Amazon and Apple? You probably think of one of the newest and hippest tech players of this moment? The company that I'll discuss in the second octopus story isn't the flashy new kid on the block—it's even the opposite. It's Barnes & Noble, the famous bookseller in the U.S. with origins that date back to 1873. Its heydays were in the 1970s and the 1980s, when under the leadership of Leonard Riggio, the company made numerous acquisitions to become a leading player in the U.S. Riggio introduced the concept of the superstore, which revolutionized the bookselling industry. The superstores combined a deep and vast selection of book titles with experienced bookselling staff and a warm, comfortable and spacious atmosphere. The product offering was not limited to books, but included music, educational toys, games and gifts.[293] Barnes & Noble continued to grow throughout the 1990s—and it was the largest bookstore in the world in 1996, with about 1,000 stores and annual sales of $2.5 billion.

**DISRUPTION CONTINUES.** The big-box villain ravaging independent bookstores eventually became lunch for another disruptor. In 1995, Amazon.com launched its bookselling website and started its online retail channel activities.

A few years later, the industry faced another disruption. At the end of the 1990s, the first e-book readers were launched in the market. Many publishers and technology firms had watched what had happened in the music industry, where customers downloaded MP3 music files. Everybody believed that this was going to happen in the bookselling market too. But the early part of the decade saw the e-book industry struggle to find a foothold for several reasons. Reading on computer screens was uncomfortable at that time: screen resolutions were bad, which caused eyestrain and dry eyes. On top of that, there were many conflicting sets of e-book standards, and publishers were still reluctant to make their content available for digitization.[294]

That changed when Sony entered the market in 2006 with its Portable Reader System (PRS 500). The PRS 500 was a huge technological improvement in the market: it made the screen easy to read (even in full sunlight), used very little battery power, and was also cheaper than the earlier e-book readers. The company had also engaged in partnerships with major publishing houses so it could offer a broad range of books. Amazon reacted and introduced the Kindle and the Kindle store in 2007. The battle in the e-book industry had begun, with a few players who vied for market dominance: Sony, Amazon and Michael Serbinis, a Toronto-based entrepreneur who launched the low-cost 'Kobo' reader in 2010. In 3.5 years, e-book sales surpassed bound-book sales on Amazon.

**BARNES & NOBLE REACTS.** When Amazon entered the book retail market in 1995, Barnes & Noble followed almost immediately with the launch of its own online store, bn.com. This was a successful move, as the Barnes & Noble website grew to become the second-largest bookseller on the internet.[295] But the e-book revolution—and the overall digital transformation of the book retail industry—forced Barnes & Noble to come up with a more solid strategic answer. The company decided to launch a corporate transformation strategy.

First, it transformed its core by adding a business line of college bookstores— Barnes & Noble acquired the company College Booksellers in 2009. Although the brick-and-mortar booksellers faced a significant drop in sales, the Barnes & Noble management team believed that the textbook industry was a growth opportunity as more schools introduced computers and e-books into the classroom. The new unit was called Barnes & Noble Education, and it adopted a different business model than the parent company and other regular main street bookstores. The education market was more a business-to-business market with a different value proposition, focused on selling larger volumes at good prices rather than on providing a great customer experience. The core now consisted of B&N Retail and B&N Education. This was the first part of the company's strategic answer.

In 2009, Barnes & Noble started with the second part of its octopus strategy. The company recruited e-commerce executive William Lynch and a team of engineers on the American West Coast. In a secret location, far away from the headquarters in New York, the team built a new e-book reader. Eight months later, the Nook entered the market. The new business model leapfrogged Amazon's Kindle technology and used the chain's brick-and-mortar stores to give customers physical access to the product in a way that Amazon couldn't match. Industry observers considered this a winning combination.[296] In 2011, shipments of e-readers had risen to 26.4 million units, an increase of more than 100% compared to the year before.[297]

But then the e-reader market collapsed. Apple had entered the scene and introduced the iPad in 2010. It didn't take long before consumers began reading e-books on tablets and smartphones—and all of the leading players in the e-book market—Kindle, Nook, PRS and Kobo—suffered.[298]

**A FAILING STRATEGY.** Figure 56 shows that Barnes & Noble suffered a lot. Although the traditional core business (B&N Retail) survived, the move to the college bookstore business—a strategic move to transform the core—was short-lived, and in 2015, the company spun off its education division. When it acquired B&N College Booksellers five years earlier, the management team believed that the combination of textbooks and trade books on a single-branded platform would help cross-promote print and digital offerings to their customers. But those synergies never materialized: Barnes & Noble was never able to improve the moderate profit margins of the education unit.[299] And despite many restructuring efforts, the company struggled with profitability in its traditional retail business too.

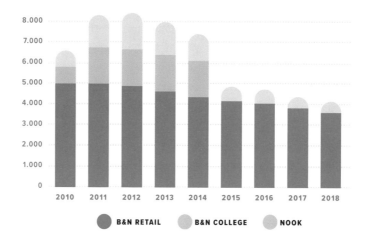

Source: Barnes & Noble Annual Reports & Form 10-K (2010–18)

**Figure 56** • Evolution of revenues

What was even worse, its digital business (Nook)—which included e-books, digital newsstands, and the sale of Nook devices—was accumulating huge losses. Revenues stalled for several years after a promising 2011 and declined significantly from 2014 onwards—the Nook division contributed only marginally to the sales volume. In its 2017 annual report, the company was still committed to offering customers any digital book, newspaper or magazine, anytime, and on any device. But in 2018, the losses of the digital division had reached $1.5 billion. Clearly, this was a company struggling on two fronts, and many predicted the end of this iconic brand. One journalist commented: "Barnes & Noble's collapse spanned the 2010s: Its online store lagged behind, while its physical stores got overrun by gadgets, blankets and trinkets in pursuit of any kind of sale."[300] Another journalist added: "Slumping sales, closing stores, and a big swing and a miss on digital have hurt the book chain."[301]

Barnes & Noble's profitability suffered: in the period 2010–18, the average return on equity was -7.8%. In those nine years, the company had only three years with positive results, indicating the challenges of competing in two different markets. Barnes & Noble had clearly lost the battle with Amazon and Apple—and this would normally be the end of the story.

**LIGHT AT THE END OF THE TUNNEL?** In August 2019, Barnes & Noble was acquired by the hedge fund Elliott Management. This investment company wanted to build an empire with bookstore companies in the English-speaking world, and it had already acquired British bookstore chain Waterstones. Under the leadership of James Daunt, this company had resurrected as a profitable bookstore chain again, after some tumultuous years of cost cutting and closing stores. The plan was to repeat this trick with Barnes & Noble. The recipe? A fundamental transformation of the core—not a corporate transformation! "Barnes & Noble needs investment, not further cost cuts. The simple fact is that Barnes & Noble needs money: people want to shop in places that look modern, clean, and inviting. The Barnes & Noble stores look tired and need a little botox," said Daunt.[302] His turnaround strategy was built on the hypothesis that "in a world where Amazon offers unbeatable convenience and prices, big book chains will only survive if they act more like independents. A good independent bookshop is something pretty special... it has personality and character."[303]

All this was lacking at Barnes & Noble. This was an undifferentiated company stuck in the middle and, unlike its competitors, unable to adapt. One analyst compared Barnes & Noble with a public library that serves Starbucks coffee.[304] Barnes & Noble had to revive its core business and get customers back in the store. It improved its merchandising offerings, increased promotional activities, and narrowed its product assortments, making navigation in the stores better and enhancing product discovery. It increased the number of in-store events and collected more information on its customers.

A more fundamental strategic reaction was to give each branch manager more autonomy to order what, to their mind, their readers wanted. This higher level of decentralization was a huge shift for the bookseller. Daunt aimed at getting away from cookie-cutter stores and making each bookstore unique, one at a time. The pandemic lockdowns forced Barnes & Noble to rationalize the chain, but they also offered the company the time to renovate the stores and recalibrate the business. Retail bankruptcies offered opportunities by creating cheaper space for new stores.[305]

Although Barnes & Noble no longer publishes financials, there are indications that this new strategy works. While the chain has continued to close unprofitable stores, it has also expanded and opened some new ones. Daunt has also confirmed that Barnes & Noble's online business has improved: that segment was up 35% over its pre-pandemic level, making up about 10% of the chain's overall sales.[306] After two turbulent decades, the company can start focusing on growth again.

## Octopus story #3: How does an asset-heavy company fight with asset-light companies?

The media and book retail industries are not the only ones that experienced heavy turbulence—the hospitality industry also had its fair share of disruption and disturbance. The third and last octopus story sheds some light on how Accor, the European market leader in the hospitality industry, has dealt with turbulence. This company embarked on a significant corporate transformation, led by Sébastien Bazin, who was appointed CEO in 2013. At that time, the company was a pure hotel company and had redefined its business model around two strategic business divisions—HotelServices, which was the hotel operator and brand franchisor, and HotelInvest, the property owner and investor. The HotelServices division managed 3,600 hotels spread over ten brands in the luxury, upscale, midscale and economy segment. About 80% of Accor's revenues, however, originated from the HotelInvest division. The company's revenues amounted to 5.5 billion EUR, and after some bad financial years, partially caused by years of turbulence in the board room, the return on equity was 5%.

**TURBULENCE IN THE HOSPITALITY INDUSTRY.** In 2013, hotel firms were getting worried about the digital disruption in the industry. Hospitality firms had already seen digital firms overtaking them—in 2005, online travel agencies like Booking.com and Expedia had taken significant market share from the traditional agencies. Due to their dominant positions, these companies could charge higher commissions to the hotels. A second disruption took place when price comparison websites like TripAdvisor emerged, facilitating customers' selection decisions. These two disruptions, however, triggered little reaction from the hotel companies.[307]

All that changed when the sharing economy found its way to the hotel industry. Airbnb was founded in 2007 and set its first steps in Europe in 2011. In the beginning, hotel managers also neglected this trend: they argued that home sharing didn't replace hotel stays and, if it did, it was in the budget and leisure segment. When Airbnb created a new division focused on business travel in 2015, it had launched a frontal attack on the large hotels' core segment.

**ACCORHOTELS REACTS.** Sébastien Bazin had not waited until 2015 to react. When he was appointed, he made a clear point, 'For the last 15 years, we've been sleeping. I said that publicly and I got yelled at by my peers.'[308] 'The company was a sleeping giant, but we were too introverted, too shy… If we were to continue over the next 50 years only offering [hotel rooms], we were going to have a tough wake-up call in ten years.'[309] Bazin clearly was not planning to sit back and relax—he began divesting Accor's real estate portfolio. Competitors like Marriott and Intercontinental had also transitioned to an asset-light model, where the focus was more on providing hotel services rather than on managing hotel properties. In 2018, Accor sold a large part of the HotelInvest portfolio, which turned Accor into an almost pure hotel operator and franchisor. Bazin also engineered some changes in Accor's core business hotel portfolio, expanding from primarily European economy hotels towards a more global presence skewed towards the luxury and premium segment.[310]

**FUNDAMENTAL CHANGES IN THE CORE.** Bazin didn't stop at reshuffling his portfolio. He wanted his company to embrace the digital revolution and radically improve the customer experience. He admitted that the hotel industry—including AccorHotels—had been too transaction- and product-driven and wanted to collect as much information about the customer as possible to deliver a fully personalized customer experience.[311] Customer-centricity starts with understanding your customer. Therefore, Accor wanted to increase the number of touch points with the customers and improve the interaction with the guests. Bazin was convinced that he could counter the threats imposed by Airbnb and other online marketplaces. He took some strong elements of Airbnb's value proposition and integrated them with some of the hotel's traditional strengths (see Figure 57). Bazin commented:

> "Airbnb is growing. By definition, they are taking away some of our clientele. Those clients, which are extremely price sensitive are the budget economy low scale—because they actually get an offer that is cheaper, they feel it is more spacious, with a better experience [...] Put yourself into the shoes of who is using Airbnb. If you understand the reason, then why don't you basically recreate what they want within your hotel space? Which you can. Can I get more leisure capacity in my hotel? Of course. Can it be cheaper? Of course. Can you have a better food and beverage experience? You're going to give them exactly the same thing, plus a better security system, better comfort, better hygiene, without the agony of not knowing where the kids are going to be there before you leave, or when you get in."[312]

**AccorHotel's Digital Transformation**

| Value proposition | VERY SIMILAR TO COMPETITORS | | SOMEWHAT SIMILAR TO COMPETITORS | | VERY SIMILAR FROM COMPETITORS |
|---|---|---|---|---|---|
| Product performance | ○ | ○ | ● | ○ | ○ |
| Price level of the offering | ● | ○ | ○ | ○ | ○ |
| Accessibility of the offering | ○ | ○ | ○ | ● | ○ |
| Service level associated with the offering | ○ | ○ | ○ | ● | ○ |
| Sustainability of the offering | ● | ○ | ○ | ○ | ○ |
| **Key process and activities** | VERY SIMILAR TO COMPETITORS | | SOMEWHAT SIMILAR TO COMPETITORS | | VERY SIMILAR FROM COMPETITORS |
| Front-end activities | ○ | ● | ○ | ○ | ○ |
| Back-end activities | ○ | ○ | ● | ○ | ○ |
| Support and management activities | ○ | ○ | ○ | ● | ○ |
| **Key resources** | VERY SIMILAR TO COMPETITORS | | SOMEWHAT SIMILAR TO COMPETITORS | | VERY SIMILAR FROM COMPETITORS |
| Core resources and capabilities | ○ | ○ | ○ | ● | ○ |
| Network of suppliers and partners | ○ | ○ | ○ | ● | ○ |
| Role in the entire ecosystem | ○ | ○ | ○ | ● | ○ |
| **Profit Model** | VERY SIMILAR TO COMPETITORS | | SOMEWHAT SIMILAR TO COMPETITORS | | VERY SIMILAR FROM COMPETITORS |
| Revenue structure | ○ | ● | ○ | ○ | ○ |
| Cost structure | ○ | ○ | ● | ○ | ○ |

**Figure 57** · AccorHotel's business model innovation in the core

Like many of its competitors, AccorHotels introduced innovative technologies to further increase the service levels and personalization for the guests. This included a Google Home voice assistant, a connected tablet, and a special LED lighting system, in combination with sleep and aromatherapy aids.[313]

In 2014, Accor invested 225 million EUR in the 'Leading Digital Hospitality' program, set up to make customers 'feel welcome'—which was the name for the new customer value proposition. This program included tracks like 'mobile first', 'customer-centric', and 'seamless journey'—and it was not just limited to the guests but also included projects to improve the satisfaction of employees and partners.

Bazin relied extensively on external partnerships and acquisitions of digital players to bring in new expertise, such as ResDiary (management and distribution of restaurant tables), VeryChic (private sales of hotel accommodation and luxury holidays), Gekko (hotel bookings for business travelers), D-EDGE (online distribution for independent hotels), and more. These companies remained independent, a deliberate choice according to Sébastien Bazin, 'We're turning the company from the culture of a very large matrix pyramid structure to an entrepreneur structure. Those acquisitions and investments must remain self-standing. The more we have autonomous self-standing units, the more it will benefit us.'[314]

Transforming the core also required a cultural transformation for the hotel giant's 250,000 employees. Innovation had to play a more prominent role in the corporate culture, and Bazin hired Thibault Viort, a serial digital entrepreneur, as Chief Disruption and Growth Officer. His role was to identify new growth opportunities and new entrepreneurs, oversee investments and acquisitions, and reinforce interactions with startups. Bazin also installed a Shadow Executive Committee with young managers between 25 and 35 years old as a think tank for innovation projects. And the company also set up a Marketing Innovation Lab, which focused on the creation of new lifestyle brands aimed at millennials.[315]

One of the Lab's inventions was Jo&Joe, a new accommodation solution for millennials who wanted to blend the originality of private rental spaces like Airbnb with the social experience of hostels, along with the comfort and security of hotels. Jo&-Joe was an urban concept designed for a new generation of travelers who were seeking modern design and a variety of room options at affordable prices.

**AUGMENTED HOSPITALITY.** Sébastien Bazin also thought about business model innovations outside the traditional core business. He saw two major growth paths: the first was entering the sharing economy; the second, reaching out to the non-travelers segment and bringing hospitality outside the hotel. These diversification moves positioned Accor as a leader in 'augmented hospitality', going beyond the provision of accommodation. Accor would enable new ways to live, work, and play.[316] 'Live' was done with the group's 40 hotel brands, 'work' meant bringing the group's coworking offers to center stage, and 'play' implied offering customers entertainment services from specialized Accor companies, such as Potel & Chabot, Paris Society, and the thousands of restaurants and bars in its hotels around the world.


**ENTERING THE SHARING ECONOMY.** Bazin did not just watch how private home rental companies like Airbnb emerged as significant substitutes for hotel companies, he decided to fight back: "We do believe the hospitality industry is going through a profound transformation, and that serviced homes will be a growing part of the larger hospitality business in the midterm."[317] In 2016, AccorHotels opened a new chapter in its history by expanding into luxury serviced private rentals. Accor acquired the company OneFineStay and took equity participations in Squarebreak, Oasis Collections and Travel Keys. Bazin explains:

> "Why did we go into the sharing economy? Airbnb did it successfully, and we should have thought about it 15 years ago, except we were so product-minded. 90% of my business is fewer than two nights, 90% of Airbnb's business is more than three nights. It's not the same mix—70% of my business is business-to-business corporate, while 90% of Airbnb is business-to-consumer leisure. So, we've been impacting each other but we're basically not in the same field. Airbnb is not service-oriented, so we decided to go into the upscale chain of the sharing economy."[318]

The new acquisitions were matchmaking companies that linked homeowners who offered their property to travelers looking for upmarket accommodation. This business model was very similar to Airbnb's business model, but it was different in the service level that was offered.[319] For example, OneFineStay managed the entire booking process but also provided hotel-style services to the guests such as toiletries, bed furnishings, cleaning services and full 24/7 phone support. Hosts and travelers did not rate each other and didn't interact.[320] Figure 58 shows that this was a fundamentally new business model compared to its traditional core business.

**One FineStay**

| Value proposition | VERY SIMILAR TO COMPETITORS | | SOMEWHAT SIMILAR TO COMPETITORS | | VERY SIMILAR FROM COMPETITORS |
|---|---|---|---|---|---|
| Product performance | ○ | ● | ○ | ○ | ○ |
| Price level of the offering | ○ | ○ | ○ | ● | ○ |
| Accessibility of the offering | ○ | ○ | ○ | ● | ○ |
| Service level associated with the offering | ○ | ● | ○ | ○ | ○ |
| Sustainability of the offering | ● | ○ | ○ | ○ | ○ |

| Key process and activities | VERY SIMILAR TO COMPETITORS | | SOMEWHAT SIMILAR TO COMPETITORS | | VERY SIMILAR FROM COMPETITORS |
|---|---|---|---|---|---|
| Front-end activities | ○ | ○ | ○ | ● | ○ |
| Back-end activities | ○ | ○ | ○ | ● | ○ |
| Support and management activities | ○ | ○ | ○ | ○ | ● |

| Key resources | VERY SIMILAR TO COMPETITORS | | SOMEWHAT SIMILAR TO COMPETITORS | | VERY SIMILAR FROM COMPETITORS |
|---|---|---|---|---|---|
| Core resources and capabilities | ○ | ○ | ○ | ● | ○ |
| Network of suppliers and partners | ○ | ○ | ○ | ● | ○ |
| Role in the entire ecosystem | ○ | ○ | ○ | ● | ○ |

| Profit Model | VERY SIMILAR TO COMPETITORS | | SOMEWHAT SIMILAR TO COMPETITORS | | VERY SIMILAR FROM COMPETITORS |
|---|---|---|---|---|---|
| Revenue structure | ○ | ○ | ○ | ○ | ● |
| Cost structure | ○ | ○ | ○ | ○ | ● |

**Figure 58** • OneFineStay business model innovation outside the core

Accor invested in other hospitality companies such as John Paul and Travel Keys. John Paul was a relatively young French company that merged with American company Les Concierges in 2015 to create the world leader in premium customer and employee loyalty services. Travel Keys was a leading player in the American private vacation rental market. With these acquisitions, Accor confirmed its commitment to expand the portfolio with new business models, not just in Europe but also in America.

**REACHING OUT TO THE NON-TRAVELER.** Bazin introduced another business model innovation by focusing on an atypical customer segment for the hotel industry, the non-traveler,

> 'Ninety-five percent of what we have done for 50 years has been based on the guy coming from outside of town. A traveler, from a different city, from a different country, which I think is interesting, but not too smart. Because we missed a population which is 100 times greater and better and easier: the guy living next door. The local inhabitants. They live around the hotel, or they work in an office around the hotel—and 90% of them never dare to come into the property, because they are afraid that we're going to ask for their room number. They don't need a room, but they might need a service.'[321]

In 2017, Accor acquired Nextdoor—later renamed Wojo—a social network company that offered companies, entrepreneurs and freelancers nice places to work, with extra coworking facilities. This company jumped on the need for flexible offices and workspaces and had more than 600 companies using their services. Wojo initially opened in Accor hotels, which helped optimize the availability of the hotel infrastructure—most travelers were only using the hotel infrastructure from 8 p.m. to 8 a.m.[322]

That same year Accor also launched AccorLocal, an application allowing residents who live near an Accor property to access the services of local artisans and companies.[323] Locals could use the app to book yoga classes, pick up dry cleaning, order flowers and pick up breakfast on their way to work. In this way, Accor diversified its income base by charging a commission to the merchants (the dry cleaners, florists, and other service providers).[324]

---

**PERFORMANCE EVALUATION.** All these strategic moves have transformed AccorHotels from a pure hotel company to a world leading hospitality group with a broad range of hotels—ranging from luxury to economy—entertainment and nightlife venues, restaurants and bars, branded private residences, shared accommodation properties, concierge services, and coworking spaces. This fundamental transformation was achieved in less than ten years.

How did all those strategic initiatives affect Accor's performance? Was this a high-risk, high-return strategy? Accor's financial results for the last 12 years indicate that Bazin did a good job restoring Accor's profitability. The results after 2013 were significantly better than the years before.[325] Accor published some performance figures for its new businesses: revenues for this division increased from 44 million EUR (2016) to 159 million EUR (2020). As was expected, the company did not make a profit with that division, but the EBITDA improved significantly. During and after the Covid years, Accor no longer published financial information on this unit. There were, however, indications that Accor struggled to make the OneFineStay acquisition—one of its more prominent investments in the sharing economy—profitable. In its first two years in the Accor group, OneFineStay saw four CEO changes, which clearly points to some struggles in the boardroom.

The Covid years also impacted Accor's results heavily—Accor reported significantly worse results than major competitors Intercontinental and Marriott in those years. Nevertheless, 2022 marked a year of full recovery for the whole sector, and that was the case for Accor as well. Time will tell who will emerge as the winner in the hospitality industry and to what extent business model innovation was a crucial recipe for success.

# Transformation inside the core

An octopus strategy is a strategy that consists of a double business model innovation, one inside and one outside the core. This double business model innovation can only occur if the top management is prepared to change the corporate identity.

**A FUNDAMENTALLY NEW VALUE PROPOSITION IN THE CORE.** All 3 companies—Schibsted, Barnes & Noble, and AccorHotels—had to withstand heavy turbulence. All three companies reacted with fierce transformations inside their core. I've already outlined in great detail what such a core transformation entails, so I will just repeat some key messages from Chapter 6 and illustrate them with some examples from our octopus stories.

Schibsted transformed from a traditional newspaper company into a multimedia company, offering media content via multiple platforms. This change affected many departments—from sales to marketing to news production. Barnes & Noble added an education unit, focusing on the textbook market—a market with different key success factors requiring different capabilities. And AccorHotels launched a digital transformation in its core hotel business, bringing the level of service and customization to a much higher level than before.

**MORE THAN COPY/PASTE.** The three companies were ready to create new value propositions for their renewed core business. Those new value propositions incorporate elements from the disruptors but are more than pure copies—all three octopus companies also relied on the strengths of their old traditional models. Schibsted's multimedia unit borrowed a lot from what the online news providers offered—constantly updated news, more concise stories with links to other websites, and more co-creation with readers. But the multimedia unit also had access to Schibsted's journalistic content and brand, something that the new online players didn't have. Accor also integrated elements of the online marketplaces but upgraded them with more and better services, made possible by the introduction of many new innovative technologies.

**CREATION OF APOLLO UNITS.** Another common feature of these core transformations is the use of what I called 'Apollo units' in the previous chapter—separate structures that help create the new value propositions. It's key to grant sufficient autonomy to such an Apollo team. For example, Schibsted separated its multimedia unit from its newspaper unit for a considerable time. Says Sverre Munck, who was manager of the Multimedia division that time:

> "We spun out VG.no very early on, and allowed it to compete with its parent brand, the print newspaper. It was a separate digital company for 13 years—for reasons that made a lot of sense editorially and commercially. Then, we integrated them again—but we spun out a new mobile subsidiary. The thinking was the same as before: forcing the mobile unit to operate in the parent brand would end up with them being squashed, and the budgets that they are going after wouldn't be deemed worthwhile inside the larger operation."[326]

The same applied to Barnes & Noble and AccorHotels. B&N Education was kept separate, as were the digital acquisitions of AccorHotels. You need to build a separate structure for your strategic innovation team and keep it free from interference from the core, although the format can be different—ranging from 'commando teams' to 'tugboat structures'. I refer to Chapter 6 for more information on these structures.

**A STRATEGIC AND A CULTURAL CHANGE.** This core transformation impacts the entire organization: this is not a small innovation project but a fundamental strategic change that is best tackled profoundly and substantially. In the previous chapter, I presented the *Six Batteries of Change* model, which covers the ingredients of such a strategic change. The main message of this change model is that you should focus as much attention on the rational side of change—strategy, structures, systems, processes and projects—as on the emotional side of change—which is about the dynamics in the top team, the culture and the connection with your employees.

If you want to change something as fundamental as your value proposition, you need to put a change structure in place—larger organizations typically use a program management office (PMO). The more successful transformers also create sound project management methodologies to help employees with all of the change projects. But structural initiatives that are not accompanied by a cultural shift are likely to be ineffective. Two of the three octopus cases emphasized the importance of cultural transformation. This cultural transformation should be driven from the top. Core transformations ask for tough decisions and drastic resource allocations. Without active support and commitment and visible sponsorship from senior top management, it's impossible to finish such a big challenge successfully.

The managers of Schibsted and AccorHotels were well aware of all this: the digital transformations in both companies were also supported with cultural transformations. Becoming a digital company requires an open mindset, whereby you continuously challenge the status quo. It's about moving away from the traditional hierarchical structures to a more agile organization, where the focus is on fast decision-making, continuous monitoring, and fast adaptation.

## Innovation outside the core

An octopus strategy is not finished after you've transformed your core. An equally important part is the creation of a new business model, next to your adapted core. Schibsted moved into classified advertising, creating a new company (Adevinta). Barnes & Noble set up the Nook division, and Accor built new business models to move into the sharing economy and to target the non-traveler. These are all nice examples of corporate innovations, a topic that I described extensively in Chapter 5 regarding the salmon strategy. Here, I will restrict myself to repeating some key messages from that chapter.

**SIGNIFICANT COMMITMENTS TO BUILD SOMETHING NEW.** Schibsted, Barnes & Noble, and AccorHotels were all very ambitious in how they dealt with turbulence. They didn't only see threats, but they also believed that turbulence brought opportunities, and they embarked on business model innovations outside their core. The three companies all launched strategic experiments and were not afraid to commit significant investments to the new ventures even though outcomes were very uncertain. At the time of their investments, it was not clear to what extent the classified advertising business, the e-reader business, and the luxury private rental business would become attractive industries.

**A NEW VALUE PROPOSITION WITH A NEW ORGANIZATION.** The three companies also set up new businesses with dedicated management teams that were allowed to build a new value proposition with a dedicated organization. The new units got the autonomy needed to grow, but could also leverage the strengths of the existing core.

It's clear that the classified ad business of Schibsted benefited from this freedom. It was allowed to cannibalize the core business and make the investments needed to become a leader in its market. Accor formulated a powerful strategic answer to the disruptors from the online private rental market. They did more than just copy the value proposition of companies like Airbnb and Vrbo and integrated some of their traditional strong points in the new value proposition. But it's clear that Accor struggled to build a good management team for the new unit, a crucial element for success.

The company that struggled most was Barnes & Noble. The Nook division was a nightmare for the bookstore giant. The main reason was that the e-reader companies were disrupted by another technological innovation: Apple's iPad. Barnes & Noble never found an appropriate answer to this new competitor—it was really stuck in the middle between Google's Kindle (which was the cheaper alternative) and the more expensive multipurpose iPad. The Nook team was never able to maneuver itself out of this bad strategic position, and Nook became a financial disaster for Barnes & Noble.

All this shows that it's one thing to set up a new business—but simply building a new business model is no guarantee of success. Scaling the new venture into a profitable business is equally important yet far from obvious.

## Changing the corporate identity

The octopus strategy is the most challenging of the four turbulence strategies because it requires a fundamental transformation of your core and the creation of a new growth path outside your core. Both strategic moves require significant investments, while the outcomes are very uncertain. This cannot be done without a top team committed to changing the organization's corporate identity and strategy.

**WILLINGNESS TO CHANGE THE BUSINESS MIX.** Implementing an octopus strategy starts with formulating an ambition to radically transform the company. Your leadership team needs to acknowledge and support the idea that the business mix needs to change and that the corporation will be different in the future. It's good to check the readiness of your top team to transform the company.

In Schibsted, the top management team and the board members saw the change of digital disruption coming early on, and they decided to take the internet business into the core of the company and "let it drive and shine, cannibalize and transform".[327] Barnes & Noble was also willing to redefine its core business as selling reading—not just books. And Sébastien Bazin, the CEO of AccorHotels, launched the concept of augmented hospitality.

There are other nice examples of companies who changed the business mix to counter turbulence. Unlike Kodak, Fujifilm's CEO Shigetaka Komori was ready to delete the word 'film' from the company name. In the 1980s, the management team had already decided that the core business was imaging, not film. Later, that became imaging and information.

**Corporate goal.** Sébastien Bazin from AccorHotels went a step further than redefining the core business: he formulated a specific ambition to create a group in which 30% of the activities were new and where 70% would come from the classical hotel business.[328] It's important to formulate a clear goal that the group wants to achieve within say ten years from now.

Axel Springer, the German media company, also used an octopus strategy to transform itself from a German newspaper company into a leading international digital publisher focusing on digital classifieds and journalism. CEO Mathias Döpfner also set a clear ambition for his company: he challenged it to generate half of its revenue and profits from digital products within the next ten years.[329] He set that ambition in 2006, when digital products represented less than 1% of Axel Springer's revenues. In 2015, digital media constituted 61.7% of the total revenues.

Of course, formulating a strong ambition is not sufficient. Desire is not a strategy. But desire is a powerful starting point for the implementation of your octopus strategy—you need to start off with the right mindset. And that mindset is that you need to be ready to stretch the confines of your traditional core business. This is a difficult thing to do, especially when your core business is in decline. In that case, there is often so much focus on mitigating the impact of that decline that managers become narrow-minded. Force yourself to consider the opportunities of turbulence, inside and outside your core.

**INNOVATION INITIATIVES STEERED FROM THE TOP.** A second element needed to succeed with a corporate transformation strategy is that you need to put innovation at the top of the strategic agenda. This won't come as a surprise: the octopus strategy is about simultaneously pursuing a business model *innovation* inside and outside the core.

Some firms have created an innovation unit directly reporting to the group CEO, with an innovation manager who is familiar with the startup community or at least has experience in creating new companies. AccorHotels appointed Thibault Viort, a serial digital entrepreneur, as Chief Disruption and Growth Officer. Fuji also put innovation on the corporate agenda. One of the key elements of Fuji's corporate transformation was the establishment of a centralized R&D Lab and an R&D headquarters to coordinate R&D efforts and centralize allocation of R&D expenditures.

Innovation units help you build new units, but they can also be used to buy promising ventures that possess the capabilities needed for your corporate transformation. This is the approach that AccorHotels adopted. It's also the preferred strategy of Axel Springer. One manager explains: "We are not launching our own new brands, like Schibsted. We decided on a policy of investing in new business models if they seemed to be sustainable. We invested mostly in companies with a clear track record and huge growth potential." This growth strategy has worked well so far—all of the companies that Axel Springer has acquired have grown after the investment.[330] Setting up dedicated M&A or corporate venturing units are strategic initiatives that help reinforce the importance of innovation for the group. If these initiatives are taken at the corporate level, and not somewhere in one of the businesses, this sends a strong signal to the rest of the organization.

**SUPPORTED BY A POWERFUL INNOVATION CULTURE.** Of course, these structural initiatives must be supported by a strong innovation culture. The fact that Schibsted was able to launch so many disruptive ideas came from the fact that disruption and entrepreneurship were part of the company's DNA. But what do you do if your organization is lacking an innovation culture? According to Alex Osterwalder and his colleagues from the consulting firm *Strategyzer*, you install an innovation culture by working in three areas: leadership behavior, organizational behavior, and innovation team behavior.[331]

First, it's important to get sufficient leadership support for innovation. Your leaders should understand how innovation works and they should invest sufficient time in innovation efforts. Only when they provide strategic guidance for innovation projects and are involved in screening the organization's strategic innovation portfolio do they steer towards more and better innovation. They should take up leading and visible roles when new important innovation ventures are launched.

The second lever is organizational design. In companies with a strong innovation culture, exploration is stimulated, not punished. It gets a prominent place on the strategic agenda and people choose innovation as a career path. Innovators understand the challenges of the business managers, but leaders of the existing business are also supportive for the innovators—this allows for a perfect blend of exploration and exploitation.

And finally, you create an innovation culture by having good innovation practice. Innovation is a profession, and you should build a team dedicated to building innovation processes and performance indicators. It's also important for you to think how innovation projects are tackled. Innovation ideas should be created based on disciplined experimentation. This means that projects start with cheap and quick experimentation. And then you increase your bets with increasing evidence and decreasing uncertainty. The best innovation teams take time to learn from successes and failures.[332]

**DON'T NEGLECT THE IMPORTANCE OF A STRONG CORE.** An octopus strategy requires core transformation and business model innovation outside the core. Both strategic projects require significant commitments and tough choices.

While it's important to pay a lot of attention to your speedboats outside the core, it's equally important to make sure that you look at the profitability of the current core business. It's your core business that generates the cash you can invest in new ventures. And it's the core that provides some key resources and capabilities that give your new venture a head start relative to the disruptors.

In the introduction of this chapter, I referred to the story of LEGO, a company that got lost in corporate innovation. The company introduced several business model innovation initiatives and almost went bankrupt. In hindsight, LEGO suffered from two problems: first, they launched too many corporate innovation initiatives, taking too much risk for what the company could absorb; the second problem was that the company neglected its core business—the bricks business. Most of the LEGO sets that were launched were unprofitable. Building an innovation machine on a weak and unprofitable core is a recipe for disaster. When you pursue an octopus strategy, never lose sight of the strength of your core. But remember: a declining core doesn't mean an unprofitable core!

## Well-equipped for an octopus strategy?

This chapter has shown you what it takes to implement an octopus strategy. If change drivers force you to change your core and offer you opportunities to build something new, it's important to check whether you have the skills to finish this endeavor with a high probability of success. I've created not one but two checklists—one for your core transformation initiative, and one for your corporate innovation initiative(s). The questionnaires are very similar to the questionnaires presented in Chapters 5 and 6.

Implementing an octopus strategy well requires that you have good scores for the head (core transformation) and for the arms (corporate innovation). Check out your scores in Figure 59—and see whether you are ready to start an octopus strategy.

| BUSINESS MODEL INNOVATION INSIDE THE CORE | STRONGLY DISAGREE | NEITHER AGREE NOR DISAGREE | STRONGLY AGREE |
|---|---|---|---|
| 1. The value proposition of our new (set of) product(s) and service(s) is very different from the competitors' (including the disruptors') value proposition. | 1 ○ ○ ○ ○ ○ 5 | | |
| 2. We have developed a very different profit model for our new (set of) product(s) and service(s). | 1 ○ ○ ○ ○ ○ 5 | | |
| 3. The key processes needed to deliver our value proposition are fundamentally different from the competitor's value chain. | 1 ○ ○ ○ ○ ○ 5 | | |
| 4. We have created a set of new capabilities and/or resources that help us differentiate ourselves from the competitors. | 1 ○ ○ ○ ○ ○ 5 | | |
| 5. We have leveraged some of our traditional strengths in our new business model. | 1 ○ ○ ○ ○ ○ 5 | | |

| TRANSFORMATION CAPABILITIES | STRONGLY DISAGREE | NEITHER AGREE NOR DISAGREE | STRONGLY AGREE |
|---|---|---|---|
| 6. In our organization, the top team is determined to change the business portfolio during the next ten years. | 1 ○ ○ ○ ○ ○ 5 | | |
| 7. Our organization has committed significant resources to invest in business model innovation. | 1 ○ ○ ○ ○ ○ 5 | | |
| 8. We have created a separate structure for our innovation unit that can operate freely and autonomously from our traditional business. | 1 ○ ○ ○ ○ ○ 5 | | |
| 9. The change story behind our new business model is framed both as a threat and as an opportunity. | 1 ○ ○ ○ ○ ○ 5 | | |
| 10. We do regular screening and sensing exercises to check out how new disruptive offerings are affecting our current business model. | 1 ○ ○ ○ ○ ○ 5 | | |
| 11. We have set up a program management office with dedicated managers to run a portfolio of projects to renew our value proposition. | 1 ○ ○ ○ ○ ○ 5 | | |
| 12. We have developed clear roadmaps that help us in the prioritization and resource allocation of our projects. | 1 ○ ○ ○ ○ ○ 5 | | |
| 13. We systematically measure the progress of our transformation projects portfolio. | 1 ○ ○ ○ ○ ○ 5 | | |
| 14. We have developed a sound project methodology that helps us deliver our individual projects on time and within budget. | 1 ○ ○ ○ ○ ○ 5 | | |
| 15. Our employees receive sufficient training and support for dealing with a changing business environment. | 1 ○ ○ ○ ○ ○ 5 | | |
| 16. We employ an arsenal of communication tactics to get our organization moving in the right direction. | 1 ○ ○ ○ ○ ○ 5 | | |
| 17. We regularly celebrate change successes and praise our people for their change efforts. | 1 ○ ○ ○ ○ ○ 5 | | |
| 18. Our organization has an entrepreneurial culture that stimulates innovation and challenges the status quo. | 1 ○ ○ ○ ○ ○ 5 | | |
| 19. The exploration unit is characterized by a collaborative, performance-driven, and courageous culture. | 1 ○ ○ ○ ○ ○ 5 | | |
| 20. We know well how to bring projects from the exploration track back into the organization. | 1 ○ ○ ○ ○ ○ 5 | | |

| BUSINESS MODEL INNOVATION <u>OUTSIDE</u> THE CORE | STRONGLY DISAGREE | NEITHER AGREE NOR DISAGREE | STRONGLY AGREE |
|---|---|---|---|
| 1. The value proposition of our new product(s) and service(s) is very different from the competitors' (including the disruptors') value proposition. | 1 ○ ○ ○ ○ ○ | | 5 |
| 2. We have developed a very different profit model for our new (set of) product(s) and service(s). | 1 ○ ○ ○ ○ ○ | | 5 |
| 3. We have developed a very different profit model for our new (set of) product(s) and service(s). | 1 ○ ○ ○ ○ ○ | | 5 |
| 4. We have created a set of new capabilities and/or resources that help us differentiate ourselves from the competitors. | 1 ○ ○ ○ ○ ○ | | 5 |
| 5. We have leveraged some of our traditional strengths in our new business model. | 1 ○ ○ ○ ○ ○ | | 5 |

| INNOVATION CAPABILITIES | STRONGLY DISAGREE | NEITHER AGREE NOR DISAGREE | STRONGLY AGREE |
|---|---|---|---|
| 6. In our company, there is a willingness to set up new units outside the core to experiment with new business models. | 1 ○ ○ ○ ○ ○ | | 5 |
| 7. From time to time, we challenge our core business's existing strategy and business model. | 1 ○ ○ ○ ○ ○ | | 5 |
| 8. Our corporate strategy presentations always highlight the importance of our business model innovation(s) outside the core. | 1 ○ ○ ○ ○ ○ | | 5 |
| 9. Our top management believes in building innovative ventures (e.g., speedboats, moonshots) as a crucial driver of future success. | 1 ○ ○ ○ ○ ○ | | 5 |
| 10. Building a new business model happens through a process of rapid experimentation, constant evaluation, and continuous learning (see e.g. Lean Startup methodology). | 1 ○ ○ ○ ○ ○ | | 5 |
| 11. We work with 'minimum viable products' when building new business models outside our core business. | 1 ○ ○ ○ ○ ○ | | 5 |
| 12. When scaling the new business, we pay attention to structuring the operations and setting up repeatable processes. | 1 ○ ○ ○ ○ ○ | | 5 |
| 13. We actively use mergers and acquisitions or partnerships to grow the new venture and/or to gain access to critical resources. | 1 ○ ○ ○ ○ ○ | | 5 |
| 14. We have created an autonomous organization for the new venture with its own general manager, who reports to a senior executive. | 1 ○ ○ ○ ○ ○ | | 5 |
| 15. The new unit hires new employees from outside the company, for both operational and management roles. | 1 ○ ○ ○ ○ ○ | | 5 |
| 16. The new unit has the freedom to build an entirely new management infrastructure, with new roles and responsibilities to perform new activities. | 1 ○ ○ ○ ○ ○ | | 5 |
| 17. The new unit has built a culture that is significantly different from the culture of the core business. | 1 ○ ○ ○ ○ ○ | | 5 |
| 18. The new unit can leverage some key resources from the core business. | 1 ○ ○ ○ ○ ○ | | 5 |
| 19. Our corporate top team actively arbitrates when there are conflicts between managers from the core business and the managers from the new venture. | 1 ○ ○ ○ ○ ○ | | 5 |
| 20. The corporation applies performance measures for the new unit that are different than those for the established businesses. | 1 ○ ○ ○ ○ ○ | | 5 |

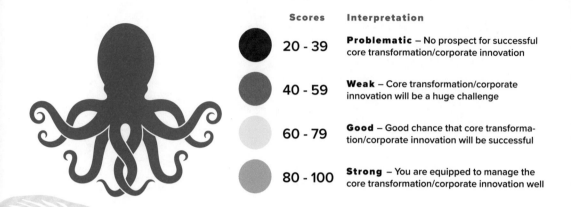

| Scores | Interpretation |
|---|---|
| 20 - 39 | **Problematic** – No prospect for successful core transformation/corporate innovation |
| 40 - 59 | **Weak** – Core transformation/corporate innovation will be a huge challenge |
| 60 - 79 | **Good** – Good chance that core transformation/corporate innovation will be successful |
| 80 - 100 | **Strong** – You are equipped to manage the core transformation/corporate innovation well |

**Figure 59** • How well are you equipped for an octopus strategy?

STRATEGY IN TURBULENT TIMES

# KEY TAKEAWAYS

- The octopus is the right strategy if change drivers force you to fundamentally transform your core business and if you see new opportunities outside your core.
- It's a dual strategy: it's about simultaneous transformation and innovation. It's also the most challenging of the four turbulence strategies.
- The stories of Schibsted Media Group, Barnes & Noble, and AccorHotels show you how corporations simultaneously transform the core and add a new business model outside their core. The case studies also show that success is not guaranteed.
- For the core transformation part, you can apply the messages that were outlined in the chapter on the chameleon strategy.
- For the corporate innovation part, you can borrow all the insights from the chapter on the salmon strategy.
- More than the other turbulence strategies, the octopus strategy requires the top team of the corporation to commit to changing the organization's corporate identity and business mix.

# References

1   This is a quote from American baseball player Yogi Berra.
2   McGrath, R. (2013) The End of Competitive Advantage: *How to Keep Your Strategy Moving as Fast as Your Business*, Harvard Business Review Press, Boston, MA.
3   Teece, D. & Pisano, G. (1994) "The Dynamic Capabilities of Firms: An Introduction," *Industrial and Corporate Change*, 3 (3), 537-556.
4   Grant, R.M. & Jordan, J. (2015) *Foundations of Strategy*, 2nd Edition, John Wiley & Sons Ltd, Chichester.
5   Bennis, W. & Nanus, B. (1985) *Leaders: The Strategies for Taking Charge*, Harper, New York, NY.
6   Emery, F.E. & Trist, E.L. (1965) "The causal texture of organizational environments," *Human Relations*, 18, 21-32.
7   Kipley, D., Lewis, A. & Jewe, R. (2012) "Entropy—Disrupting Ansoff's Five Levels of Environmental Turbulence," *Business Strategies Series*, 13 (6), 251-262.
8   Klein, F., Puck, J. & Weiss, M. (2020) "Chapter 10: Macroenvironmental Dynamism and Firm Risk Management—An Exploratory Investigation," in Van Tulder, R., Verbeke, A. & Jankowska, B., *International Business in a VUCA World: The Changing Role of States and Firms*, Emerald Publishing Limited, Bingley, 173-197.
9   Reed, J.H. (2021) "Operational and Strategic Change During Temporary Turbulence: Evidence from the Covid-19 Pandemic," *Operations Management Research*, 15, 589-608.
10  Sheffi, Y. (2015) *The Power of Resilience: How the Best Companies Manage the Unexpected*, The MIT Press, Cambridge, MA.
11  Detection lead times can also be negative, which means that the detection takes place after the disruption has taken place. That could be the case for example with a product contamination or a design defect.
12  Reed, J.H. (2021) "Operational and Strategic Change During Temporary Turbulence: Evidence from the Covid-19 Pandemic," *Operations Management Research*, 15, 589-608.
13  Martin, R. (2022) "What End of Advantage? It's Time to Look at the Evidence," *Medium*, February 21, https://rogermartin.medium.com/what-end-of-advantage-7ec34b2bded4, Website Accessed May 29th, 2023.
14  Ibid.
15  Reeves, M., Love, C. & Mathur, N. (2012) "The Most Adaptive Companies 2012: Winning in an Age of Turbulence," *The Boston Consulting Group Report*, August, 1-40.
16  Reeves, M. & Pueschel, L. (2015) "Die Another Day: What Leaders Can Do About the Shrinking Life Expectancy of Corporations," *BCG Perspectives*, The Boston Consulting Group, 1-9.
17  Sull, D.N. (2009) The Upside of Turbulence: Seizing Opportunity in an Uncertain World, HarperCollins Publishers, New York, NY.
18  Birkinshaw, J. (2022) "How Incumbents Survive and Thrive," *Harvard Business Review*, January-February, 36-42.
19  Birkinshaw, J. (2022) "How Incumbents Survive and Thrive," *Harvard Business Review*, January-February, 36-42.
20  Allen, J. & Zook, C. (2022) "When Your Business Needs a Second Growth Engine," *Harvard Business Review*, May-June, 76-85.
21  Boswell, L., Dekel, S., Johnson, E. & Moore, C. (2023) "Winning Today's Race While Running Tomorrow's," *PwC's 26th Annual Global CEO Survey*, PwC Research, 1-24.
22  O'Reilly, C.A. & Tushman, M.L. (2016) *Lead and Disrupt: How to Solve the Innovator's Dilemma*, Stanford Business Books, Stanford, CA; Govindarajan, V. (2016) *The Three-Box Solution: A Strategy for Leading Innovation*, Harvard Business Review Press, Boston, MA.
23  Viki, G., Toma, D. & Gons, E. (2017) *The Corporate Startup*, Vakmedianet, Deventer.
24  Yates, L.K. (2022) *The Unicorn Within: How Companies Can Create Game-Changing Ventures at Startup Speed*, Harvard Business Review Press, Boston, MA.
25  Leten, B. & Van Dyck, W. (2012) "Corporate Venturing: Strategies and Success Factors," *Review of Business and Economic Literature*, 242-256.
26  Anthony, S.D., Gilbert, C.G. & Johnson, M.W. (2017) *Dual Transformation: How to Reposition Today's Business While Creating the Future*, Harvard Business Review Press, Boston, MA.
27  Jacobides, M.G. (2021) "What Drives and Defines Digital Platform Power?," *Evolution Ltd. White Paper*, April 19, 1-57.
28  Pidun, U., Reeves, M. & Schüssler, M. (2020) "Why Do Most Business Ecosystems Fail?," *Report Boston Consulting Group/BCG Henderson Institute*, https://www.bcg.com/publications/2020/why-do-most-business-ecosystems-fail, Website Accessed June 3rd, 2023.
29  Setili, A. (2014) *The Agility Advantage: How to Identify and Act on Opportunities in a Fast-Changing World*, John Wiley & Sons, Inc., San Francisco, CA; Doz, Y. & Kosonen, M. (2008) *Fast Strategy: How Strategic Agility Will Help You Stay Ahead of the Game*, Pearson Education, Harlow.
30  Sull, D.N. (2009) *The Upside of Turbulence: Seizing Opportunity in an Uncertain World*, HarperCollins Publishers, New York, NY; Setili, A. (2014) *The Agility Advantage: How to Identify and Act on Opportunities in a Fast-Changing World*, John Wiley & Sons, Inc., San Francisco, CA; Doz, Y. & Kosonen, M. (2008) *Fast Strategy: How Strategic Agility Will Help You Stay Ahead of the Game*, Pearson Education, Harlow.
31  Natale, A., Poppensieker, T. & Thun, M. (2022) "From Risk Management to Strategic Resilience," *McKinsey Risk & Resilience Practice Report*, March, 1-7.

32    Baron, D. (1995) "Integrated Strategy: Market and Nonmarket Components," *California Management Review*, 37 (2), 47-65; Bach, D. & Blake, D.J. (2016) "Frame or Get Framed: The Critical Role of Issue Framing in Nonmarket Management," *California Management Review*, 58 (3), Spring, 66-87.

33    Wikipedia (2023) 'Brent Spar,' https://en.wikipedia.org/wiki/Brent_Spar, Website Accessed June 5th, 2023.

34    Youtube video: "United Breaks Guitars," https://www.youtube.com/watch?v=5YGc4zOqozo, Website Accessed June 11th, 2023.

35    De Wit, B. & Meyer, R. (2010) *Strategy: Process, Content, Context: An International Perspective*, 4th Edition, Cengage Learning EMEA, Andover, Hampshire.

36    Stadler, C., Hautz, J., Matzler, K. & von den Eichen, S.F. (2021) *Open Strategy: Mastering Disruption From Outside the C-Suite*, The MIT Press, Cambridge, MA.

37    Pearce, J.A. & Robinson, R.B. (2005) *Strategic Management: Formulation, Implementation, and Control*, 9th Edition, McGraw-Hill/Irwin, New York, NY.

38    Treacy, Michael, and Wiersema, Fred (1993) "Customer Intimacy and Other Value Disciplines," *Harvard Business Review*, January-February, p. 84; Treacy, Michael, and Wiersema, Fred (1995) The Discipline of Market Leaders, *Perseus Publishing*, New York, NY.

39    Verweire, K. (2014) *Strategy Implementation*, Routledge, Abingdon; De Prins, P., Letens, G. & Verweire, K. (2017) *Six Batteries of Change*, LannooCampus Publishers, Leuven.

40    Campbell, A., Whitehead, J., Alexander, M. & Goold, M. (2014) *Strategy for the Corporate Level: Where to Invest, What to Cut Back and How to Grow Organisations with Multiple Divisions*, Jossey-Bass, San Francisco, CA.

41    One of the best books on the topic of corporate strategy and growing beyond the core is: Campbell, A., Whitehead, J., Alexander, M. & Goold, M. (2014) *Strategy for the Corporate Level: Where to Invest, What to Cut Back and How to Grow Organisations with Multiple Divisions*, Jossey-Bass, San Francisco, CA; Pidun, U. (2019) *Corporate Strategy: Theory and Practice*, Springer Gabler, Wiesbaden.

42    De Prins, P., Letens, G. & Verweire, K. (2017) *Six Batteries of Change*, LannooCampus Publishers, Leuven.

43    Scores range from 0 to 5: a score of 0 means everybody indicated 'fully disagree' with the statement, a score of 1 means everybody indicated 'disagree' with the statement, a score of 2 means everybody indicated 'tend to disagree,' and then up to 'tend to agree' (score 3), 'agree' (score 4), or 'fully agree' (score 5). The scores are the averages of the 284 international management teams.

44    Lawton, T., Rajwani, T. & Reinmoeller, P. (2012) "Do You Have a Survival Instinct? Leveraging Genetic Codes to Achieve Fit in Hostile Environments," *Business Horizons*, 55, 81-91.

45    Yates, L.K. (2022) *The Unicorn Within: How Companies Can Create Game-Changing Ventures at Startup Speed*, Harvard Business Review Press, Boston, MA; Woodword, I.C., Padmanabhan, V., Hasija, S. & Charan, R. (2021) *The Phoenix Encounter Method: Lead Like Your Business Is On Fire!*, Mc-Graw Hill Education, New York, NY; Hinssen, P. (2020) *The Phoenix and the Unicorn: The Why, What and How of Corporate Innovation*, Peter Hinssen & Nexxworks, Ghent.

46    Day, G.S. & Schoemaker, P.J.H. (2019) *See Sooner, Act Faster: How Vigilant Leaders Thrive in an Era of Digital Turbulence*, MIT Press, Cambridge, MA.

47    Mintzberg, H., Ahlstrand, B. & Lampel, J. (1998) *Strategy Safari: A Guided Tour Through the Wilds of Strategic Management*, The Free Press, New York, NY.

48    Day, G.S. & Schoemaker, P.J.H. (2006) "Leading the Vigilant Organization," *Strategy & Leadership*, Vol. 34 (5), 4-10.

49    National Commission on Terrorists Attacks Upon the United States (2004) *The 9/11 Commission Report: Final Report of the National Commission on Terrorists Attacks Upon the United States*, https://govinfo.library.unt.edu/911/report/911Report_Exec.pdf, Website accessed January 29, 2022.

50    Durst, C., Durst., M., Kolonko, T., Neef, A. & Greif, F. (2015) "A Holistic Approach to Strategic Foresight: A Foresight Support System for the German Federal Armed Forces," *Technological Forecasting & Social Change*, Vol. 97, 91-104.

51    Debruyne, M. & Tackx, K. (2019) *Customer Innovation: Delivering a Customer-Led Strategy For Sustainable Growth*, KoganPage, New York, NY.

52    Day, G.S. & Schoemaker, P.J.H. (2016) "Adapting to Fast-Changing Markets and Technologies," *California Management Review*, Vol. 58 (4), 59-77.

53    Nestik, T. (2018) "The Psychological Aspects of Corporate Foresight," *Foresight and STI Governance*, Vol. 12 (2), 78-90.

54    Rohrbeck, R., Battistella, C. & Huizingh, E. (2015) "Corporate Foresight: An Emerging Field With a Rich Tradition," *Technological Forecasting & Social Change*, 101, 1-9.

55    Gordon, A.V., Ramic, M., Rohrbeck, R. & Spaniol, M.J. (2020) "50 Years of Corporate and Organizational Foresight: Looking Back and Going Forward," *Technological Forecasting & Social Change*, 154, 1-14.

56    Future preparedness is a measure that captures to what extent a firm has adopted sensing and probing skills that match the environmental uncertainty. Rohrbeck and Kum (2018) identified four types of companies: (1) *vigilant* companies have corporate foresight practices that are adequate for their given environment, (2) *neurotic* companies have corporate foresight practices that exceed the need for their environment, (3) *vulnerable* companies have corporate foresight practices that fall short of what would be required to match the need, and (4) *in danger* companies who lack even more corporate foresight practices than what their environment prescribes. The last three categories are grouped in the overall category 'deficiencies' [Rohrbeck, R. & Kum, M.E. (2018) "Corporate Foresight and its Impact on Firm Performance: A Longitudinal Analysis," *Technological Forecasting & Social Change*, 129 (4), 105-16].

57    Rohrbeck, R. & Kum, M.E. (2018) "Corporate Foresight and its Impact on Firm Performance: A Longitudinal Analysis," *Technological Forecasting & Social Change*, 129 (4), 105-16.

58 Grant, R.M. & Jordan, J. (2015) *Foundations of Strategy*, 2ⁿᵈ Edition, John Wiley & Sons Ltd, Chichester.
59 Farrington, T., Henson, K. & Crews, C. (2012) "The Use of Strategic Foresight Methods for Ideation and Portfolio Management," *Research-Technology Management*, March-April, 26-33.
60 Rohrbeck, R. & Boe-Lillegraven, S. (2017) "Corporate Foresight at Cisco: Introduction of the Technology Radar," *Case Study Aarhus University Department of Management*, 317-0286-1, 1-19.
61 Setili, A. (2014) *The Agility Advantage: How to Identify and Act on Opportunities in a Fast-Changing World*, Jossey-Bass, San Francisco, CA, p. 101-104.
62 Rhydderch, A. (2017) *Scenario Building: The 2x2 Matrix Technique*, Futuribles International, Paris, 1-19.
63 Durst, C., Durst., M., Kolonko, T., Neef, A. & Greif, F. (2015) "A Holistic Approach to Strategic Foresight: A Foresight Support System for the German Federal Armed Forces," *Technological Forecasting & Social Change*, Vol. 97, p. 91-104.
64 Vlerick Energy Center (2015) *Who Will Lead the Energy Market in 2030*, Vlerick Business School White Paper, Brussels, 1-20.
65 Shell International (2021) *The Energy Transformation Scenarios: An Overview*, https://www.shell.com/energy-and-innovation/the-energy-future/scenarios/the-energy-transformation-scenarios.html, Website Accessed March 3ʳᵈ, 2022.
66 Kosow, H. & Gassner, R. (2008) *Methods of Future and Scenario Analysis: Overview, Assessment, and Selection Criteria*, German Development Institute, Bonn, 1-120.
67 Schirrmeister, E., Göhring, A.-L. & Warnke, P. (2020) "Psychological Biases and Heuristics in the Context of Foresight and Scenario Processes," *Futures & Foresight Science*, 1-18.
68 Fergnani, A., Hines, A., Lanteri, A. & Esposito, M. (2020) "Corporate Foresight in an Ever-Turbulent Era," *The European Business Review*, September-October, 26-33.
69 Schirrmeister, E., Göhring, A.-L. & Warnke, P. (2020) "Psychological Biases and Heuristics in the Context of Foresight and Scenario Processes," *Futures & Foresight Science*, 1-18.
70 Erdmann, D., Sichel, B. & Yeung, L. (2015) "Overcoming Obstacles to Effective Scenario Planning," McKinsey Strategy and Corporate Finance Report, https://www.mckinsey.com/business-functions/strategy-and-corporate-finance/our-insights/overcoming-obstacles-to-effective-scenario-planning, Website accessed March 30, 2022.
71 Nestik, T. (2018) "The Psychological Aspects of Corporate Foresight," *Foresight and STI Governance*, Vol. 12 (2), 78-90.
72 Debruyne, M. & Tackx, K. (2019) *Customer Innovation: Delivering a Customer-Led Strategy For Sustainable Growth*, KoganPage, New York, NY.
73 Montibeller, G. & von Winterfeldt, D. (2018) "Individual and Group Biases in Value and Uncertainty Judgments," in Dias, L.C., Morton, A. & Quigley, J. (Eds.) *Elicitation, The Science and Art of Structuring Judgment*, Springer, Cham, Switzerland, 377-92.
74 Schirrmeister, E., Göhring, A.-L. & Warnke, P. (2020) "Psychological Biases and Heuristics in the Context of Foresight and Scenario Processes," *Futures & Foresight Science*, 1-18.
75 Rohrbeck, R., Kum, M.E., Jissink, T. & Gordon, A.V. (2018) "Corporate Foresight Benchmarking Report 2018: How Leading Firms Build a Superior Position in Markets of the Future," *Research Report Strategic Foresight Research Network*, School of Business and Social Sciences at Aarhus Universitet, 1-18.
76 Rohrbeck, R., Battistella, C. & Huizingh, E. (2015) "Corporate Foresight: An Emerging Field With a Rich Tradition," *Technological Forecasting & Social Change*, 101, 1-9.
77 Day, G.S. & Schoemaker, P.J.H. (2006) "Leading the Vigilant Organization," *Strategy & Leadership*, Vol. 34 (5), 4-10.
78 Ancona, D., Williams, M. & Gerlach, G. (2020) "The Overlooked Key to Leading Through Chaos," *MIT Sloan Management Review*, Vol. 62 (1), 34-39.
79 Ibid.
80 Woodward, I.C., Padmanabhan, V.P., Hasija, S. & Charan, R. (2021) *The Phoenix Encounter Method: Lead Like Your Business Is On Fire*, McGraw-Hill Education, New York, NY.
81 Wade, M., Shan, J., Bjerkan, H. & Yokoi, T. (2021) *Digital Vortex 2021: Digital Disruption in a COVID World*, Global Center for Digital Business Transformation, IMD Business School, 1-24.
82 Ibid., p. 14.
83 Zook, C. & Allen, J. (2010) *Profit From the Core: A Return to Growth in Turbulent Times* (Updated Edition), Harvard Business Press, Boston, MA.
84 Verweire, K. (2014) Strategy Implementation, Routledge, Abingdon.
85 Christensen, C.M. & Raynor, M.E. (2003) *The Innovator's Solution: Creating and Sustaining Successful Growth*, Harvard Business School Press, Boston, MA.
86 Crawford, R. & Mathews, R. (2001) *The Myth of Excellence: Why Great Companies Never Try to Be the Best at Everything*, Crown Business, New York, NY.
87 Treacy, M. & Wiersema, F. (1993) "Customer Intimacy and Other Value Disciplines," *Harvard Business Review*, January-February, p. 84; Treacy, M. & Wiersema, F. (1995) The Discipline of Market Leaders, *Perseus Publishing*, New York, NY.
88 Even a corporation, a multi-business firm, needs to ask itself the question: what kind of companies do fit my corporate portfolio? Corporations with a strong corporate parent have a set of corporate capabilities that make their businesses better. And these corporations know when and how to use these corporate capabilities. Corporations like Danahar, Berkshire Hathaway, and Cisco have bought many companies and increased the performance of these units over time. When they no longer see that they can add corporate value, then it's time to make shifts to the corporate portfolio.

89  Teece, D.J. (2010) "Business Models, Business Strategy, and Innovation," Long Range Planning, 43, 172-194.

90  Osterwalder, A. & Pigneur, Y. (2009) *Business Model Generation*, Self-Published Book.

91  Johnson, M.W., Christensen, C.M. & Kagermann, H. (2008) "Reinventing Your Business Model," *Harvard Business Review*, December, 51-59.

92  Markides, C.C. (2008) Game-Changing Strategies: How to Create New Market Space in Established Industries by Breaking the Rules, John Wiley & Sons, San Francisco, CA.

93  Markides, C.C. (2008) Game-Changing Strategies: How to Create New Market Space in Established Industries by Breaking the Rules, John Wiley & Sons, San Francisco, CA.

94  Hallowell, R. (2020) "Handelsbanken," *HEC Case Study*, 320-0141-1, 1-15.

95  Handelsbanken (2021) "Annual and Sustainability Report 2020," Handelsbanken, Stockholm.

96  Allen, J. & Zook, C. (2022) "When Your Business Needs a Second Growth Engine," *Harvard Business Review*, May-June, 76-85.

97  Mari, A. (2018) "Next: Building a Digital Bank For Brazilian Millennials," *Forbes*, October 30, https://www.forbes.com/sites/angelicamarideoliveira/2018/10/30/next-building-a-digital-bank-for-brazilian-millienials/, Website Accessed October 20th, 2021.

98  Ibid.

99  Sotto, L. (2021) "What Do a Chameleon's Colors Mean?," *ReptileKnowHow*, https://reptileknowhow.com/lizards/chameleons/colors/, Website accessed September 28th, 2022.

100 Johnson, M.W. (2010) *Seizing the White Space: Business Model Innovation for Growth and Renewal*, Harvard Business Review Press, Boston, MA, p. 66.

101 Hendry, L. "Octopuses Keep Surprising Us—Here Are Eight Examples How," National History Museum, https://www.nhm.ac.uk/discover/octopuses-keep-surprising-us-here-are-eight-examples-how.html, Website accessed September 28th, 2022.

102 Anthony, S.D., Gilbert, C.G. & Johnson, M.W. (2017) *Dual Transformation: How to Reposition Today's Business While Creating the Future*, Harvard Business School Press, Boston, MA.

103 Gilbert, C.G., Eyring, M. & Foster, R.N. (2012) "Two Routes to Resilience: Rebuild Your Core While You Reinvent Your Business Model," *Harvard Business Review*, December, 1-9

104 Ibid.

105 Anderson, J., Kollenz-Quétard, K. & Tavassoli, N.T. (2021) "Dollar Shave Club: Disrupting the Shaving Industry—Teaching Note," *Antwerp Management School & EDHEC Case Study*, 518-0137-8, 1-25.

106 Blodgett, S. (2018) "Black-owned Company That Makes Shaving Brand Bevel Gets Acquired by Procter & Gamble," *The Black Enterprise*, December 12, Website Accessed June 14th, 2022.

107 Allen, J. & Zook, C. (2022) "When Your Business Needs a Second Growth Engine," *Harvard Business Review*, May-June, 76-85.

108 Linz, C., Müller-Stewens, G. & Zimmerman, A. (2021) Radical Business Model Transformation: How Leading Organizations Have Successfully Adapted to Disruption, 2nd Edition, KoganPage, London.

109 These case studies include Airbnb, Amazon, Colby College, easyJet (dealing with flight shaming), General Motors (dealing with the 2011 Japan earthquake and tsunami), Handelsbanken, LEGO, Unilever, and WNBA. The four case studies described in the chapter are Fender, Starbucks, Brahma (predecessor of AB InBev), and Intel.

110 Woods, B. (2020) "Fender Sales Boom as Guitar Playing Surges During the Pandemic," *CNBC Evolve*, November, https://www.cnbc.com/2020/11/21/fender-sales-boom-as-guitar-playing-surges-during-the-pandemic.html, Website Accessed April 30th, 2023.

111 Williams, A. (2020) "Guitars Are Back, Baby!," *The New York Times*, September 8, https://www.nytimes.com/2020/09/08/style/guitar-sales-fender-gibson.html, Website Accessed April 30th, 2023.

112 Edgers, G. (2017) "Why My Guitar Gently Weeps," *The Washington Post*, June 22, https://www.washingtonpost.com/graphics/2017/lifestyle/the-slow-secret-death-of-the-electric-guitar/, Website Accessed April 30th, 2023.

113 Simonnot-Lanciaux, S. & Cantas, D.C. (2021) "Fender vs. Gibson—(B) Fender: Turbulence, Differentiation, and Adaptation," *International Journal of Case Studies in Management*, 19 (3), September, 1-10.

114 Woods, B. (2021) "Fender Hits the Right Notes," *Strategy+Business (PWC)*, February 25, https://www.strategy-business.com/article/Fender-hits-the-right-notes, Website Accessed April 30th, 2023.

115 Woods, B. (2021) "Fender Hits the Right Notes," *Strategy+Business (PWC)*, February 25, https://www.strategy-business.com/article/Fender-hits-the-right-notes, Website Accessed April 30th, 2023.

116 Simonnot-Lanciaux, S. & Cantas, D.C. (2021) "Fender vs. Gibson—(B) Fender: Turbulence, Differentiation, and Adaptation," *International Journal of Case Studies in Management*, 19 (3), September, 1-10.

117 Woods, B. (2020) "Fender Sales Boom as Guitar Playing Surges During the Pandemic," *CNBC Evolve*, November, https://www.cnbc.com/2020/11/21/fender-sales-boom-as-guitar-playing-surges-during-the-pandemic.html, Website Accessed April 30th, 2023.

118 Woods, B. (2020) "Fender Sales Boom as Guitar Playing Surges During the Pandemic," *CNBC Evolve*, November, https://www.cnbc.com/2020/11/21/fender-sales-boom-as-guitar-playing-surges-during-the-pandemic.html, Website Accessed April 30th, 2023.

119 Chou, C. (2020) "Still Rocking On: Fender Hits Record Year during Pandemic," *Alizila Website*, September 11, https://www.alizila.com/fender-tmall-record-year-pandemic/, Website Accessed April 30th, 2023.

120 Ibid.

121 Woods, B. (2020) "Fender Sales Boom as Guitar Playing Surges During the Pandemic," *CNBC Evolve*, November, https://www.cnbc.com/2020/11/21/fender-sales-boom-as-guitar-playing-surges-during-the-pandemic.html, Website Accessed April 30th, 2023.

122 Starbucks Fiscal 2020 Annual Report.

123 Netessine, S. (2021) "What Covid Teaches Us About Innovating Fast," *Financial Times*, May 9, https://www.ft.com/content/4c69a6e5-8bb3-4be0-9674-11f2c21976b7, Website Accessed May 1st, 2023.

124 Walton, C. (2020) "3 Ways Starbucks Will Emerge From Covid-19 Stronger Than Before," Forbes, April 3, https://www.forbes.com/sites/christopherwalton/2020/04/03/3-ways-starbucks-will-emerge-from-covid-19-stronger-than-before, Website Accessed May 2nd, 2023.

125 Karaca, H.S., Zagorsky, J.L. & The Conversation (2023) "Two Business School Professors Break Down the Deeper Reasons Why Starbucks Customers Were so Enraged When the Company Changed its Loyalty Program," *Fortune*, January 25, https://fortune.com/2023/01/25/customers-angry-starbucks-customer-loyalty-program-professors-explain-why/, Website Accessed May 2nd, 2023.

126 Wilson, M. (2020) "Starbucks Is About to Look a Lot Different—and Covid-19 Is Only Part of the Reason Why," *FastCompany*, June 10, https://www.fastcompany.com/90514230/starbucks-is-about-to-look-a-lot-different-and-covid-19-is-only-part-of-the-reason-why, Website Accessed May 2nd, 2023.

127 Ibid.

128 Sull, D.N. & Escobari, M. (2005) *Success Against the Odds: What Brazilian Companies Teach Us About Thriving in an Unpredictable Market*, Elsevier Campus, London.

129 Sull, D.N. & Escobari, M. (2004) "Brahma versus Antarctica: Reversal of Fortune in Brazil's Beer Market, London Business School Case Study, CS04-015-001, 1-33.

130 Sull, D.N. (2009) *The Upside of Turbulence: Seizing Opportunity in an Uncertain World*, HarperCollins Publishers, New York, NY.

131 Ibid.

132 Ibid.

133 Ibid., p. 181.

134 Ibid.

135 This case study is entirely based on the Intel story described in: Sheffi, Y. (2017) *The Power of Resilience: How the Best Companies Manage the Unexpected*, The MIT Press, Cambridge, MA—Chapter 1: A Quake Breaks a Supply Chain.

136 Sheffi, Y. (2015) "Preparing for Disruptions Through Early Detection," *MIT Sloan Management Review*, 57 (1), 31-42.

137 Johnson, M.W., Christensen, C.M. & Kagermann, H. (2008) "Reinventing Your Business Model," *Harvard Business Review*, December, 51-59.

138 Bundy, J., Pfarrer, M.D., Short, C.E. & Coombs, W.T. (2017) "Crises and Crisis Management: Integration, Interpretation, and Research Development," *Journal of Management*, 43 (6), 1661-1692.

139 Pedersen, C.L., Ritter, T. & Di Benedetto, C.A. (2020) "Managing Through a Crisis: Managerial Implications for Business-to-Business Firms," *Industrial Marketing Management*, 88, 314-322.

140 Sheffi, Y. (2015) "Preparing for Disruptions Through Early Detection," *MIT Sloan Management Review*, 57 (1), 31-42.

141 Hinssen, P. (2022), "The Never Normal—Peter Hinssen at USI," *USI Events*, January 6th, https://www.youtube.com/watch?v=sfifYEq31Es, Website Accessed May 18th, 2023.

142 All three concepts are ill-defined and it's good to know that the management literature recognizes that there are definition problems with each of the three concepts. The management literature has introduced many more related concepts like robustness, absorption, adaptability, flexibility, and corporate vitality. For the sake of simplicity, I've chosen to concentrate on the concepts of risk management, resilience, and agility to make the advice digestible for the hands-on manager.

143 Pearson, C.M. & Clair, J.A. (1998) "Reframing Crisis Management," *Academy of Management Review*, 23 (1), 59-76.

144 Linnenluecke, M.K. (2017) "Resilience in Business and Management Research: A Review of Influential Publications and a Research Agenda," *International Journal of Management Reviews*, 19, 4-30.

145 Charbonnier-Voirin, A. (2011) "The Development and Partial Testing of the Psychometric Properties of a Measurement Scale of Organizational Agility," *M@n@gement*, 14 (2), 119-156.

146 In this section, I have defined crisis management rather narrowly, i.e., mainly focusing on the crisis response phase. Crisis management is a reaction to an emergency. In the crisis management literature, crisis management can also be defined more broadly, i.e. adopting a crisis as a process perspective that highlights the importance of pre-event, in-event, and post-event crisis management. When you incorporate the pre-event and post-event phase, you come close to building resilience, a topic that I will discuss later in this chapter. That's why I have opted for this more narrow view of crisis management.

147 Renjen, P. (2020) "The Heart of Resilient Leadership: Responding to Covid-19," *Deloitte Insights*, Deloitte Touche Tohmatsu Ltd., 1-22.

148 Nathanial, P. & Van der Heyden, L. (2020) "Crisis Management: Framework and Principles with Applications to Covid-19," *Insead Working Paper*, 2020/17/FIN/TOM, 1-8.

149 Renjen, P. (2020) "The Heart of Resilient Leadership: Responding to Covid-19," *Deloitte Insights*, Deloitte Touche Tohmatsu Ltd., 1-22.

150 Finn, P., Mysore, M. & Usher, O. (2020) "When Nothing Is Normal: Managing in Extreme Uncertainty," *McKinsey Risk Practice Report*, November, 1-8.

151 Ibid.

152 Sellnow, T. (2010) "BP's Crisis Communication: Finding Redemption Through Renewal," *Communication Currents*, August 1st, National Communication Association, https://www.natcom.org/communication-currents/bps-crisis-communication-finding-redemption-through-renewal, Website Accessed May 18th, 2023.

153 Hale, J., Dulek, R. & Hale, D. (2005) "Crisis Response Communication Challenges," *Journal of Business Communication*, 42 (2), 112-134.

154  IMD (2022) "IMD Report Ranks Top Companies by Resilience to Crisis," *Yahoo! Finance*, May 4, https://sg.finance.yahoo.com/news/imd-report-ranks-top-companies-090000196.html, Website Accessed May 23rd, 2023.

155  Hepfer, M. & Lawrence, T.B. (2022) "The Heterogeneity of Organizational Resilience: Exploring Functional, Operational and Strategic Resilience," *Organization Theory*, 3, 1-29.

156  Linnenluecke, M.K. (2015) "Resilience in Business and Management Research: A Review of Influential Publications and a Research Agenda," *International Journal of Management Reviews*, 19, 4-30.

157  Sheffi, Y. (2015) *The Power of Resilience: How the Best Companies Manage the Unexpected*, The MIT Press, Cambridge, MA.

158  Risk managers usually swap the axes and use the X-axis for the severity or impact of a risk (negligible, minor, moderate, significant, severe) and the Y-axis for the likelihood (from (very) unlikely to possible to (very) likely). I've changed the axes to make the link with the Uncertainty-Impact Matrix that was introduced in Chapter 2.

159  Sheffi, Y. (2015) "Preparing for Disruptions Through Early Detection," *MIT Sloan Management Review*, 57 (1), 31-42.

160  Sheffi, Y. (2015) *The Power of Resilience: How the Best Companies Manage the Unexpected*, The MIT Press, Cambridge, MA.

161  Nauck, F., Pancaldi, L., Poppensieker, T. & White, O. (2021) "The Resilience Imperative: Succeeding in Uncertain Times," *McKinsey Risk & Resilience Practice Report*, May, 1-6.

162  Meeus, L. (2021) "The Issues That Shape Strategy," *The European Business Review*, March-April, 67-73; Bach, D. & Allen, D.B. (2010) "What Every CEO Needs to Know about Nonmarket Strategy," *MIT Sloan Management Review*, Spring, 41-48; Bach, D. & Blake, D.J. (2016) "Frame or Get Framed: The Critical Role of Issue Framing in Nonmarket Management," *California Management Review*, 58 (3), 66-87.

163  Fink, S. (1986) Crisis Management: Planning for the Inevitable, *American Management Association*, New York, NY.

164  Jaques, T. (2007) "Issue Management and Crisis Management: An Integrated, Non-Linear, Relational Construct," *Public Relations Review*, 33, 147-157.

165  Ibid.

166  Sull, D. (2010) "Competing Through Organizational Agility," *McKinsey Quarterly*, 1, 1-9.

167  Nafei, W. (2016) "Organizational Agility: The Key to Organizational Success," *International Journal of Business and Management*, 11 (5), 296-309; Sali, O. (2017) "How to Create an Agile Organization," *McKinsey People & Organizational Performance Report*, October, 1-16.

168  Sull, D. & Sull, C. (2022) "Preparing Your Company for the Next Recession," *MIT Sloan Management Review*, December, 1-8.

169  Thadamalla, J.S. & Bhagyalakshmi, K. (2022) "Airbnb Inc.'s Resilience Pays Off for a Successful Turnaround," *Amity Research Centers Headquarter Case Study*, 322-0112-1, 1-5.

170  Aghion, P., Bloom, N., Lucking, B., Sadun, R. & Van Reenen, J. (2021) "Turbulence, Firm Decentralization, and Growth in Bad Times," *American Economic Journal: Applied Economics*, 13 (1), January, 133-169.

171  Salo, O. (2017) "How to Create an Agile Organization," *McKinsey People & Organizational Performance Report*, October, 1-16.

172  Sull, D.N. (2009) *The Upside of Turbulence: Seizing Opportunity in an Uncertain World*, HarperCollins Publishers, New York, NY.

173  Sull, D. & Sull, C. (2022) "Preparing Your Company for the Next Recession," *MIT Sloan Management Review*, December, 1-8.

174  Sull, D.N., Homkes, R. & Sull, C. (2015) "Why Strategy Execution Unravels—and What to Do About It," *Harvard Business Review*, March, 58-67.

175  Sull, D.N. (2009) "How to Thrive in Turbulent Markets," *Harvard Business Review*, February, 1-10.

176  https://en.wikipedia.org/wiki/The_Rumble_in_the_Jungle, Website Accessed May 21st, 2023.

177  Hamel, G. & Prahalad, C.K. (1994) *Competing for the Future*, Harvard Business School Press, Cambridge, MA; Kim, W.C. & Mauborgne, R. (2005) *Blue Ocean Strategy: How to Create Uncontested Market Space and Make the Competition Irrelevant*, Harvard Business Review Press, Cambridge, MA.

178  Furstenthal, L., Roth, E. & Brown, S. (2021) "Innovation-The Launchpath Out of the Crisis," *McKinsey & Company Strategy & Corporate Finance Practice Report*, 1-6.

179  The case studies that I analyzed were: Bradesco (Next), Daimler (car2go and Moovel), Disney (Streaming business), Dow Corning (Xiameter), House of HR/Accent Jobs (NowJobs), Klöckner (XOM Materials), Nestlé (Nespresso), Ørsted (wind-power business), Qantas (Jetstar), and Singapore Airlines (Scoot).

180  This case study is based on interviews with the members of the NowJobs founding team Peter Ingelbrecht, Frédéric Pattyn, and Eline David, and Accent/House of HR director Lindsay Demuynck. The interviews were done on November 18th and December 16th, 2022.

181  House of HR (2022) "Our 2021 House Report," p. 34.

182  Ibid., p. 35.

183  Ibid., p. 2.

184  Redactive Media Group (2017) "Responding to Structural Change: Goh Choon Phong, Singapore Airlines," *CEO Interview Asia & Pacific*, https://airlines.iata.org/ceo-interviews/responding-to-structural-change-goh-choon-phong-singapore-airlines-0, Website Accessed October 24th, 2022.

185  Singapore Airlines (2017) *Annual Report FY2016/17*, Singapore Airlines Ltd., Singapore, p. 16.

186  Smit, W. & Dula, C. (2013) "Singapore Airlines Scoots into the Low-Cost Long-Haul Category," *Singapore Management University Case Study*, SMU-13-0026, 1-21.

187  Schifrin, D. & Carroll, G. & Sorensen, J. (2020) "Scoot: Singapore Airlines' Low-Cost Carrier Strategy," *Stanford Business School Case Study*, Case SM-321, p. 7.

188    Ibid.

189    Smit, W. & Dula, C. (2013) "Singapore Airlines Scoots into the Low-Cost Long-Haul Category," *Singapore Management University Case Study*, SMU-13-0026, p. 5.

190    Michael Page (2016) "Scoot CEO Campbell Wilson: How to Sustain Growth in a Fast-Growing Company," https://www.michaelpage.com.my/advice/management-advice/leadership/scoot-ceo-campbell-wilson-how-sustain-growth-fast-growing, Website Accessed October 27th, 2022.

191    In 2020, Scoot had 2406 employees [Singapore Airlines (2020) *Annual Report FY2019/20*, Singapore Airlines Ltd., Singapore].

192    Schifrin, D. & Carroll, G. & Sørensen, J. (2020) "Scoot: Singapore Airlines' Low-Cost Carrier Strategy," *Stanford Business School Case Study*, Case SM-321, p. 8.

193    Roberts, K. (2018) "Career Profile: Campbell Wilson, CEO of Scoot," *Expat Living Singapore*, 9th Jan., https://expat-living.sg/career-profile-campbell-wilson-ceo-of-scoot/, Website Accessed October 27th, 2022.

194    Singapore Airlines (2017) *Annual Report FY2016/17*, Singapore Airlines Ltd., Singapore.

195    Doran, M. (2022) "Singapore Airlines and Scoot Inching Closer to 2019 Passenger Levels, *Simple Flying*, November 17th, https://simpleflying.com/singapore-airlines-scoot-inching-closer-2019/, Website Accessed January 4th, 2023.

196    Daimler Group Media (2017) "CASE: Networked Strategy," https://group-media.mercedes-benz.com/marsMediaSite/en/instance/ko/CASE-Networked-strategy.xhtml?oid=29182599, Website Accessed October 12th, 2022.

197    Orleans, A. & Siegel, R.E. (2017) "Daimler: Reinventing Mobility," *Stanford Business School Case Study*, Case E-642, p. 3.

198    Daimler Annual Report 2015, p. 20 & 58.

199    Daimler (2020) "How Daimler Looked into the Future," https://www.daimler-mobility.com/en/innovations/mobility-services/history-of-the-dms/, Website Accessed October 12th, 2022.

200    Linz, C., Müller-Stewens, G. & Zimmerman, A. (2021) *Radical Business Model Transformation: How Leading Organizations Have Successfully Adapted to Disruption*, 2nd Edition, KoganPage, London, p. 135

201    Daimler (2020) "How Daimler Looked into the Future," https://www.daimler-mobility.com/en/innovations/mobility-services/history-of-the-dms/, Website Accessed October 12th, 2022.

202    Linz, C., Müller-Stewens, G. & Zimmerman, A. (2021) *Radical Business Model Transformation: How Leading Organizations Have Successfully Adapted to Disruption*, 2nd Edition, KoganPage, London.

203    Orleans, A. & Siegel, R.E. (2017) "Daimler: Reinventing Mobility," *Stanford Business School Case Study*, Case E-642, 1-24.

204    Amelang, S. (2022) "BMW and Mercedes-Benz Sell Car-Sharing Joint Venture," *The Driven*, May 9, https://thedriven.io/2022/05/09/bmw-and-mercedes-benz-sell-car-sharing-joint-venture/, Website Accessed October 14th, 2022.

205    Mercedes-Benz Mobility (2022) "BMW Group and Mercedes-Benz Mobility Intend to Sell their Car-Sharing Joint Venture Share Now to Stellantis," https://www.mercedes-benz-mobility.com/en/who-we-are/stories/sell-share-now/, Website Accessed October 15th, 2022.

206    Garvin, D.A. (2004) "What Every CEO Should Know About Creating New Businesses," *Harvard Business Review*, July-August, 18-21; Zook, C. & Allen, J. (2012) *Repeatability: Build Enduring Businesses for a World of Constant Change*, Harvard Business Review Press, Boston, MA.

207    Christensen, C.M., Bartman, T. & van Bever, D. (2016) "The Hard Truth About Business Model Innovation," *MIT Sloan Management Review*, Vol. 58 (1),31-40.

208    These figures are based on statistics from early-stage venture capital investments into startups in the US from 2004-13. See Osterwalder, A., Pigneur, Y., Etiemble, E. & Smith, A. (2020) *The Invincible Company*, John Wiley & Sons, Inc., Hoboken, NJ, p. 55.

209    Markides, C.C. (2021) Organizing for the New Normal: Prepare Your Company for the Journey of Continuous Disruption, KoganPage, London, p. 107.

210    Johnson, M.W. (2010) *Seizing the White Space: Business Model Innovation for Growth and Renewal*, Harvard Business Review Press, Boston, MA.

211    Johnson, M.W. (2010) *Seizing the White Space: Business Model Innovation for Growth and Renewal*, Harvard Business Review Press, Boston, MA.

212    Markides, C.C. (1998) "Strategic Innovation in Established Companies," *MIT Sloan Management Review*, Spring, 31-42.

213    Linz, C., Müller-Stewens, G. & Zimmerman, A. (2021) *Radical Business Model Transformation: How Leading Organizations Have Successfully Adapted to Disruption*, 2nd Edition, KoganPage, London, p. 120.

214    Govindarajan, V. & Trimble, C. (2005) "Organizational DNA for Strategic Innovation," *California Management Review*, Vol. 47 (3), 45-76.

215    Furstenthal, L., Roth, E. & Brown, S. (2021) *Innovation-The Launchpath Out of the Crisis*, McKinsey & Company Strategy & Corporate Finance Practice Report, McKinsey, 1-6.

216    Ries, E. (2011) *The Lean Startup: How Today's Entrepreneurs Use Continuous Innovation to Create Radically Successfully Businesses*, Crown Business, New York, NY.

217    Eisenmann, T., Ries, E., Dillard, S. (2013) "Hypothesis-Driven Entrepreneurship: The Lean Startup," *Harvard Business School Note*, 9-812-095, 1-26.

218    Garvin, D.A. (2004) "What Every CEO Should Know About Creating New Businesses," *Harvard Business Review*, July-August, 18-21.

219    Pisano, G.P. (2019) *Creative Construction: The DNA of Sustained Innovation*, PublicAffairs (Hachette Book Group), New York, NY.

220 Eisenmann, T., Ries, E., Dillard, S. (2013) "Hypothesis-Driven Entrepreneurship: The Lean Startup," *Harvard Business School Note*, 9-812-095, 1-26.

221 O'Reilly III, C.A. & Tushman, M.L. (2016) *Lead and Disrupt: How to Solve the Innovator's Dilemma*, Stanford Business Books, Stanford, CA.

222 Hinssen, P. (2017) *The Day After Tomorrow: How to Survive in Times of Radical Innovation*, Lannoo Campus, Leuven & Van Duuren Management, Culemborg.

223 Govindarajan, V. & Trimble, C. (2005) "Building Breakthrough Businesses Within Established Organizations," *Harvard Business Review*, May, 58-68; Markides, C.C. (2008) *Game-Changing Strategies: How to Create New Market Space in Established Industries by Breaking the Rules*, John Wiley & Sons, San Francisco, CA.

224 Anthony, S.D., Gilbert, C.G. & Johnson, M.W. (2017) *Dual Transformation: How to Reposition Today's Business While Creating the Future*, Harvard Business Review Press, Boston, MA.

225 Gilbert, C., Eyring, M. & Foster, R.N. (2012) "Two Routes to Resilience," *Harvard Business Review*, December, 1-9.

226 Anthony, S.D., Gilbert, C.G. & Johnson, M.W. (2017) *Dual Transformation: How to Reposition Today's Business While Creating the Future*, Harvard Business Review Press, Boston, MA.

227 Ibid., p. 86.

228 Black, J.S. & Gregersen, H. (2014) *It Starts With One: Changing Individuals Changes Organizations*, 3rd Ed., Pearson Education, Upper Saddle River, NJ; Kotter, J.P. (2012) "Accelerate! How The Most Innovative Companies Capitalize on Today's Rapid-Fire Strategic Challenges—And Still Make Their Numbers," *Harvard Business Review*, November, 1-13.

229 The case studies that were examined are: DBS Bank, Het Financieele Dagblad Media Group, Hilti, John Deere, KBC, Michelin, New York Times, Tag Heuer, and Rolls-Royce.

230 Michel, S. (2013) "Hilti Fleet Management: Strategically Moving from Products to B2B Solutions," *IMD Case Study*, IMD-3-2354, 1-14.

231 Johnson, M.W. (2010) *Seizing the White Space: Business Model Innovation for Growth and Renewal*, Harvard Business School Review Press, Boston, MA, p. 65.

232 Casadesus-Masanell, R., Gassman, O. & Sauer, R. (2017) "Hilti Fleet Management (B): Towards a New Business Model," *Harvard Business School Case Study*, 9-717-564, p. 1.

233 Ibid., p. 1.

234 Michel, S. (2013) "Hilti Fleet Management: Strategically Moving from Products to B2B Solutions," *IMD Case Study*, IMD-3-2354, p. 5.

235 Casadesus-Masanell, R., Gassman, O. & Sauer, R. (2017) "Hilti Fleet Management (B): Towards a New Business Model," *Harvard Business School Case Study*, 9-717-564, p. 2.

236 Casadesus-Masanell, R., Gassman, O. & Sauer, R. (2017) "Hilti Fleet Management (B): Towards a New Business Model," *Harvard Business School Case Study*, 9-717-564, p. 2-3.

237 Ibid., p. 4.

238 Ibid., p. 5.

239 Monteiro, F. (2017) "How TAG Heuer Pivoted to Digital," *Knowledge at Wharton*, October 5th, https://knowledge.wharton.upenn.edu/article/tag-heuer-connected-watch/, Website accessed August 20th, 2022.

240 Monteiro, F. (2017) "The TAG Heuer Carrera Connected Watch (A): Swiss Avant-Garde for the Digital Age," *Insead Case Study*, 317-0113-1, 1-19.

241 Ibid., p. 6.

242 Markides, C.C. (2021) *Organizing for the New Normal: Prepare Your Company for the Journey of Continuous Disruption*, KoganPage, London.

243 Ibid., p. 93.

244 Monteiro, F. (2017) "The TAG Heuer Carrera Connected Watch (A): Swiss Avant-Garde for the Digital Age," *Insead Case Study*, 317-0113-1, p. 14.

245 Touchot, A. (2017) "The TAG Heuer Connected Modular 45, The Company's First 'Swiss Made' Smartwatch," *Hodinkee*, March 14th, https://www.hodinkee.com/articles/tag-heuer-connected-modular-45-swiss-made-smartwatch, accessed November 12th, 2017.

246 Ibid., p. 14.

247 Naas, R. (2020) "For TAG Heuer, Smartwatch is 'Additional Business' Beyond Core," *Bloomberg Europe Edition*, March 14th, https://www.bloomberg.com/news/articles/2020-03-14/tag-heuer-s-connected-watch-is-purely-additional-business, Website accessed August 22nd, 2022.

248 Cumps, B., Verweire, K. & Viaene, S. (2023) "KBC Dealing with Continuous Turbulence," *Vlerick Business School Case Study*, 1-20.

249 Faridi, OM (2020) "Brussels based KBC Bank to Adopt Digital-First Distribution Model by Offering AI enabled Virtual Assistant for Core Banking Services," *Crowdfund Insider*, https://www.crowdfundinsider.com/2020/11/169131-brussels-based-kbc-bank-to-adopt-digital-first-distribution-model-by-offering-ai-enabled-virtual-assistant-for-core-banking-services/, Website accessed May 26th, 2022.

250 Cumps, B., Verweire, K. & Viaene, S. (2023) "KBC Dealing with Continuous Turbulence," *Vlerick Business School Case Study*, 1-20.

251 International Banker (2020) "Interview with Mr. Johan Thijs, Group Chief Executive Officer of KBC Group," *International Banker Online Magazine*, https://internationalbanker.com/banking/interview-with-mr-johan-thijs-group-chief-executive-officer-kbc-group/, Website accessed July 14, 2022.

252 Birkinshaw, J. & Gibson, C. (2004) "Building Ambidexterity Into an Organization," *MIT Sloan Management Review*, Summer, 47-55; Osterwalder, A., Pigneur, Y., Smith, A. & Etiemble, F. (2020) *The Invincible Company*, John Wiley & Sons, Inc., Hoboken, NJ.

253   Osterwalder, A., Pigneur, Y., Smith, A. & Etiemble, F. (2020) *The Invincible Company*, John Wiley & Sons, Inc., Hoboken, NJ.

254   Markides, C.C. (2021) *Organizing for the New Normal: Prepare Your Company for the Journey of Continuous Disruption*, KoganPage, London, p. 107.

255   Personal interview with Erik Luts, KBC Chief Innovation Officer, and Sigrid De Wever, KBC General Manager Corporate Strategy and Innovation, on February 2nd, 2022.

256   Thompson, M., Taqqu, Y. & Narisetti, R. (2020) "Building a Digital New York Times: CEO Mark Thompson," *McKinsey & Company Technology, Media & Telecommunications Practice*, McKinsey & Company, 1-10.

257   Markides, C.C. (2021) Organizing for the New Normal: Prepare Your Company for the Journey of Continuous Disruption, KoganPage, London.

258   Johnson, M.W. (2010) *Seizing the White Space: Business Model Innovation for Growth and Renewal*, Harvard Business Review Press, Boston, MA.

259   De Prins, P., Letens, G. & Verweire, K. (2017) *Six Batteries of Change*, Lannoo Publishers, Tielt.

260   Ibid.

261   Our research showed that change success was correlated significantly with the number of batteries charged. The higher the number of batteries charged, the more likely executives are to rate the transformation a success. Only 30 percent of the companies that had only 1 or 2 batteries charged (out of the 6) reported a moderately successful change. That figure increased to 69 percent if 3 or 4 batteries were charged. And 95 percent of the companies reported a successful change if 5 or 6 batteries were charged.

262   Monteiro, F. (2017) "The TAG Heuer Carrera Connected Watch (A): Swiss Avant-Garde for the Digital Age," *Insead Case Study*, 317-0113-1, p. 14.

263   Casadesus-Masanell, R., Gassman, O. & Sauer, R. (2017) "Hilti Fleet Management (B): Towards a New Business Model," *Harvard Business School Case Study*, 9-717-564, p. 2-3.

264   Hamel, G. (2000) *Leading the Revolution*, Harvard Business School Press, Boston, MA.

265   Thompson, M., Taqqu, Y. & Narisetti, R. (2020) "Building a Digital New York Times: CEO Mark Thompson," *McKinsey & Company Technology, Media & Telecommunications Practice*, McKinsey & Company, p. 5.

266   Gilbert, C. (2003) "The Disruption Opportunity," *MIT Sloan Management Review*, Summer, 27-31.

267   De Prins, P., Letens, G. & Verweire, K. (2017) *Six Batteries of Change*, Lannoo Publishers, Tielt.

268   Ibid.

269   Markides, C.C. (2008) *Game-Changing Strategies: How to Create New Market Space in Established Industries by Breaking the Rules*, John Wiley & Sons, San Francisco, CA.

270   Monteiro, F. (2017) "The TAG Heuer Carrera Connected Watch (A): Swiss Avant-Garde for the Digital Age," *Insead Case Study*, 317-0113-1, p. 5.

271   Anthony, S.D., Gilbert, C.G. & Johnson, M.W. (2017) *Dual Transformation: How to Reposition Today's Business While Creating the Future*, Harvard Business Review Press, Boston, MA.

272   Bell, D., Gabrieli, F. & Beyersdorfer, D. (2020) "Danone Changing the Food System," *Harvard Business School Case Study*, 9-520-053, 1-29; Anthony, S.D. & Schwartz, E.I. (2017) "The Transformation 10: Strategic Change Rankings for 2017," *Innosight Publication*, https://www.innosight.com/wp-content/uploads/2017/05/Innosight_Transformation-10.pdf, Website Accessed March 14th, 2023.

273   Anthony, S.D. & Schwartz, E.I. (2017) "The Transformation 10: Strategic Change Rankings for 2017," *Innosight Publication*, https://www.innosight.com/wp-content/uploads/2017/05/Innosight_Transformation-10.pdf, Website Accessed March 14th, 2023.

274   Anthony, S.D., Gilbert, C.G. & Johnson, M.W. (2017) *Dual Transformation: How to Reposition Today's Business While Creating the Future*, Harvard Business Review Press, Boston, MA.

275   Anand, B. & Hood, S. (2007) 'Schibsted,' *Harvard Business School Case Study*, 9-707-474, 1-36.

276   Ibid., p. 8.

277   Weverbergh, R. (2013) "Eight Lessons in How to Disrupt Yourself from Schibsted," Whiteboard Magazine, http://www.whiteboardmag.com/8-lessons-in-how-to-disrupt-yourself-from-schibsted/, Website Accessed February 8th, 2019.

278   Doctor, K. (2012) "Looking to Europe for News—Industry Innovation, Part 2: Schibsted's Stunning Classifieds and Services Business," *NiemanLab Website*, https://www.niemanlab.org/2012/02/looking-to-europe-for-news-industry-innovation-part-2-schibsteds-stunning-classifieds-and-services-business/, Website Accessed March 1st, 2023.

279   Anand, B. & Hood, S. (2007) 'Schibsted,' *Harvard Business School Case Study*, 9-707-474, 1-36.

280   Weverbergh, R. (2013) "Eight Lessons in How to Disrupt Yourself from Schibsted," Whiteboard Magazine, http://www.whiteboardmag.com/8-lessons-in-how-to-disrupt-yourself-from-schibsted/, Website Accessed February 8th, 2019.

281   Anand, B. & Hood, S. (2007) 'Schibsted,' *Harvard Business School Case Study*, 9-707-474, 1-36.

282   Anand, B. & Hood, S. (2007) 'Schibsted,' *Harvard Business School Case Study*, 9-707-474, p. 10.

283   Weverbergh, R. (2013) "Eight Lessons in How to Disrupt Yourself from Schibsted," Whiteboard Magazine, http://www.whiteboardmag.com/8-lessons-in-how-to-disrupt-yourself-from-schibsted/, Website Accessed February 8th, 2019.

284   Anand, B. & Hood, S. (2007) 'Schibsted,' *Harvard Business School Case Study*, 9-707-474, p. 10.

285   Ibid., p. 10.

286   Ibid., p. 10.

287   Schibsted Annual Report 2009, p. 4.

288   Anand, B. & Hood, S. (2007) 'Schibsted,' *Harvard Business School Case Study*, 9-707-474, p. 11.

289    WAN-IFRA Staff (2017) "How Schibsted Media Group Makes Disruption Seem Hip," World Association of News Publishers Website, https://wan-ifra.org/2017/05/how-schibsted-media-group-makes-disruption-seem-hip/, Website Accessed March 3rd, 2023.

290    Schibsted Annual Report 2013, p. 3.

291    Anand, B. & Hood, S. (2007) 'Schibsted,' *Harvard Business School Case Study*, 9-707-474, p. 11.

292    Doctor, K. (2012) "Looking to Europe for News—Industry Innovation, Part 2: Schibsted's Stunning Classifieds and Services Business," *NiemanLab Website*, https://www.niemanlab.org/2012/02/looking-to-europe-for-news-industry-innovation-part-2-schibsteds-stunning-classifieds-and-services-business/, Website Accessed March 1st, 2023.

293    Barnes & Noble Website, https://www.barnesandnobleinc.com/about-bn/history/, Website Accessed March 15th, 2023.

294    Ibid., p. 4.

295    MacCormack, A., Kimball Dunn, B. & Kemerer, C. (2014) "Barnes & Noble: Managing the E-Book Revolution," *Harvard Business School Case Study*, 9-613-073, 1-21.

296    Gilbert, C., Eyring, M. & Foster, R.N. (2012) "Two Routes to Resilience," *Harvard Business Review*, December, 1-9.

297    Statistica (2013) "E-reader Sales Worldwide from 2009-2012," https://www.statista.com/statistics/273700/sales-of-e-readers-worldwide-since-2009/, Website Accessed March 15th, 2023.

298    Grant, R.M. & Jordan, J. (2015) *Foundations of Strategy* (2nd Edition), John Wiley & Sons Ltd, Chichester.

299    In the years 2011-15, operating profit margins (= EBIT/sales) were 4.0%, 4.0%, 3.7% and 3.8% (own calculations based on financial data from annual reports). In 2015, B&N Education was split off. The operating profit margin for B&N Retail for that period was 1.9%, 3.2%, 5.0 and 5.3%. After the split-off, the operating profit margin for B&N Retail dropped to 5.2% (2015), 2.8% (2016), 2.4% (2017) and -3.3%. In 2019, Barnes & Noble was acquired.

300    Selyukh, A. (2023) "How Barnes & Noble Turned a Page, Expanding for the First Time in Years," *NPR*, March 7th, https://www.npr.org/2023/03/07/1161295820/how-barnes-noble-turned-a-page-expanding-for-the-first-time-in-years?, Website Accessed March 15th, 2023.

301    Wiener-Bronner, D. (2018) "5 Things Barnes & Noble Can Do Right Now to Save Itself," *CNNMoney*, January 7th, https://money.cnn.com/2018/01/17/news/companies/save-barnes--noble/index.html, Website Accessed March 15th, 2023.

302    Knowledge at Wharton (2019) "What's the Next Chapter for Barnes & Noble?," *Knowledge at Wharton Podcast*, June 18th, https://knowledge.wharton.upenn.edu/podcast/knowledge-at-wharton-podcast/whats-next-chapter-barnes-noble/, Website Accessed March 16th, 2023.

303    Bhatnagar, M. & Bhagyalakshimi, K. (2022) "Barnes & Noble Weaves Turnaround Plans," *Amity Research Centers Headquarter Case Study*, 322-0291-1, p. 6.

304    Knowledge at Wharton (2018) "Can Barnes & Noble Survive?," *Knowledge at Wharton Podcast*, June 7th, https://knowledge.wharton.upenn.edu/podcast/knowledge-at-wharton-podcast/can-barnes-noble-survive/, Website Accessed March 16th, 2023.

305    Selyukh, A. (2023) "How Barnes & Noble Turned a Page, Expanding for the First Time in Years," *NPR*, March 7th, https://www.npr.org/2023/03/07/1161295820/how-barnes-noble-turned-a-page-expanding-for-the-first-time-in-years?, Website Accessed March 15th, 2023.

306    Bhatnagar, M. & Bhagyalakshimi, K. (2022) "Barnes & Noble Weaves Turnaround Plans," *Amity Research Centers Headquarter Case Study*, 322-0291-1.

307    Keller-Birrer, V. & Jelassi, T. (2017) "AccorHotels' Digital Transformation: A Strategic Response to Hospitality Disruptor Airbnb," *IMD Case Study*, IMD-7-1915, 1-25.

308    Ting, D. (2016) "AccorHotels CEO to the Hotel Industry: 'You Have an Obligation to Be Bold,'" *Skift.com*, August 5th, https://skift.com/2016/08/05/accorhotels-ceo-to-the-hotel-industry-you-have-an-obligation-to-be-bold/, Website Accessed March 7th, 2023.

309    Sheivachman, A. (2018) "AccorHotels CEO Gets Candid About Moving Hospitality Beyond Hotels," *Skift.com*, April 27th, https://skift.com/2018/04/27/accorhotels-ceo-gets-candid-about-moving-hospitality-beyond-hotels/, Website Accessed March 8th, 2023.

310    O'Neill, S. (2023) "Accor CEO Defends Hotel Giant's Latest Reorg," *Skift.com*, January 24th, https://skift.com/2023/01/24/accor-ceo-defends-hotel-giants-latest-reorg/, Website Accessed March 8th, 2023.

311    Ting, D. (2016) "AccorHotels CEO to the Hotel Industry: 'You Have an Obligation to Be Bold,'" *Skift.com*, August 5th, https://skift.com/2016/08/05/accorhotels-ceo-to-the-hotel-industry-you-have-an-obligation-to-be-bold/, Website Accessed March 7th, 2023

312    Ting, D. (2016) "AccorHotels CEO to the Hotel Industry: 'You Have an Obligation to Be Bold,'" *Skift.com*, August 5th, https://skift.com/2016/08/05/accorhotels-ceo-to-the-hotel-industry-you-have-an-obligation-to-be-bold/, Website Accessed March 7th, 2023.

313    Ting, D. (2017) "AccorHotels Is Working on a Smart Room That's Accessible and Personalized," *Skift.com*, November 22nd, https://skift.com/2017/11/22/accorhotels-is-working-on-a-smart-room-thats-both-accessible-and-personalized/, Website Accessed March 8th, 2023.

314    Ting, D. (2017) "Accor CEO: We Want to Transform the Way Everyone Uses Hotels," *Skift.com*, February 23rd, https://skift.com/2017/02/23/accor-ceo-we-want-to-transform-the-way-you-use-hotels/, Website Accessed March 8th, 2023.

315    Keller-Birrer, V. & Jelassi, T. (2017) "AccorHotels' Digital Transformation: A Strategic Response to Hospitality Disruptor Airbnb," *IMD Case Study*, IMD-7-1915, 1-25.

316    Accor Annual Report 2019, p. 7.

317   Hamdi, R. (2016) "Bazin Seeks Startups to Accelerate AccorHotels Transformation," *Forbes*, April 25th, https://www.forbes.com/sites/hamdiraini/2016/04/25/bazin-seeks-startups-to-accelerate-accorhotels-transformation/?sh=4eab17144a8e, Website Accessed March 10th, 2023.
318   Ting, D. (2016) "AccorHotels CEO to the Hotel Industry: 'You Have an Obligation to Be Bold,'" *Skift.com*, August 5th, https://skift.com/2016/08/05/accorhotels-ceo-to-the-hotel-industry-you-have-an-obligation-to-be-bold/, Website Accessed March 7th, 2023.
319   Smithson, B. (2019) "What's the Difference between OneFineStay and Airbnb?," *The Points Guy UK website*, https://thepointsguy.co.uk/guide/difference-onefinestay-airbnb/, Website Accessed March 14th, 2023.
320   Lewis, A. (2015) "OneFineStay," https://www.businessmodelzoo.com/exemplars/onefinestay/, Website Accessed March 11th, 2023; OneFineStay website, https://www.onefinestay.com/, Website Accessed March 11th, 2023.
321   Ting, D. (2017) "Accor CEO: We Want to Transform the Way Everyone Uses Hotels," *Skift.com*, February 23rd, https://skift.com/2017/02/23/accor-ceo-we-want-to-transform-the-way-you-use-hotels/, Website Accessed March 8th, 2023.
322   Accor Annual Report 2018.
323   Mest, E. (2017) "AccorHotels Celebrates 50 Years with Launch of AccorLocal," *Hotel Management*, November 15th, https://www.hotelmanagement.net/tech/accorhotels-celebrates-50-years-launch-accorlocal, Website Accessed March 10th, 2023.
324   Ting, D. (2017) "Accor CEO: We Want to Transform the Way Everyone Uses Hotels," *Skift.com*, February 23rd, https://skift.com/2017/02/23/accor-ceo-we-want-to-transform-the-way-you-use-hotels/, Website Accessed March 8th, 2023.
325   This statement is based on my extensive analysis of Accor's financial results for the period 2011-22 and of the financial results of Intercontinental and Marriott.
326   Weverbergh, R. (2013) "Eight Lessons in How to Disrupt Yourself from Schibsted," *Whiteboard Magazine*, http://www.whiteboardmag.com/8-lessons-in-how-to-disrupt-yourself-from-schibsted/, Website Accessed February 8th, 2019.
327   Lystimäki, J. (2014) "Schibsted: Strategic Digital Transformation," *Presentation in Aalto University—Professional Diploma in Business and Information Systems Engineering*, May, https://www.slideshare.net/torifi/digital-transformation-and-what-you-can-learn-from-schibsted-34509416, Website Accessed March 24th, 2023.
328   Keller-Birrer, V. & Jelassi, T. (2017) "AccorHotels' Digital Transformation: A Strategic Response to Hospitality Disruptor Airbnb," *IMD Case Study*, IMD-7-1915, 1-25.
329   Kissick, R., Burgelman, R.A. & Siegel, R. (2016) "Axel Springer in 2016: From Transformation to Acceleration," *Stanford Business School Case Study*, E-610, 1-28.
330   Buche, Y. & Piskorski, M.J. (2016) "Digital Transformation at Axel Springer," *IMD Case Study*, IMD-7-1733, 1-18.
331   Osterwalder, A., Pigneur, Y., Etiemble, F. & Smith, A. (2020) *The Invincible Company*, John Wiley & Sons, Inc., Hoboken, NJ.
332   Ibid., p. 310.